SKILLS FOR LAWYERS

SKILLS FOR LAWYERS

Annabel Elkington, MA (Hons), Dip Law, Barrister

John Holtam LLB (Southampton), LLM (Edinburgh), Solicitor

Gemma M Shield LLB (Hons), Solicitor

Stephanie Verlander LLB (Hons), MA, MCLIP

Published by

College of Law Publishing, Braboeuf Manor, Portsmouth Road, St Catherines, Guildford GU3 1HA

British Library Cataloguing-in-Publication Data

A catalogue record for this book is available from the British Library.

ISBN: 978 1 911269 84 7

Typeset and Designed by Style Photosetting Ltd, Mayfield, East Sussex

Index by Moira Greenhalgh, Carnforth, Lancashire

Printed in Great Britain by The Irongate Group, Derby

Preface

Knowledge of how the internal combustion engine works and what the Highway Code states does not necessarily make a good driver. In the same way, knowledge of the law does not necessarily make a good lawyer. The practice of law requires not merely an understanding of law and procedure but also the skills necessary to utilise that knowledge effectively.

The purpose of this book is to help prospective practitioners to develop fundamental skills which will prove essential in their later careers. Those skills are as follows:

(a)   writing and drafting;

(b)   legal research;

(c)   interviewing and advising clients;

(d)   negotiation; and

(e)   advocacy.

The chapters covering each of these skills are essential preparatory reading for practice of the relevant skill on the Legal Practice Course. It is hoped that they will also prove useful in later years for the trainee or qualified solicitor, both to monitor one's own development and to evaluate others, learning from their successes and their failures.

Contents

Case Scenarios

ROAD TRAFFIC ACCIDENT / PERSONAL INJURY CASE STUDY

Summary

An accident occurred at the junction of Larkhall Road and Forest Road on Tuesday, 15 January 2016. A white van heading south on Forest Road was turning right into Larkhall Road. As the van was turning right it collided with a car heading north up Forest Road. The collision also involved a cyclist who was travelling alongside the car at the moment of impact.

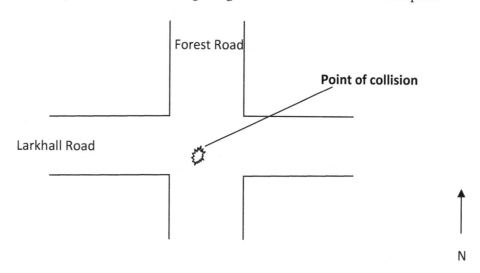

Vehicles and drivers involved

Van White Ford company van owned by Armitage Deliveries and driven by Adam Worcik. Mr Worcik is a Polish national living in the UK and working as a driver for Armitage Deliveries. He sustained minor whiplash as a result of the accident.

Car Silver Vauxhall Zafira owned and driven by Caroline Marsh, a senior midwife who works for her local NHS trust. Ms Marsh suffered serious whiplash, a broken collar bone and a cut to her forehead which required seven stitches as a result of the accident. She has serious ongoing symptoms in relation to the whiplash injury, and the cut has left a permanent scar on her forehead (there is the possibility of further surgery to improve the appearance of this scar).

Cycle Red Trek 200 ridden by Paul Chester, a freelance musician. Mr Chester suffered a broken left wrist and a cut to his arm which required 13 stitches.

Liability

Liability is disputed. Mr Worcik claims that Ms Marsh was driving far too fast and that she was using her mobile phone when the accident happened. Ms Marsh claims that Mr Worcik suddenly pulled into her path without indicating as she pulled out of the junction. Mr Chester, the cyclist, does not have a clear recollection of what happened.

Solicitors for the parties

Acting for Mr Worcik, the van driver	Acting for Ms Marsh, the car driver	Acting for Mr Chester, the cyclist
Shea & De Sousa 67 Longbridge Road Stockwell London SW9 4RT 0207 479 4791	Alexa Hughes & Co 33 Millennium House Teddington KT4 6RB 0208 221 3445	Marshalls 114–116 Market Street Kingston KT1 4RT 0208 566 3228 inquiries@marshalls.co.uk

POTENTIAL TRANSACTION

Robert Grove Ltd is a large company specialising in restaurants/retail food outlets. Toast & Tea is a small chain of upmarket cafes owned by two brothers, Mark and Dominic Flowers, and a friend of theirs, Florence Lowe. The Toast & Tea owners are seeking to find a buyer for their company, and Robert Grove Ltd has expressed an interest in purchasing the chain.

Sellers

The owners of Toast & Tea have decided to sell, as their interests in the business are beginning to diverge. The chain has been very successful and currently owns 16 outlets in prime locations in central London. The cafes are old fashioned in design with a focus on service and quality which is reflected in the prices. Each cafe offers a children's room where under-8s enjoy supervised play. The cafes have won many awards for both food provided and provision for children/families.

The owners are keen for the transaction to progress quickly, as two of them have other ventures in which they would like to invest. They hope to achieve a purchase price of £22 million, but accept that in the current economic climate and given the current property market they may have to accept a figure closer to £18 million. Most of the value of the company is in ownership of cafe properties which have been purchased as freeholds/long leaseholds and in most cases have undergone valuable development work. The Flowers brothers were the major investors in the company and have a bigger stake, but Florence Lowe has acted as CEO and has been very hands-on in managing the chain.

Solicitors for the seller:
Mace McKenzie
Frobisher House, City Road, London EC2 5BR
0207 422 2134

Buyer

Robert Grove Ltd owns a range of pubs, restaurants and retail food outlets across the UK and Ireland. It has been looking to expand into the 'luxury' market. Toast & Tea's award-winning combination is attractive to it as a complement to its existing portfolio, and Robert Grove Ltd believes that given greater economies of scale it can make the business highly profitable.

Robert Grove Ltd would like to see Florence Lowe continue in her role or accept a position as an advisor for an agreed handover period. It is happy to proceed quickly but would ideally like any deal to include structured payments over a 12-month period. The current suggested purchase price of £22 million is based on valuation of Toast & Tea including its premises made at a time when commercial property prices were significantly higher.

Solicitors for the buyer:
Salinger & Rye
40–47 City House, Cornhill Square, London EC1 4RT
0207 836 9368

WRITING AND DRAFTING

WRITING AND DRAFTING

LEARNING OUTCOMES

After reading this chapter you will be able to:

- plan and draft a range of legal documents
- identify and use different structures when drafting a clause
- correctly use definitions within legal documents
- identify and avoid using archaic language, jargon, tautology and other common errors
- draft clear, precise and unambiguous documents
- understand the critical importance of checking and proofreading documents.

1.1 INTRODUCTION TO WRITING AND DRAFTING

Much of your professional work will require you to communicate in writing. The ability to write clearly, concisely and professionally under time pressure is a core skill for every solicitor. Every type of written communication needs to be effective, unambiguous and well drafted, whether it is an e-mail, letter or formal legal document.

Modern working practices mean that we often send tens of e-mails every day. You will have to reply promptly to e-mails and letters, and will frequently be asked to draft legal documents quickly. Set out below are some of the fundamental rules of good writing and drafting practice, together with some of the most common errors. In each section, there are examples and exercises with recommended times for completion. The answers to exercises can be found in the **Appendix to Part I**.

Good writing and drafting requires a four-stage process:

(a) *preparation and research*   take full instructions, undertake any further enquiries which are needed, identify the objective(s)/purpose of the document, research the law;

(b) *planning*   decide on the best structure and necessary content;

(c) *drafting*   clearly and concisely set out the information/points following your plan;

(d) *checking*   cross-check your document to ensure that it is correct, unambiguous and meets the objectives you identified.

1.2 PREPARATION AND RESEARCH

1.2.1 Taking instructions

The first step will always be to take instructions from your client. You must have a clear understanding of what your client wishes to achieve and of all the relevant facts. Part of your role at this stage will be to ensure that you identify everything you need to know. Your client may not be aware of all the information you might need.

EXAMPLE

Your client instructs you to impose an obligation on a buyer of part of his land to put up a 2.5 metre fence along what will become the common boundary. You must identify the need for further information as to:

(a)   what type of fence is required;

(b)   the time limit to be imposed;

(c)   who will be required to maintain the fence; and

(d)   who will obtain planning permission and what happens if planning permission is not granted.

1.2.2 Researching the law

Before you can decide how best to advise your client and/or how to draft any necessary documentation, you must research the relevant law.

1.3 PLANNING

Once you have full instructions and have mastered the current legal position, you can begin to plan your advice.

Identify your client's objectives and decide how they can best be met. You will then need to select the most appropriate structure.

1.3.1 Common document structure

Many documents will contain the following elements:

- commencement;
- date;
- parties;
- recitals;
- operative part;
- testimonium;
- schedules;
- execution and attestation.

1.3.1.1 Commencement, date and parties

A document will normally begin with a 'commencement' which describes the nature of the document, for example 'This Agreement', 'This Conveyance'. Alternatively, the document's title can simply be set out as a heading. Deeds may also use the word 'deed' in the title, for example 'This deed of Conveyance'.

A space should be left for insertion of the date when the document is completed.

The full names and addresses of the parties should be inserted. (In the case of a company, the address of its registered office should be inserted.)

> **EXAMPLE**
>
> <u>SERVICE AGREEMENT</u>
>
> DATE:
>
> PARTIES: (1) Weyford Products Limited whose registered office is at 32 Bridge House, Wharf Road, Milton, Berefordshire.
>
> (2) Joan Alice Bennet of 8 High Street, Milton, Berefordshire.
>
> A long and complicated document can benefit from an index or table of clauses (preferably at the front).

1.3.1.2 Recitals

Recitals clauses are not essential and you should consider carefully whether or not to include them. You can use them to set out the background facts to the document and so make it more self-explanatory. For example, in a conveyance of land by a personal representative, the date of the deceased's death and the date on which a grant of representation was obtained could be recited.

Recitals are also sometimes used to introduce and summarise the contents of the operative part of the document but, except in complicated documents, this is generally not necessary and increases the risk of introducing ambiguities.

1.3.1.3 Operative part

The operative part of a document is the part which creates the legal rights and obligations.

The contents of the operative part of a document depend on the nature of the document. For example, a commercial agreement will generally contain:

(a) conditions precedent (conditions which have to be satisfied before the agreement comes into force);

(b) agreements (the rights and obligations of the parties);

(c) representations and warranties (ie, statements about factual and legal matters which one of the parties requires to be made to him or her in a legally binding way);

(d) 'boiler-plate' clauses (ie, standard clauses inserted into all agreements of such a type and dealing with, for example, the service of notices under the agreement, or the jurisdiction for action where the agreement has an international element).

1.3.1.4 Testimonium

A testimonium clause is not essential but, if used, it introduces the signatures of the parties and may describe a particular method of executing where, for example, a company is using its seal as part of its execution, or an attorney is signing on behalf of a party.

1.3.1.5 Schedules

Use schedules where appropriate to avoid breaking the continuity of a document with too much detail. The operative part of the document then refers to the schedule, and the schedule contains the detail.

> **EXAMPLE**
>
> <u>TENANT'S COVENANTS</u>
>
> The Tenant covenants with the Landlord to observe and perform the covenants set out in Schedule 1.

SCHEDULE 1

1.   To pay the rent ... etc.

Note that the obligation or right is created in the operative part of the document. Only the detail of the obligation or right is put in the schedule.

1.3.1.6 Execution and attestation

A document will end with an execution clause. This will refer to the signatures of the parties and any other formalities necessary to give the document legal effect. The wording of this clause will vary depending on the nature of the party executing, whether the document is executed as a deed, and whether the party's signature is witnessed ('attested').

For a document executed by an individual and not intended to take effect as a deed, the clause could read:

Signed by ALAN JONES)   (Alan Jones signs here)

in the presence of:)

(Witness signs here)

If the document is intended to take effect as a deed the clause could read:

Executed as a deed   )   (Alan Jones signs here)

by ALAN JONES   )

in the presence of:)

(Witness signs here)

1.3.2 Order of clauses in the operative part

It is difficult to lay down rules as to the order of clauses. It will vary according to the nature of the document, but it is often a matter of common sense and logic.

1.3.2.1 Common structures for operative clauses

Deciding on the best structure to adopt when drafting the operative clauses of a document is the most important stage in planning your document.

1.3.2.2 Chronological order

One possibility is to list topics in chronological order. This is often particularly suitable for a document that deals with one simple transaction.

Imagine a contract for the hire of a car. The order of topics could be:

- parties;
- definitions;
- agreement by Owner to hire out car to Hirer on the terms set out in the agreement;
- payment;
- insurance;
- promises by Owner as to the state of the car at the start of the hire;
- duration of hire;
- what the car can be used for;
- who may drive;
- Hirer's promises as to the return of the car;
- remedies for breach of the agreement.

For a contract such as this, a chronological structure will produce a simpler and less repetitive document than if you try to divide topics into Owner's Obligations and Hirer's Obligations.

1.3.2.3 Categorical order

A categorical structure sets out the duties and responsibilities in categories. An example of this is a lease.

The structure of a typical lease is:

- parties;
- definitions;
- the grant of the term by Landlord to Tenant;
- Tenant's covenants;
- Landlord's covenants;
- provisos, eg, the Landlord's power to forfeit the lease.

Here, the division into landlord's obligations and tenant's obligations is essential. The obligations have to be performed throughout the entire term of the lease. There is no chronological order to them.

1.3.2.4 Order of importance

This could be the order used in a simple contract, where the obligations are not to be carried out in any chronological order. An example could be an agreement between employer and employee on severance of employment.

1.3.2.5 Combinations

A document may use a combination of the above structures. A contract with a firm of furniture removers could list the firm's obligations in chronological order, for example:

- to pack the contents of the house;
- to transport to storage;
- to store;
- to transport to new house;
- to unpack;

and then list the owner's obligations.

In a lease, all the tenant's covenants will be put together, but will appear in order of importance.

1.3.3 Structuring a clause

1.3.3.1 Structuring clauses and sub-clauses within the operative part

(a) Use a separate clause for each separate matter.

(b) Use sub-paragraphing to avoid long, cumbersome clauses and provisos.

(c) Number each clause and sub-clause.

(d) Give each clause or group of clauses a heading that correctly defines the subject matter of the clauses, eg:

Tenant's Covenants

Look at the following two examples and decide which you think is easier to understand.

> **EXAMPLE 1**
>
> The Licensee shall purchase exclusively from the Grantor all materials used in making the Invention provided that the licensee shall be entitled to relieve itself of its liability to observe this obligation upon giving the Grantor three months' notice in writing.

> **EXAMPLE 2**
>
> 1.   Subject to Clause 2, the Licensee must purchase exclusively from the Grantor all materials used in making the Invention.
>
> 2.   The Licensee may end the obligation contained in Clause 1 by giving the Grantor three months' notice in writing.

Both examples contain the same provisions, but the second is easier to understand because it uses separate numbered clauses for each point.

1.3.3.2   Structuring a clause according to Coode

Read the following clause and think about the structure. Do you think the structure adopted helps to make the meaning clear?

> **Clause X**
>
> The Company shall reimburse the Replacement Value of lost or damaged goods provided that the value of the claim does not exceed £1,000 and the Policyholder notifies the loss within 7 days from (but excluding) the date of its occurrence PROVIDED ALWAYS THAT the above shall not apply to claims made under Clause 10 of this Policy.

This clause starts with a statement of a legal obligation which at first sight appears absolute. The conditions and exceptions attaching to the obligation are not stated until afterwards, so that it is necessary to reconsider the obligation in the light of them. This kind of clause construction is very common in legal drafting, but it is not the most logical way to structure a clause and it makes it more difficult to understand.

In 1843, George Coode wrote a treatise on 'Legislative Expression'; or, 'The Language of The Written Law'. His general principle is that a clause should be structured in the following order:

- circumstances/exceptions (ie, circumstances where the right or obligation does or does not exist);
- conditions (ie, conditions on which the right or obligation depends);
- obligation or right (ie, who **must** do what or who **may** do what).

Words suitable for introducing an exception are 'except where ...'.

Words suitable for introducing circumstances are 'where ...' 'if ... then' or 'when ...' or 'on ...'.

Words suitable for introducing conditions are 'if ...' or 'provided that ...'.

These are two examples of Coode in legislation:

Section 2(1) of the Land Registration and Land Charges Act 1971

If any question arises as to whether a person is entitled to an indemnity under any provision of the Land Registration Act 1925 [*circumstance*] [...] **he** [*person*] **may apply** to the court to have that question determined [*the right*].

Section 23(1) of the Matrimonial Causes Act 1973

On granting a decree of divorce ... [*circumstance*] **the court** [*person*] **may make** any one or more of the following orders ... [*right*].

This is an example of Coode in a document:

> **15   Compensation on termination of contract**
>
> Except where otherwise provided [exception], if before 1 December 2017 this contract is terminated by the Buyer [circumstance], then provided the Seller is not in breach of any of his obligations under this contract [condition] the Buyer must pay the Seller the sum of £5000 [obligation].

The rule produces a logical and, to lawyers, a familiar structure, but it does not have to be followed invariably.

Imagine that an owner of land has employed consultants to design and build an amusement park. The consultants want to control the use of their name in any advertising material issued by the landowner. Their name is to be used only if certain conditions are met.

If the clause were drafted using Coode's rule, it would read:

> Only where
> (a)   the Landowner has given the Consultants advance details of any advertising material it plans to use; and
> (b)   the Consultants have given their express written approval; and
> (c)   the Consultants have not ended this Agreement under subclause 11(1)
> may the Landowner use the Consultants' name in advertising material.

The clause could make the point in a more natural and in a stronger manner if Coode were ignored and the clause were drafted to read:

> The Landowner may only use the Consultants' name in advertising material where:
> (a)   the Landowner has given the Consultants advance details of any advertising materials it plans to use; and
> (b)   the Consultants have given their express written approval; and
> (c)   the Consultants have not ended this Agreement under subclause 11(1).

EXAMPLE

Coode's structure can be a useful tool in preparing documents. The clause set out at the start of **1.3.3.2** has been redrafted below using Coode's structure and other techniques to improve its clarity.

Clause X   Claims for lost or damaged goods

Where:

(a)   a claim does not exceed £1,000; and

(b)   the Policyholder notifies the loss within 7 days from (but excluding) the date of its occurrence; and

(c)   the claim is not one made under Clause 10 of this Policy

the Company shall reimburse the Replacement Value.

1.3.4   Use of precedents

Using a precedent can help in the planning of your document by giving an example of:

(a)   suitable structure;

(b)   provisions that you have not thought of and that will benefit your client;

(c)   suitable wording; and/or

(d)   legal problems you had not considered.

However, precedents should be used with caution.

1.3.4.1 Guidelines for using precedents

(a) Look for a precedent only after you have researched and planned your document.

(b) Always check that the precedent is up to date and legally correct.

(c) Adapt the precedent to your transaction, not your transaction to the precedent.

(d) Do not copy words from a precedent unless you are sure of their legal effect.

(e) Do not change words in a precedent unless you are sure that the change will not have an unexpected legal effect. This is particularly true of precedents for wills.

(f) Never assume a precedent cannot be improved.

(g) Do not copy clauses that are irrelevant or, worse, are to the disadvantage of your client;

(h) Do not adopt inappropriate or archaic wording.

1.4 DRAFTING

Having carefully planned the content and structure of your document, you can confidently begin to draft. Your document should be as easy as possible to read and understand. It is essential that everything you draft is precise and unambiguous. You should try to be as concise as possible. Concise documents are easier and quicker to read. Set out below are a number of rules and guidelines which can help you to keep your documents precise and concise.

1.4.1 Use definitions

A definition can do two things.

First, it can create a 'tag' or 'nickname'. This avoids repetition of lengthy names or phrases. This use is often seen in the description of parties to a document.

> **EXAMPLE**
>
> This agreement is made between
>
> (1) Everett Kingdom Finance plc ('Everett')
> (2) Samuel Luke Stowe ('SLS')

In the rest of the document it is only necessary to refer to Everett and SLS.

> **EXAMPLE**
>
> In this agreement
>
> 1. 'the Period of Hire' means from 9am on 1 November 2009 until noon on 23 November 2009.
>
> A subsequent clause might then say something such as 'if the Hirer does not return the Car at or before the end of the Period of Hire ...'.

Secondly, a definition can also create a private dictionary for the document by giving a word something other than its ordinary meaning, or by giving a word an unusually extended or restricted meaning.

> **EXAMPLE**
>
> In this agreement
>
> 'Boat' includes a sailboard.

1.4.1.1   Where to put the definitions

Definitions that are to apply throughout the document should be put in alphabetical order in a definitions clause at the start of the operative part of the document.

> **EXAMPLE**
> Definitions
> In this Agreement
> (1)   'Arbitration' means ...
> (2)   'Balance Sheet' means ... etc.

If a definition will be used only in one part of a document or in one clause, you can put the definition at the start of the relevant part or clause.

> **EXAMPLE**
> 4.1   In this clause, 'Promotional Material' means ...
> 4.2   The Landowner must ensure that all Promotional Material is ...

In a simple document, a 'tag' may be given to a name or phrase the first time that it is used, and the tag may then be used throughout the rest of the document. For example, in a contract for the sale of land, a clause may say:

> The Seller, for the benefit of his adjoining property, 10 Smith Avenue, Morton, N. Yorks ('the Retained Land') reserves a right of way on foot ...

Later clauses can then refer to the Retained Land.

This method should be used only for simple short documents. In a long document, it wastes time to have to search through the clauses to find the one in which the tag was first adopted.

1.4.1.2   Guidelines for using definitions

(a)   It is usual to give the definition a capital letter and to use it with the capital letter throughout the document. This alerts anybody reading it to the fact that a particular word or expression has been given a particular meaning by the document.

(b)   A definition should only define. It should not be used to create a substantive right or obligation. The right or obligation should be created in the clause that uses the definition.

(c)   If you have a definition, do not forget to use it when you are drafting the rest of the document.

(d)   When you use a defined term in a clause, check that it makes sense within the clause.

(e)   In a definition, do not define by reference to other, undefined terms.

1.4.2   Padding/superfluous words

Cut out unnecessary phrases which lengthen the sentence while adding nothing to its meaning. For example:

- 'in the circumstances';
- 'in this instance';
- 'the fact that';
- 'of course'.

1.4.3   Tautology

Tautology or saying the same thing twice using different words should be avoided. For example:

- 'unfilled vacancy';
- 'true facts';
- 'now current'.

Similarly, avoid excessive use of adjectives which do not make the meaning more precise. For example:

- 'grave and fatal error';
- 'careful and detailed consideration'.

1.4.4 Compound prepositions

Use single prepositions instead of compound prepositions. For example:

- 'in accordance with'   under/by
- 'by reason of'   by/through
- 'with reference to'   about
- 'in order to'   to

1.4.5 Nouns derived from verbs

Use the verb itself rather than a noun derived from it. This helps create a more immediate effect.

- 'make an admission' (admit);
- 'give consideration to' (consider);
- 'effect a termination' (terminate or end).

1.4.6 Archaic language

Twenty-first century documents should be drafted using contemporary language. Delete or replace archaic words and phrases such as:

- 'crave leave';
- 'the said';
- 'hereinbefore';
- 'aforementioned';
- 'whereof'.

1.4.7 Keep sentences and paragraphs short

In long sentences, the verb, subject and object may be separated by too many subclauses. This places a strain on the reader's memory and understanding. Always try to keep the sentence core together.

> **EXAMPLE**
>
> The evidence, including evidence from independent surveys as well as that gathered personally by the writers of this report and the results of investigations formally commissioned by this department, suggests that the public, while acknowledging an overall increase in the actual level of government spending on health, by which is meant on health care both at the doctor–patient level and in hospitals, still views the problems and defects in the National Health Service and in particular in National Health hospitals as the result of a general lack of funding.

The subclauses break up the main thought of the paragraph so that it is difficult to follow. The paragraph would be better rewritten in separate sentences with the main thought first, even though this may increase its length. Brackets may be used for subsidiary points where appropriate. For example:

> The evidence suggests that the public still views the problems and defects in the National Health Service and in particular in National Health hospitals as the result of a general lack of funding. This is so even though it acknowledges an overall increase in the actual level of government spending on health care both at the doctor–patient level and in hospitals. (Evidence on this issue includes evidence from independent surveys, that gathered personally by the writers of this report and the results of investigations formally commissioned by this department.)

1.4.8 Use the active and not the passive tense where possible

In a sentence where the verb is in the active voice, the subject of the sentence acts upon the object of the sentence. Where the verb is in the passive voice, the object of the sentence is acted upon by the subject. Compare:

> The defendant struck the claimant (active voice).

> The claimant was struck by the defendant (passive voice).

1.4.8.1 Problems with the passive

Over-use of the passive voice lengthens a sentence and can make it sound weak. In the worst cases, it obscures meaning. For example:

> It is hoped that resources will be relocated so that changes may be made in the methods by which the system is administered.

Where the verb is in the passive, you may accidentally omit the phrase which indicates who or what is doing the acting. For example:

> The claimant was struck.

In a legal context, the effect of this omission may be important. For example:

> Notice will be served. By whom?

> **EXERCISE 1**
>
> Try rewriting the following using the active tense.
>
> (i)   A final warning letter is to be written by the line manager.
> (ii)   The matter will be considered by the committee at the next meeting.
> (iii) Notice was given by the solicitor.

1.4.8.2 Some uses for the passive

The passive can sound more objective and detached, and therefore more appropriate in certain legal contexts. For example:

> The allegations are denied

sounds better than:

> Our client denies the allegations (which introduces a personal note).

It is correct to use the passive where the subject of the legal action is irrelevant. For example:

> The common seal of X Co was affixed ... It does not matter who affixed it.

The passive may also be used in a legal context to cover the possibility of action by a number of different persons, some of whom are unknown. For example:

> If the goods are damaged we will refund the cost. This could cover damage by the supplier, the carrier, or any third party.

1.4.9 Precision

It is particularly important to ensure that what you write is not ambiguous and expresses exactly your client's objectives. An ambiguous document may at best cause your client to have to make further enquiries; at worst it can result in an expensive dispute and litigation.

1.4.9.1 Ambiguity

Take care with word order

Words or phrases in the wrong place may create ambiguity. Consider the sentence:

> We undertake to repair or replace goods shown to be defective *within six months of the date of purchase*.

It is not clear whether the phrase in italics governs the repair/replacement or the notification of defect. It could be rewritten as:

> Where, within six months of the date of purchase, goods are shown to be defective, we will repair or replace them.

(assuming this was the intended meaning).

Do you mean 'and' or 'or'?

Consider:

> The Seller may serve notice of termination, recover goods already delivered and retain all instalments already paid.

The use of 'and' in this sentence suggests that the list is conjunctive, ie that the seller may do all of the things in it. But can he or she choose to do only some of them?

Compare:

> The Seller may serve notice of termination, recover goods already delivered or retain all instalments already paid.

The use of 'or' here suggests that the list is disjunctive, ie that the seller may do only one of the things in the list. But it could also mean that he or she might both serve notice and either recover goods or retain instalments.

To avoid such ambiguity, consider (depending on the meaning required) using phrases such as:

> The Seller may do all or any of the following:
>
> or
>
> The Seller may exercise one only of the following rights:

The 'undistributed middle'

Take care with provisions 'before/after' a particular date or 'over/under' a particular weight or measure. Consider the following examples:

> Where the company delivers the goods before 1 January ... /Where the company delivers the goods after 1 January ...

What happens if it delivers them *on* 1 January?

> Goods over 20kg must be sent by rail ... /Goods under 20kg may be sent by air

What about goods weighing *exactly* 20kg?

Expressions of time

Take care to avoid ambiguity. Consider:

> The Buyer must pay a deposit within 7 days of today's date.

Does the 7 days include or exclude today?

For legal and practical reasons, avoid expressing periods of time in the following ways:

- from [a date];
- by [a date];
- within [so many days of] or from [a date];
- until [a date].

It is safer to be clear by using one of the following:

- from but excluding/not including;
- from and including;
- on or after;
- on or before;
- within a period of 7 days commencing with;
- until but excluding/not including;
- until and including.

Are you creating an obligation or a discretion?

An obligation is created by the phrase:

> The Customer shall pay a deposit on signing this Agreement.

A discretion is created by the phrase:

> The Company may retain the deposit if the Customer does not collect the goods on or before 30 June.

Take care when using 'shall'. It is grammatically correct to use it in the third person to indicate an obligation ('the Tenant shall pay the Rent'), but it is also used in the first person to indicate simple future ('I shall go to London'). Alternatively, you could use 'must' to create an obligation.

Avoid words of similar sound or appearance

Words of similar sound or appearance are easily confused and may also confuse a lay client. For example:

Avoid	*Use instead*
'mortgagee/mortgagor'	'lender/borrower'
'lessor/lessee'	'landlord/tenant'

Ambiguous pronouns

Consider:

> Where the Supplier fails to deliver the Goods to the Customer in accordance with Clause 9 or the Goods delivered do not correspond with the sample he may terminate this Agreement.

Who may terminate the agreement?

Where it is not clear to which noun a pronoun refers, the noun should be repeated.

The ejusdem generis rule

Consider:

> In consequence of war, disturbance or any other cause.

Unless a contrary intention appears, 'any other cause' will be construed as meaning only causes in the same category as those previously listed.

To avoid ambiguity, add (as appropriate):

> whether of the same kind as [the causes] previously listed or not
>
> or
>
> or any other [cause] provided it is of the same kind as the [causes] previously listed.

1.4.9.2   Shall/will

In the first person, 'shall' simply looks to the future. In the second and third person, 'will' looks to the future.

> I shall interview the client tomorrow. I hope that you will sit in. Afterwards we shall discuss the problem and consider the next steps.

In the first person, 'will' expresses determination. In the second or third person, 'shall' expresses determination or obligation.

> I will make you do this.
>
> The Buyer shall pay £500 on 1 December.

This means that you create problems if your document says 'the Buyer will pay ...'. Is this what he or she intends to do, or is it what he or she is obligated to do?

Many documents use expressions such as, 'If the Company shall breach this term ...'. The clause is looking to the future but is using 'shall' incorrectly. It could be redrafted to say, 'In the event of the company breaking ...'. Better still, 'If the Company breaks ...'.

1.4.10   Layout and presentation

Use the layout and presentation of your document to enhance its readability and usefulness. Use headings and bullet points to break up text. Use diagrams, tables, colours and different fonts where they are necessary or helpful. Where a document is likely to be annotated, leave wide margins and use double spacing. For many court documents there are very detailed requirements as to how you should present your document. Check that you have followed any relevant rules/guidelines. For example, under the Civil Procedure Rules (PD 32) it is recommended that witness statements should be 'produced on durable quality A4 paper with a 3.5cm margin'.

1.4.10.1   Paragraphs

Using paragraphs makes prose more readable and helps to avoid cumbersome clauses and subclauses. Always number your paragraphs if possible as this aids navigation and will help anyone using the document.

1.4.10.2   Tabulation

Tabulation aids clarity and can help to avoid ambiguity. Consider the sentence:

> Any trainee solicitor is entitled to paid leave to attend a conference, lecture, or seminar *provided by The Law Society.*

How much of the sentence is the phrase in italics intended to qualify? Does it apply only to 'seminar', or to 'conference' and 'lecture' as well?

Compare:

> Any trainee solicitor is entitled to paid leave to attend:
>
> (a)   a conference; or
>
> (b)   a lecture; or

(c)   a seminar,

provided by The Law Society.

Care should be taken, however, not to indent the final phrase 'provided by The Law Society' to the same margin as 'a seminar' or the ambiguity would remain.

A useful basic rule is that any sentence longer than three lines is a good candidate for tabulation if it includes a compound or series.

1.4.10.3   Numbering

Where a series of points is being made, numbering may improve clarity and aid later cross-referencing.

Examples of numbering systems:

4.5.1   The system adopted in this book and known as the decimal system.

4(5)(a)(i)   A system based on the legislative approach and known as the alphanumeric system.

4.5(a)(i)   A combination system using elements of both decimal and alphanumeric systems.

1.4.11   Jargon

Jargon is a broad term and may include specialised language of a professional, occupational or other group which is often meaningless to outsiders. It may also include slang. While jargon can be a useful professional shorthand, it should never be used where it might obscure meaning.

EXAMPLE

- *Bilateral probital hematoma*   medical terminology for a black eye
- *Ab initio*   Latin/legal terminology for 'at the beginning'
- HTH, *web cookie*   computer/Internet jargon for 'Hope this Helps', and the name for a small text file that is sent to your computer via your web browser when you visit certain websites

---

Similarly, avoid using acronyms which might be unfamiliar or have several different meanings, eg CPR (Civil Procedure Rules, cardiopulmonary resuscitation, Canadian Pacific Railway, etc).

If appropriate, consider providing a plain English translation of any legal or technical terms. It is worth noting that in June 2006 the Coroner Reform Bill became the first Bill to feature a plain English translation alongside every legal clause.

1.5   CHECKING

Always check your work.

(a)   If possible leave the document for a while and then come back to it.

(b)   Ideally get someone else to check it.

(c)   Reading the document aloud can be a good way of identifying mistakes/poorly-drafted material.

(d)   Print out your work and read from hard copy rather than trying to check it on screen.

(e)   Do not read from the beginning of the document. Try starting from the middle or towards the end. The later parts of documents tend to be less familiar and less well checked.

(f)   Always confirm names, figures, dates, addresses and page numbers.

(g)   Do not rely on automated spelling or grammar checks.

(h)   Check all cross-references in the document to other clauses or to schedules.

(i)   Above all check that your document reflects your client's objectives.

1.6   PRACTICAL AND ETHICAL CONSIDERATIONS

1.6.1   Good practice when submitting a draft

Out of courtesy, you should always supply to the other side an additional copy of any draft sent for approval.

1.6.2   Good practice when amending the other side's draft

Make sure that all amendments are clearly identifiable.

1.6.3   Ethical considerations when negotiating a draft

The SRA Code of Conduct sets out the principles of professional conduct which apply to all aspects of practice and includes the requirement to:

(a)   act with integrity; and

(b)   behave in a way that maintains the trust the public places in you and in the provision of legal services.

Breach of these rules renders the solicitor liable to disciplinary action.

Do not attempt to mislead the other side by concealing amendments you have made to their draft, for example by writing a covering letter which draws attention to some amendments and not to others. Any deliberate attempt to mislead could be criminally fraudulent as well as amounting to professional misconduct.

Do not attempt to take advantage of a mistake made by the other side. Point it out to them. They may otherwise be able to claim rectification of the document to incorporate an omitted provision or to allege that the agreement is a nullity, so enabling them to resist specific performance.

1.6.4   Female addressees

Where possible, try to find out a woman's preferred form of address in advance, for example 'Miss', 'Mrs' or 'Ms'. As an alternative some writers use the addressee's full name, eg 'Dear Sarah Wills'.

1.6.5   Gender neutral language

Use gender neutral language where possible. There are several techniques that may be used to make your writing gender neutral. Words which imply gender, eg workman, chairman, policeman, may simply be replaced with gender-neutral words such as worker, chair or chairperson, police officer. Gender specific pronouns (he or his) may be replaced by the nouns they represent, or by the use of 'he or she' or 'his or her' or the plural, or by replacing with the, *a* or *an*.

EXERCISE 2

Rewrite the following using gender neutral language.

(i)   A businessman should exercise caution when extending his financial liabilities.

(ii)   The draftsman must use his skills to write concisely.

(iii)   A good statesman is able to make his points clear and assert his authority.

1.7   WRITING LETTERS

1.7.1   Who is the addressee?

Consider the needs of the reader and try to adapt your style accordingly.

1.7.1.1   The lay client

Avoid jargon and legalese when writing to a lay client. Explain all unfamiliar terms, but do not patronise. How familiar is the client with the subject?

1.7.1.2   The business client and other professionals

The business client will generally be familiar with solicitors' letters. Avoid padding and get to the point quickly. Where necessary, explain legal terminology or process.

1.7.1.3   Other solicitors

What kind of matter are you dealing with? Are you writing from a position of strength or weakness? Do you want to adopt a conciliatory or non-conciliatory stance? Consider which is more likely to persuade the addressee. Remember that the other solicitor may send a copy of your letter to his or her client.

1.7.2   'Ghosting'

You may be asked to write letters to be signed in a partner's own name. Read the file and consider the partner's style. Check how well the partner knows the addressee; for example, if you are writing to a client, is the partner on first-name terms with him or her?

1.7.3   Starting and ending the letter

Letters beginning 'Dear Sirs/Sir/Madam' all end 'Yours faithfully'.

A letter addressed to a person by surname, for example 'Dear Mr Smith', ends with 'Yours sincerely'.

A letter beginning 'Dear John' may end with 'Yours sincerely' or 'Yours'.

1.7.4   Content

1.7.4.1   Consider overall structure

An initial heading identifying the matter is conventional. For example:

> **Sale of 25 Acacia Avenue, Bristol**

A complex letter will be easier to understand (and reply to) if you give each paragraph a number and a heading.

1.7.4.2   Form and style

If you are writing in the firm's name (eg, a formal letter to the other side), write in the first person plural ('we') and be consistent.

Acknowledge the addressee's last communication.

If it is your first letter to the addressee, explain your involvement.

State the purpose of the letter.

Carry out that purpose using:

- logical sequence;
- separate paragraphs;
- short sentences;
- active voice.

Write in a restrained tone. Avoid overemphasis (eg, unnecessary adverbs – 'totally unhappy', 'completely inaccurate'). Use exclamation marks sparingly. Do not express surprise, amazement, outrage, etc.

Avoid jokes and witticisms.

1.7.5 Some practical points

1.7.5.1 Second thoughts and improvements

- Try to be detached about your document.
- How would it sound if read out in open court in the future?
- Try not to write a letter in anger or when emotional. If you do, do not post it until you have had a chance to re-read it or a colleague has reviewed it.
- Consider giving a deadline for a reply (eg, if the matter is urgent or if the letter might be unwelcome).
- If you have asked a client to do something, make sure your instructions are clear. Consider ending with a list or table summarising the action points.
- Check the grammar and spelling.

1.7.5.2 Final checks

Check that the letter:

- carries the correct references (ie, yours and those of the other side);
- is dated;
- is signed;
- is accompanied by the right enclosures;
- is put into the right envelope, and is properly addressed.

1.8 WRITING REPORTS AND MEMORANDA

1.8.1 Reports

1.8.1.1 Purpose

Reports usually cover a specific subject and serve a particular purpose. In the office, you may have to write a report on some legal research or fact-finding you have been asked to undertake.

1.8.1.2 Is your research complete?

Consider whether you have all the necessary information and identify any gaps.

1.8.1.3 Edit your material

Consider how much information should go into the report. Brevity increases the likelihood of the report being read, but too little information and your conclusions may not be adequately supported and the document may be less persuasive.

1.8.1.4 Planning your report

Plan the text of your report carefully to produce a logical argument.

Consider what will be the most useful structure for the reader. For example, if you were asked to answer specific questions, could you use these to head paragraphs of your report?

Consider including:

- a contents page or an index;
- an introduction explaining why the report was commissioned;

- a brief summary of the report before the main text for quick reference;
- diagrams (if relevant);
- case or statute references (if relevant);
- a bibliography;
- appendices;
- acknowledgements of sources of information.

1.8.1.5   Style

For whom are you writing? Adapt your style appropriately.

Think about whether you should paraphrase or explain your source material, or whether you can reproduce it word for word.

1.8.1.6   Layout and presentation

Make sure the report is well set out, with clear headings and numbered paragraphs and subparagraphs if appropriate.

Is it to be used as a discussion document? If so, consider having it printed double-spaced with wide margins to leave room for annotation.

1.8.1.7   Final checks

Print the report and read it through carefully, amending and rewriting where necessary.

Check that you have:

- done what you were asked to do;
- identified any relevant options;
- reached a conclusion.

1.8.2   Memoranda

1.8.2.1   Types of memoranda

Solicitors generally have to write two types of memoranda:

- attendance notes (as a record of their meetings or telephone calls with clients, other solicitors, etc);
- internal memoranda (as a quick way of communicating with others in the firm).

1.8.2.2   Attendance notes

Attendance notes are put on a file as a record of an oral discussion, transaction or agreement and must be clear and accurate in case of any later dispute.

They are essential for anyone who takes over a file and was not present for the meeting, telephone call, etc.

They may also be needed when a client's bill is prepared as part of the record of chargeable time spent on the matter.

Write your attendance note as soon as possible after the event when everything is fresh in your mind and you are less likely to have forgotten something.

Always try to take contemporaneous notes – in a simple case, you can put them straight on the file. For more complicated matters, you can use your notes to compile your attendance note, but do not destroy them: they are important additional evidence in any dispute.

An attendance note should normally contain the following:

- the client's name;

- the subject matter;
- your reference;
- the date;
- the place (of any meeting);
- the people present (at a meeting);
- the starting and finishing times (of the meeting or phone call);
- a summary of what was discussed or agreed;
- any follow-up action to be taken by you or others.

If your attendance note records an important decision or agreement, always confirm it by letter to avoid misunderstandings.

1.8.2.3   Internal memoranda

Keep internal memoranda brief and business-like, but take care with the tone. If a memo sounds curt, you may cause offence to the recipient.

The format required is generally as follows:

MEMORANDUM

From:

To:

Fee earner's reference:

Date:

Client's name:

Client's matter:

Most firms use printed forms on which these headings already appear.

1.9   SPELLING AND GRAMMAR

Poor spelling and grammar will undermine the authority of anything that you write. Poor grammar is at best distracting and likely to leave a poor impression. At worst it may alter the meaning of a document and render it ineffective. The following exercises allow you to test your grammar. If you find that you have scored poorly then refresh your understanding using any of the books contained in the further reading section or using one of the many Internet resources on grammar which are freely available (eg, www.bbc.co.uk/skillswise/words/grammar/).

EXERCISE 3

Spelling

Which one of the following is correctly spelt?

(i)	acomodation	accommodation	accomodation
(ii)	unneccessary	unneccesary	unnecessary
(iii)	privilege	priviledge	privelige
(iv)	embarrass	embarras	embarass
(v)	professor	proffessor	profesor

Apostrophes

Add apostrophes where necessary in the following sentences:

(i)   Whos likely to be delayed by a few minutes of rain?

(ii)   Weve always valued both the local Gardening Institutes lectures.

(iii)   Im sure he said its a ten oclock train we need to catch.

(iv)   The childrens enjoyment of the fair was greater than ours.

(v)   The girls football shirts hung on pegs in the cloakrooms main aisle.

Other punctuation

Add a comma or full stop beneath the *:

(i)   MARY DAVENPORT WRITES WELL * HOWEVER, LUCIEN GRANT HATES WRITING.

(ii)   MY PRINCIPAL AREA OF SPECIALITY IS TAX * MY SECOND SPECIALITY IS FINANCE.

Add full stops and capital letters to:

(iii)   The trainee was quite clear that he needed to work harder if he wanted to get taken on it was quite possible for the firm to hire all the trainees that year his friend had already been given an indication that he would be offered a job and he had been working really long hours.

Add commas to:

(iv)   Edward O'Grady however always wanted to surf the Internet rather than do his work.

(v)   The solicitor walked up to his office opened the door took off his coat and slumped into his chair.

(vi)   For business meetings the firm offered tea coffee water fruit juices biscuits and sandwiches.

Add semi-colons to:

(vii)   I read the Legal Times before work every day it keeps me on top of changes in the law.

(viii) The employer wrote to the employee to complain about his time keeping workers ought to know that starting work on time is essential.

EXERCISE 4

(a)   Identify the errors in the following paragraph.

(b)   Then try rewriting the paragraph using the rules and recommendations set out in this chapter.

I am writing with reference to your enquiry concerning the use of the entrance area and hallway at the gallery for the purpose of displaying informational materials and presenting visual displays on the subject of recycling. In the circumstances the central question will be whether the internal content origins and visual qualities of the material hereinbefore mentioned are to be felt to be appropriate after due consideration has be given by the Gallery Board, such permissions are at the sole dicretion of the board. The Boards decision concerning any such request will be made after it has met in session on the first Thursday of each calendar month and notification will be sent within 14 days of the said meeting.

ANSWERS TO EXERCISES

Exercise 1

Answers

(i)   The line manager will write a final warning letter.
(ii)   The committee will consider the matter at the next meeting.
(iii)   The solicitor gave notice.

Exercise 2

Answers

(i)   A business person should exercise caution when extending his/her financial liabilities.
        Business people should exercise caution when extending their financial liabilities.
(ii)   The drafter must use his/her skills to write concisely.
        Draftspersons must use their skills to write concisely.
(iii)   A good statesperson is able to make his or her points clear and assert authority.

Exercise 3

Spelling

Answers

(i)   accommodation
(ii)   unnecessary
(iii)   privilege
(iv)   embarrass
(v)   professor

Apostrophes

Answers

(i)   Who's likely to be delayed by a few minutes of rain?
(ii)   We've always valued both the local Gardening Institutes' lectures.
(iii)   I'm sure he said it's a ten o'clock train we need to catch.
(iv)   The children's enjoyment of the fair was greater than ours.
(v)   The girls' football shirts hung on pegs in the cloakroom's main aisle.

Other punctutation

Answers

Add a comma or full stop beneath the *:

(i)   MARY DAVENPORT WRITES WELL. HOWEVER, LUCIEN GRANT HATES WRITING.
(ii)   MY PRINCIPAL AREA OF SPECIALITY IS TAX. MY SECOND SPECIALITY IS FINANCE.

Add full stops and capital letters to:

(iii)   The trainee was quite clear that he needed to work harder if he wanted to get taken on. It was quite possible for the firm to hire all the trainees that year. His friend had already been given an indication that he would be offered a job and he had been working really long hours.

Add commas to:

(iv)   Edward O'Grady, however, always wanted to surf the Internet rather than do his work.

(v)   The solicitor walked up to his office, opened the door, took off his coat and slumped into his chair.

(vi)   For business meetings, the firm offered tea, coffee, water, fruit juices, biscuits and sandwiches.

Add semi-colons to:

(vii) I read the Legal Times before work every day; it keeps me on top of changes in the law.

(viii) The employer wrote to the employee to complain about his time keeping; workers ought to know that starting work on time is essential.

Exercise 4

Answers

I am writing <u>with reference to</u> your enquiry concerning the use of the entrance area and hallway at the gallery for <u>the purpose of displaying informational materials and presenting visual displays</u> on the subject of recycling. <u>In the circumstances</u> the central question will be whether the internal <u>content origins</u> and visual qualities of the material <u>hereinbefore mentioned</u> are <u>to be felt to be</u> appropriate after due <u>consideration has be given</u> by the Gallery Board, such permissions are at the sole <u>dicretion</u> of the <u>board</u>. The <u>Boards</u> decision concerning any such request will be made after it has met in session on the first Thursday of each calendar month and notification will be sent within <u>14 days of the said meeting</u>.

- The structure of the paragraph is confusing and illogical, eg we are told the criteria for decisions before we are told who has authority to make them.
- The provision relating to time is ambiguous.
- Sentences are too long, use archaic terminology and unnecessarily complicated words and phrases, eg 'informational materials', 'hereinbefore mentioned'.
- There are numerous padding words and phrases and compound prepositions, eg 'with reference to'.
- There are spelling and grammatical errors.
- The paragraph uses archaic terminology.
- The paragraph uses the passive tense.

The overall effect of these errors is to make the paragraph difficult to understand and pompous in tone.

Set out below is an example of how the paragraph might be rewritten.

> 'I am writing about your request to use the entrance area and hallway at the Gallery for a display about recycling. Permission to mount a display is given by the Gallery Board ("the Board") which meets on the first Thursday of each month. The Board will decide whether the quality and content of the material is appropriate. The Board will let you know its decision within 2 weeks of and including the date of the meeting.'

The original paragraph was 120 words. The paragraph above which contains the same information is only 76 words. It is also easier to read and understand.

PART II

PRACTICAL LEGAL RESEARCH

CHAPTER 2

INTRODUCTION TO PRACTICAL LEGAL RESEARCH

LEARNING OUTCOMES

After reading this chapter you will be able to:

- explain how legal research is used in a practical context
- understand how to approach a problem presented by a client
- identify the key stages in analysing a problem
- describe the importance of selecting appropriate search terms
- understand the significance of recording your research methods
- identify how to update your research in different sources.

2.1 WHY SHOULD I READ THIS SECTION?

In a nutshell, you should read this section because trainees spend a large proportion of their time engaged in legal research. Strong research skills are therefore highly valued by firms.

You may be convinced that you can already carry out research effectively as a result of previous study. In an academic context, that may well be true. Undoubtedly at some time you will have located and summarised a primary source of law. You may also have compiled long and detailed essays on legislative history, or analysed opposing learned opinions on a contentious legal topic. These sorts of experiences are useful. But on their own they do not equip you to research the law effectively as a solicitor. The following chapters will build on your existing skills, by shifting the focus from academic to practical application.

2.2 THE ROLE OF LEGAL RESEARCH IN THE OFFICE

Law firms exist to make money. They generate fees by selling the time that lawyers spend on solving clients' problems. Practical legal research is a particularly important step in this larger process.

In a law firm, legal research entails the ability to produce work that is:

- accurate;
- timely;
- up-to-date;
- carried out efficiently;
- commercially aware;
- presented in an appropriate and succinct form.

The focus on timeliness and efficiency in the commercial world requires a shift in mindset from the academic environment, where students often have several weeks to complete a piece of research. For practising lawyers, time really is money.

In addition, many students expect that other support staff will be on hand to carry out the spadework of research when their careers get underway. The reality is very different. Bluntly, a principal task of trainees is to carry out legal research on behalf of other fee earners! So your ability to impress the people for whom you conduct research will be a key factor in whether you succeed or fail in your career as a solicitor. Therefore the time and effort you invest in learning how to research effectively on the LPC will pay dividends from the earliest stage of your training contract.

2.3 PROBLEM-SOLVING

The main purpose of a lawyer's skills and knowledge is to bridge the gap between a client's actual circumstances and what the client wants them to be: in other words, to solve clients' problems.

At any one time, a solicitor is likely to deal with a variety of case files presented by clients who are diverse in background and personality. Unsurprisingly, the problems that clients present to solicitors tend to be complex and difficult. They may have multiple strands. Often there will be a range of possible solutions, some legal and some non-legal. Each client's circumstances will generate a different set of time pressures. For all these reasons, especially for the novice, it is sensible to adopt a logical framework for problem-solving. The following model sets out such a framework.

2.3.1 Problem analysis model

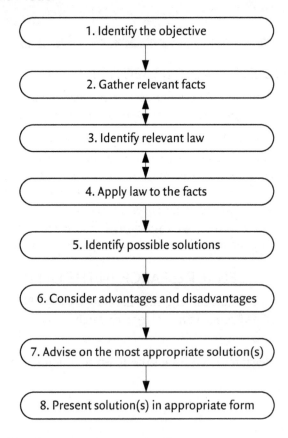

We shall now consider these steps in more detail.

Stage 1.   Identify the objective

You must clearly establish the client's objectives by discussing the circumstances that prompted him or her to seek legal advice. It is important to remember that what the client wants to achieve must drive your approach to solving legal problems (in so far, of course, as regulatory and professional conduct rules allow). Focus your preliminary discussion on the client's objectives, and then keep them at the centre of your thinking.

Stage 2.   Gather relevant facts

The client may begin with a brief explanation of his or her circumstances. You should then ask questions to obtain all the facts that may be relevant to the process of tackling the problem in order to achieve his or her objectives. Lateral thinking is a useful technique at this stage: continually review in your mind any gaps in the client's account that might hamper a rigorous legal analysis.

You will often need to gather more facts from a range of other sources besides the client. This may include:

- other participants in the matter (such as witnesses or police officers);
- documents (such as witness statements or photographs);
- experts (such as surveyors or forensic scientists);
- other lawyers (perhaps more experienced colleagues or even the solicitor for the opposing party, for example if rules oblige him or her to disclose certain documents in the course of litigation).

This phase will inevitably generate large volumes of documents, in both paper and electronic form. It is vital to have processes in place at the beginning to manage this material in an orderly way.

Stage 3.   Identify relevant law

Now you should begin to narrow your focus by highlighting those facts that will help you investigate possible solutions to the client's problem.

A series of legal issues will arise from these key facts. These will tend to divide into issues of substantive law and issues of procedure. You may already have a good grasp of the issues in the area of law in question, or the area may be outside your usual field of practice. In either case, you are likely to need to undertake further research.

Note that double arrows link stages 2 and 3 in the model. This is because they are inter-dependent. Researching the relevant law may well prompt further questions, so that you may need to go back to the client to ask for more information. Retracing your steps is nothing to worry about. The key thing is to avoid jumping to conclusions on the basis of insufficient knowledge of either the facts or the law.

Stage 4.   Apply law to the facts

In stages 2 and 3 the aim has been to build a full picture of all the possibilities of both fact and law. Now the aim is to narrow the focus by applying the law to the material facts. This phase requires the same techniques of analysis and evaluation that judges use to decide disputes. However, remember that your client's interest in the law is limited to how it relates to his or her particular circumstances. He or she is not interested in lofty statements of the law in general.

Note once again in the model that a double arrow links this stage to the previous one. Reassess regularly and be prepared to be flexible as you work between facts and law; you may well need to take a step back before progressing.

Stage 5.   Identify possible solutions

When you have established clearly the relationship of facts and law, a range of potential solutions should begin to emerge. This phase is again one of expanding options: you should try to ensure that no alternative is missed.

The technique of brainstorming can be useful: allocate a set period of time to thinking creatively and trying to generate as many solutions as possible, even solutions that seem impractical at first glance. This works well as a group activity.

Always consider the possibility of doing nothing. For example, it may be worth waiting to see what action another party may take first, or it may even be worth ignoring the problem if you have reason to expect that it will resolve itself. Sometimes a client will seek advice if he or she anticipates a problem, for example an employer may have dismissed an employee who has indicated that he intends to challenge the dismissal. In such a case it would be worth waiting to see if the employee actually does bring a challenge, rather than taking any immediate action.

Stage 6.   Consider advantages and disadvantages

Having listed all possible solutions, weigh each in terms of potential rewards and potential risks. The client's circumstances will clearly influence your analysis. Different options may carry different financial or emotional costs (for example the stress of going to court). The requirements of external regulators and the rules of professional conduct should also determine your thinking.

Some options you may eliminate at once as wholly unworkable or inappropriate. For others, this process of evaluation may be technically demanding and complex, calling for a high level of expertise and even some intuition. As a junior lawyer it will often therefore be necessary to confer with more experienced colleagues, either informally or as part of a practice team.

Stage 7.   Advise on the most appropriate solution(s)

You should now be in a position to advise on which one or more solutions will best fulfil the client's objectives. Be prepared to outline the varying costs and benefits in detail, especially the risks of things going wrong, the consequences of that outcome, and options for limiting risk.

Stage 8.   Present solution(s) in appropriate form

To end the process, you need to report the fruits of your labour. Remember to tailor your report to the recipient. This may be the client in person. If so, the client will not need all the details of your research. He or she will want practical legal solutions. More likely early in your professional life, it will be your supervising solicitor to whom you will provide a written report. He or she will then use your analysis to advise the client.

It may be useful to involve the client as early as possible in the process of sifting different courses of action. The final decision on what to do, of course, lies with the client.

2.4   PRINCIPLES OF PRACTICAL LEGAL RESEARCH

The remainder of Part II of this book will focus on the mechanics of research in legal practice. The research process underpins all of the stages in the problem-solving model. It entails finding and reporting the material that is relevant to solving a legal problem in the quickest possible time. There is no magic formula that will enable you to do this. As with all skills, it has to be learnt, and practice is the only way to build competence. As a student, you have time and resources to explore and practice that will not be available to you after your career begins: make the most of this opportunity. It is also worth noting that reading about legal research is not the easiest way to learn it. When reading the next few chapters, if possible try the examples given, use the legal databases and practise using the printed sources if you have access to a law library.

The following general principles should guide your research.

2.4.1 Devise search terms carefully

In order to exploit any legal source, you must devise appropriate search terms. These are often known as 'keywords'. They are words or phrases that enable you to find the relevant law to help find a solution to your client's legal problem. You may need to look up these keywords in a printed index, or type them into a database search engine. It is worth spending time on getting the right keywords as effective keywords will help you pinpoint the relevant area of law, saving time and ensuring you find the correct information.

When starting their research, many people make the mistake of being too specific about the information they are searching for. A particularly common mistake is to attempt to find precedent which exactly matches the detailed facts of the problem.

EXAMPLE

Imagine that your supervisor has a client who is complaining that she has ordered a 3D television from a shop but the shop has delivered an inferior model. The supervisor asks you to investigate possible remedies. One way of tackling this problem is to do a keyword search using the word 'televisions'. This is not the best way of going about the search. A better approach is to think in legal concepts and to research the underlying law that might be relevant. So the more experienced researcher would probably start his or her search with keywords such as:

- contract remedies;
- sale of goods;
- unfair terms in consumer contracts.

The published version of cases or statutes will use words preferred by the judge or draftsperson. These may be different from the words you would have chosen yourself in considering that area of law. Think along the lines of terms that lawyers might use; a legal dictionary may be useful in this respect. Be accurate. Beware slang, which is unlikely to appear in formal legal documents. Expand any abbreviations. Consider possible synonyms: all the alternative words that might describe the same concept or item or activity. Also consider different terms that may be used in European Union (EU) law. For example, in official EU documents, a bank is commonly referred to as a 'credit institution'.

The following table lists possible alternative keywords that might arise out of different sorts of legal problems:

Problem	Example
Alternative expressions for the same legal concept or topic	**employment** or **labour**
Alternative English and Latin expressions	**stare decisis** or **precedent**
Synonyms used to describe non-technical terms	**buyer and seller** or **purchaser and vendor**
Broader and narrower terms which may have been used to construct the source (ie case or statute)	**tort – negligence – professional negligence – medical negligence – psychiatric damage**
Related terms	**immigration** and **nationality** **competition** and **monopolies**
Changes in terminology over time	**exclusion clauses** or **exemption clauses**
Abbreviations	**BBC** or **British Broadcasting Corporation**

2.4.2   Knowing where to look

You might now be thinking that you have to have considerable knowledge about the relevant areas of law before beginning a piece of research. This is not the case. The key to success lies not in knowing the law, but in knowing where to find it.

As a general rule, start with a source which gives a general overview of the law in a certain area. A useful starting point in this regard is *Halsbury's Laws of England* (see **4.2**). Key practitioner texts and academic textbooks are possible alternatives. These texts which provide commentary on the law are often referred to as secondary sources.

Once you have a broad grasp of the relevant law, you should consider moving on to a second layer of research tools: those which contain the primary sources. Primary sources are the raw materials of the law, such as statutes, statutory instruments and case law. Many researchers are nervous about using primary sources. There is no need to be. Although sometimes the language is difficult, primary sources are essential to your research. This is because they contain authoritative statements of what the law actually is, rather than what a commentator thinks the law is, or what it should be.

It is worth remembering that there are hundreds of different sources of legal information. Some are in paper form; some are in online form; some exist in both. Each source has different strengths and weaknesses. The following sections of this book will familiarise you with some of the main sources. Think carefully about which source to use for a particular problem. If you choose the wrong information tool, the research job will take far longer and your results may be inaccurate.

2.4.3   Using indexes

The most effective way to access the information content in a source is to use an index. Most sources (paper and online) will have one or more 'tables of primary sources', and a 'subject index'. A table of primary sources is an index that helps you to locate cases, statutes or statutory instruments appearing in a work. It is also useful for completing or correcting a flawed citation. Arrangement may be alphabetical or chronological. A subject index helps you to locate commentary on specific areas of the law. Often this commentary will refer to primary sources, either in the text itself or in footnotes.

Using a subject index in a paper source is an acquired skill. Look at any index to see how it is arranged. There may be tiered entries in this form:

county court

> jurisdiction
>> extent

The broad topic, **county court**, appears first. Subsequent entries are progressively more specific. To make best use of the index, you need to look up the most specific keyword that will lead to the answer to your problem. A good index will offer a variety of terms, including cross-references (that is, references between terms of similar meaning). However, choosing the right term will always involve a process of elimination and some inspired guesswork.

Online databases often allow you to search for terms appearing anywhere in a source. In other words, their 'subject index' is not a separate component as in a book. Instead it comprises every word appearing in the source. It is tempting to rely on this facility, known as a 'free text' search. However, it can generate large numbers of irrelevant results (for example, instances where your search term happens to appear in discussion of a different subject). For a better signal:noise ratio, it is usually more effective to search within a particular field of the documents in an online source, such as 'case party' or 'keywords' in a database of law reports.

Searching an online database also requires you to be alert to possible synonyms. For example, if you search for **employment law** but the preferred term used in the source is **labour law**, the database may return zero results even though there is actually plenty of coverage of the subject. If your initial search fails, think of alternative terms which may be preferred by the source you are using.

2.4.4 Record the research trail

When conducting legal research in practice, one or more of the following three things will often happen:

(a)   The facts available to you might change, requiring the conclusions drawn from a piece of research to be reviewed.

(b)   Your supervisor may want to check your work.

(c)   The client or the court may want proof that the work you are charging for has actually been done.

For these and other reasons, it is vital to record the progress of your research and the methods used to locate information very carefully, and using the correct citations.

2.4.5 Update your information

The law changes constantly. A new Act of Parliament or a judgment by the Supreme Court can reverse lawyers' received wisdom on an issue overnight. You must therefore take steps to make sure that the law you cite in the course of your research is as up-to-date as possible.

Consider what sorts of developments are most likely to have occurred in your area of interest. For example, is it likely that relevant new legislation has recently been enacted? Is it an area that generates a large volume of case law, affecting the status of earlier decisions or affecting the interpretation of a statute? Is it an area where the law is liable to change by way of statutory instrument? A thorough update will encompass all these possibilities, but the efficient researcher will check the most likely developments first.

PROFESSIONAL CONDUCT POINT

Solicitors have a duty to base their advice to clients on legal knowledge that is current as well as thorough. In order to give sound advice, you must keep yourself abreast of recent developments. Updating your research must therefore become a matter of routine. Update even when a source seems to provide a satisfactory answer.

Subsequent chapters will outline the mechanics of how to update the information in particular sources. However, the following broad principles should be borne in mind:

(a)   Different sources deal with the problem of currency in different ways. Many paper sources are published in 'looseleaf' format, for example, so that selected pages can be swapped on a regular basis. The title page at the front of the work will usually provide a publication date.

(b)   Do not assume that online sources are wholly up-to-date – they can be subject to editorial delays.

(c)   Note the publication date of every source that you cite in your research (often online databases are continually updated and so have no static 'publication date'; in this case, note the date that you carried out your search).

(d)   Check whether the source states a cut-off date (again this may not be explicit in relation to a database; look for links labelled 'information', or an 'i' icon).

(e)   Stay with a source until you have exhausted its value (for example, if you find relevant information in a practitioner text, check whether an updating supplement exists).

(f)   Learn how to use updating resources (for example, case and legislation citators).

(g)   When you switch from one source to another, always compare the scope of the content; look for an explanatory preface, a database user guide or an online help facility.

(h)   Continue to make methodical notes of new information as the research progresses, including full citations and references.

Current Law is a useful general updating source. The paper version comprises several components; all of the content is also available as part of the *Westlaw* subscription database. The different uses of *Current Law* will be described in the context of different research tasks in subsequent chapters.

2.4.6   Presenting your findings in an appropriate format

You should present your findings in writing where possible. It is important to remember that your supervisor is undoubtedly a busy person. You will soon learn how he or she likes reports to be presented, but it is safe to assume that he or she will not thank you for producing armfuls of law reports and statutes without at least attempting to draw some conclusions from your research. Whatever structure you adopt, it is always a good idea to put a summary of your findings at the top of the report, and to reference your sources clearly and consistently. Reporting your findings is discussed in more detail in **Chapter 9**.

2.4.7   Know when to stop and ask

With so much law out there, it is sometimes very difficult to spot that you have found the correct answer when it is right in front of you. Remember what was said right at the beginning of this chapter about accuracy and efficiency. Getting the correct answer is very important; however, so is making the most efficient use of your time. If you think that you have found the correct answer, or if you are getting stuck, then stop the research and go back to your supervisor with what you have done so far. Do not be afraid to ask for guidance; it is what your supervisor is there for! Also bear in mind the expertise of the librarians in your organisation. They are there to help and will be happy to advise you about choosing sources, or about the mechanics of how to exploit a particular source.

SUMMARY – TIPS FOR SUCCESS

(a)   Analyse the client's problem(s) carefully so that you are clear about his or her objectives.

(b)   Devise search terms based on relevant legal concepts.

(c)   Select the most appropriate research tool, and learn to use different tools and their indexes properly – do not cut corners.

(d)   Always update your information.

(e)   Present the information in an appropriate form.

(f)   Do not be afraid to ask for help.

ONLINE VERSUS PRINTED SOURCES

LEARNING OUTCOMES

After reading this chapter you will be able to:

- outline the advantages of both printed and online sources
- understand how to access legal resources online
- identify effective database search techniques
- explain the pros and cons of legal information available via free Internet sites.

3.1 INTRODUCTION

Legal information is available in paper and online versions. Sometimes the same resource is available in both formats. When carrying out your research, the resources you choose to use and their format will depend upon what sources are available to you.

Online versions via subscription databases such as *Westlaw* or *LexisLibrary* may be more up-to-date. They allow you to search quickly and print or download your results. Another advantage is that you can usually access them from anywhere, provided you have internet access.

However, printed materials continue to play a key role in research carried out in legal practice. Cost may be a limiting factor, particularly for smaller firms (subscriptions to databases are expensive). Also, it remains the case that some significant sources have no full digital equivalent (for example *The Digest*, a comprehensive encyclopedia of case law).

Students are often sceptical about this, and prefer online research, but you need to learn how to use a range of sources in paper as well as electronic format to become a competent legal researcher. Quality of information content is the most important consideration. If you have a choice, you may find it useful to use both formats. Perhaps start with a printed secondary resource (such as *Halsbury's Laws of England* or a practitioner work) to give you an overview of a subject and identify the key legislation and cases. Then move on to an online database to find and update those primary sources.

3.2 ADVANTAGES OF PRINTED SOURCES

(a) Straightforward to access (no need for passwords or training in search software).

(b) Easy on the eye (many people do not like to read more than a couple of pages of information on screen).

(c)   Costs associated with electronic information can be high.

(d)   Not affected by technological failure.

(e)   Convenience (for example, quick reference/to mark up a personal copy/to read on the train home).

(f)   Easy to compare two or more sources at the same time.

(g)   Easy to scan/browse by 'flicking through'.

(h)   Indexes compiled by experts enable you to find relevant information quickly.

3.3   ADVANTAGES OF ONLINE SOURCES

(a)   Usually accessible from anywhere with Internet access.

(b)   Simultaneous access by many users to single source.

(c)   High volumes of information can be stored efficiently.

(d)   Speed of updating by publisher.

(e)   Quick, flexible and efficient searching and retrieval.

(f)   Ability to manipulate text (for example, to cut and paste key passages from a source).

(g)   Rapid and customised current awareness in the form of e-mail updates and RSS feeds.

3.4   ACCESSING ONLINE SOURCES

Legal information (including case law and legislation) may be accessed online via both freely available and subscription (paid for) sources. Freely available sources include government websites, such as www.legislation.gov.uk, and the website of the British and Irish Legal Information Institute, www.bailii.org. Reputable free sites can be extremely useful, but you do need to exercise caution and judgement when using some of these resources (we consider this further at **3.7**).

The two major subscription sources in the UK are the online databases *LexisLibrary* and *Westlaw*. There is some overlap between the content of the two (for example, both contain the full text of the authoritative *Law Reports*), but they are in competition so most journal and case reports appear in full text on one or the other. For advice on which titles are available from which source, ask library staff or search your library catalogue.

Note that, in practice, you will have access to subscription sources only if your firm is a paid-up subscriber. Due to the significant costs involved, this may not necessarily be the case. However, the main advantage of databases such as *Westlaw* or *LexisLibrary* is the amount of added value content they provide. For example, they update legislation to show any amendments and give guidance on whether cases are still good law. They also offer access to commentary on the law, through either journal articles or legal texts such as *Chitty on Contracts* (via *Westlaw*) or *Blackstone's Criminal Practice* (via *LexisLibrary*). As a consequence, many firms will decide that a subscription is a sound commercial investment.

3.5   GUIDELINES FOR SEARCHING ONLINE DATABASES

Searching online involves thinking of keywords that are likely to feature in documents relevant to a legal problem, then typing these keywords into a database search engine. It is not all that different from using the index to a book. However, other aspects are very different, so planning in advance how to formulate and carry out searches of databases is vitally important. Typing a string of words into a database is rarely an efficient use of time, and may well not get you the results you need. In the context of legal practice, where time is a valuable commodity and you have a professional duty of care in advice given to a client, this matters more than during student days.

To add to the problem, publishers of online databases use different versions of software, so the rules for searching them may differ. However, most databases feature an on-screen 'help' facility, and some even offer on-screen tutorials; working through such a tutorial is definitely a worthwhile investment of time. You may also have the opportunity to attend training sessions organised by your library or the database provider. These sessions can help you to get the most from the databases and improve your search technique.

A number of simple techniques will make your searching of online databases more structured and precise. For example, you may be able to narrow your search at the outset by certain criteria, such as date range or level of court. In addition, certain symbols are widely understood across databases to stand for certain letters, or to combine or exclude words. These symbols can either widen your search or narrow it as you desire.

To search effectively, bear in mind the following techniques.

3.5.1   Truncation

A search with a truncated word will search for different word endings. Why is this necessary? In most databases, typing in the word **negligent** will retrieve only documents that feature exactly that word; it will not pick up occurrences of 'negligence' or 'negligently', words which might equally well be used in the case or statute you are searching for. To widen the trawl, use a truncated form of the word to perform the search.

The symbol used to truncate varies between databases; check the 'help' facility to make sure.

Truncation can be particularly useful for finding singulars and plurals. So, for example, searching *LexisLibrary* using **pollut!** will retrieve 'pollute', 'pollutes', 'polluting', 'pollution', 'pollutants', etc, in fact any word which begins with these six letters.

3.5.2   Wild card characters

These function within a word as a truncation symbol does at the end of a word. The symbol varies between databases; as with truncation, you should check the 'help' facility. So, for example, searching *LexisLibrary* using **wom★n** will retrieve instances of 'woman' and 'women'.

3.5.3   Connectors

The commands **and**, **or** and **not** are sometimes known as Boolean operators or connectors. They function as follows:

Connector	Effect	Function
and eg **Donoghue and Stevenson**	The computer will retrieve only those documents where both the first term and the second term appear	Narrows a search – to improve precision of results
or eg **fence or boundary**	The computer will retrieve all documents where the first term appears and also all documents where the second term appears	Expands a search – to search for possible synonyms, etc
not eg **pollution not air**	The computer will retrieve documents that contain the first term but do not contain the second term	Narrows a search – eliminates terms not relevant to your topic

3.5.4   Field searching

Most databases divide documents into a number of separate fields. Thus searches may be confined to a specified field or a combination of fields. For instance, if you are searching for cases on a particular topic, you could confine your search to the 'subject/keywords' field as you should get fewer, more relevant results than if you use the same term in a 'free text' search.

You can usually search across the entire database (cases, legislation, commentary, journal articles) using a 'free text' search from the home page. However, it is a scattergun approach: comprehensive, but likely to generate a large proportion of results that are irrelevant to your purpose. Use with caution. A more effective technique is to narrow your search to a particular area (cases, legislation, journal articles) and then use links from your result to link to other relevant documents.

3.5.5 Phrase searching

How systems search for phrases varies. In some databases a phrase can be entered just as it is, eg **infringement of human rights**, and will be found; others, however, will assume that the **and** operator is to be placed between each word, and retrieve the words separately. This will probably undermine the effectiveness of the search.

The most common way of searching for a phrase is to include it within double quotation marks, for instance **"breach of contract"**.

3.5.6 Avoiding stop words

Databases tend to have a list of common words (such as 'is' and 'have') that are ignored in the process of searching. Try to avoid such words; the 'help' facility will usually identify them in that particular database.

3.5.7 Refining the outcome

If your initial search retrieves a glut of results, do not immediately go back to square one. Instead look for a way to edit the search, perhaps by adding an extra keyword and then searching again within the results. Or you may have the option to rearrange the results so the most relevant appear at the top of the results list. This will save time, and in the long term it may save money too.

> **CONCLUSION**
>
> Think before you type! Remember that computers cannot do the thinking for you. They can search only according to where you tell them to search, the words you feed into them and the way you combine those words. Planning your search strategy in advance using the methods described here will pay off.

3.6 THE FREE INTERNET: GOOGLE AND BEYOND

So far our discussion of online research has revolved around commercial databases, which require payment of a subscription for access. A common, and dangerous, misconception on the part of students is that all the information they need for their legal research can be found on the free Internet, using a search engine such as Google. So why not rely just on Google, Wikipedia and so forth?

The answer may be summed up in one word: **quality.** Quality of information is a crucial consideration when you use free sites on the Internet. Anybody can publish there. Sites frequently change their appearance, or even disappear altogether. Unlike pay-to-access databases, nobody is responsible for ensuring currency, accuracy and impartiality of content. Instead you must make an assessment against these criteria for yourself. Search engines such as Google do not search all websites or databases, so much online legal information is not accessible via this route. It is recommended that you begin any legal research with an authoritative source such as an online legal database or printed legal resource.

PROFESSIONAL CONDUCT POINT

Solicitors are professionally liable for the quality of the advice that they give to their clients. Quality of advice depends upon quality of information. The following story from the *Law Society Gazette* underlines the risk to clients and to their own practices of solicitors relying upon Wikipedia, Google and other non-specialist search engines for legal research.

Net-surfing lawyers warned of compliance risk

by Jonathan Rayner

Solicitors risk breaching conduct rules and could face insurance claims if they use non-specialist online sources for legal research, a leading QC solicitor has warned.

Evidence has emerged that increasing numbers of solicitors, from trainees to senior partners, are putting clients and their own practices at possible risk by using collaboratively written online encyclopaedia Wikipedia, Google and other search engines for legal research.

This is despite having specialist libraries and subscriptions to Lawtel, Justis and other authoritative on-line resources.

Professional conduct solicitor Andrew Hopper QC said: 'Citing any authority in court other than the actual source is a recipe for disaster and an irate judge. Wikipedia and the rest are recognised and valued, but lawyers should use their common sense, filter and check everything by going back to the original.'

Frank Maher, a partner at Liverpool risk management and law firm Legal Risk, said search engine results can get facts wrong.

He added: 'They do not always update cases. An online press release, for example, might be out of date because the case has been appealed and the outcome changed. That's more than just embarrassing – you risk insurance claims and conduct issues.'

Emma Harris, Law Society librarian, told the *Gazette*: 'Today's trainees, despite the best efforts of law school librarians, don't know the world outside the internet. We had a trainee come into the library who, when given the textbook that would answer his query, asked, "What's this list at the back and what do these little numbers mean?" That would be the index.

'Qualified lawyers are also vulnerable. Twice we've had practising solicitors contact the library looking for the full text of a statute that applied to their case. One statute turned out to be Swedish law, the other American. They had done their research through a non-legal search engine.'

Harris pointed to a Wikipedia entry on intestacy rules that also highlighted the dangers of internet research. 'Whoever wrote it got the rules mixed up with inheritance tax. Anyone following its advice would make a very expensive mistake.'

Amanda McKenzie, information services manager at City firm Olswang, said: 'A fee-earner or trainee needs to use authoritative material. This is a risk and a compliance issue.'

(Reproduced with permission of the *Law Society Gazette*, 12 June 2008, vol. 105, no. 23, p. 1)

Law firms are highly competitive businesses. They spend large amounts of money on subscriptions to quality-assured commercial databases such as *Westlaw* and *LexisLibrary* (whose content is hidden from Google). If there were a safe free alternative, you can be sure they would adopt it! However, there are useful free online resources available and there are times when you may need to use them. The guidance below is intended to help you find and evaluate the best sources.

3.6.1 Search engines

Search engines do not publish information on the Internet; they work as a finding tool. There are various search engines available, the most popular being Google (www.google.co.uk). The average Google search can return over a million results. Whilst it is convenient to rely on the results on the first page, be aware that these may not be the most relevant or authoritative as commercial sponsorship allows companies to pay to place their sites near the top of the results list. In order to produce fewer, more relevant results, there are various search techniques you can use. For example:

* enclosing search terms within inverted commas will find only that phrase, eg "litigation funding"
* site: searches only a particular site, eg site:www.law.ac.uk
* -site: excludes results from a particular site, eg -site:Wikipedia.org
* intitle: words in the title of the page, eg intitle:"environment act"

Alternatively, instead of using the general search box on the home page, use the advanced search screen which makes it easier to create a focused, accurate search.

To find this function, click settings in the bottom right corner of the Google screen and select Advanced search from the list.

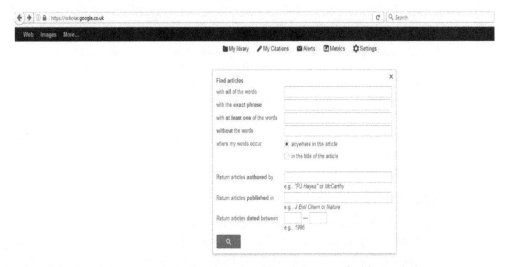

Google and Google logo are registered trademarks of Google Inc., used with permission

Another option for finding authoritative free resources is to use Google Scholar (https://scholar.google.co.uk) which specifically searches for academic material, including theses, articles, books, conference papers, etc. To use the advanced search facility, click on the drop down arrow on the search box.

Google and the Google logo are registered trademarks of Google Inc., used with permission

3.6.2 Official websites

The EU, Parliament, the courts and government all publish authoritative information on their websites. Useful official websites are:

- British and Irish Institute of Legal Information (www.bailii.org)
- EUR-Lex (eur-lex.europa.eu/homepage.html)
- legislation.gov (www.legislation.gov.uk)
- Ministry of Justice (www.justice.gov.uk)
- UK Parliament (www.parliament.uk)
- UK Supreme Court (www.supremecourt.uk)

However, whilst the information on official sites can be treated as reliable and authoritative, caution may still be needed. For example, not all the legislation on the legislation.gov site is available in an updated form.

3.6.3   Portals and directories

Portals and directories are gateways to selected free online legal information. They are useful for helping to find authoritative sites and can provide a quicker, more efficient route than search engines. A good example is www.venables.co.uk.

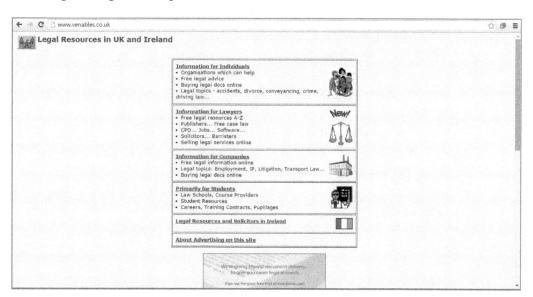

Reproduced with kind permission of Delia Venables

3.6.4   Social media and Web 2.0

Web 2.0 is an umbrella term used to describe collaborative Internet tools such as blogs, wikis and social media sites.

Wikis are collaborative websites, which allow users to create and edit information.

Blogs are online journals containing the personal opinions of the author. Over recent years many law firms, practising lawyers and law teachers have published blogs.

A useful directory of UK legal blogs is available at www.infolaw.co.uk/lawfinder.

Some content on blogs may be serious and useful (for example, a barrister may report recent developments in his or her specialist area of practice). Other content (even within the same blog) may be more frivolous. Therefore, while they may be worthwhile sources of comment about the law and legal practice, their content should not be relied upon uncritically when carrying out legal research. This same caution should be applied to all information found on social media and free websites.

3.6.5   Finding business information

Increasingly, both as part of your studies and in the workplace, you may need to find information on companies and markets. Whilst finding legal information may have become second nature, it can be difficult to know where to start when faced with this challenge. Fortunately there are some extremely useful and authoritative free resources you can use, such as:

- *The Financial Times* (www.ft.com): you can search the site for information on a specific company or on general commercial sectors such as banking or retail. Some of the content is freely available and some is restricted to subscribers.

- Companies House (www.gov.uk/government/organisations/companies-house) allows you to search for a range of information on companies, and links to https://beta.companieshouse.gov.uk.
- *The Gazette* (www.thegazette.co.uk) publishes online profiles of every UK business registered with Companies House.

3.6.6   Evaluating websites

When using free online resources, it is vitally important that you establish whether the information you have found online is authoritative, accurate and up to date. To do so, consider the following:

- Who is the author or publisher of the material? Do they have expertise in this area?
- When was it published? Is the information current?
- What is the jurisdiction of the source – is it applicable to the UK? The domain name of the site can be useful in establishing this.
- Who is the intended audience?
- Is it objective? Is it published by a commercial organisation, a political party or an organisation with a specific objective?

If you consider these factors, it should enable you to determine whether the information can be relied upon.

GETTING STARTED

LEARNING OUTCOMES

After reading this chapter you will be able to:

- explain the difference between primary and secondary sources
- understand how to use *Halsbury's Laws of England* in printed and online format
- identify practitioner works and describe how to use them
- select appropriate primary sources for your research.

4.1 INTRODUCTION

When you have completed your initial analysis of the relevant facts and identified the legal issues involved in your problem, you need to move on to the next step – researching the law in detail and applying it to the problem.

Rather than going straight to primary sources, it is often advisable to start with secondary sources such as a general legal encyclopedia (for example *Halsbury's Laws of England*) or a good practitioner text. These will give you an overview of the law and highlight any key legislation and case law.

4.2 HALSBURY'S LAWS OF ENGLAND

The printed version of *Halsbury's Laws of England* runs to around 100 volumes. The same content is available online on the *LexisLibrary* subscription database.

Halsbury's Laws of England provides commentary upon the present state of all areas of English law. (Note that the word 'laws' in the title denotes laws of the land in a general sense; it is not limited to Acts of Parliament.) It is arranged alphabetically by subject. Each subject is divided into numbered paragraphs that summarise the law in a particular area. Footnotes direct you to related cases and statutes.

4.2.1 Using the paper version

To find out the law using the paper version of *Halsbury's Laws of England*, you must take four steps:

- index;
- main volume(s);
- Cumulative Supplement; and
- Noter-Up.

4.2.1.1 Consolidated index

The index volumes identify and give references to keywords. Think of subject terms that identify the problem you are researching. The index will refer you from those terms to discussion of the law in one or more of the main volumes.

PERSONAL INJURY CASE STUDY

For example, our road traffic case study involves a car whose driver was on the telephone at the time of a collision. Searching the Consolidated Index produces the following reference:

MOBILE TELEPHONE

  driving while using, breach of construction and use requirements, **89** (5th), 68

  . . .

  vehicle, use in **89** (5th), 427

Each reference indicates the context in which mobiles are being discussed, followed by the number in **bold** of the main volume where the discussion appears, and then the edition to which this main volume belongs (4th or 5th – the publisher has been moving from the 4th to the 5th edition over recent years – this process is now complete so all main volumes are available in the 5th edition), and then one or more paragraph (*not* page) numbers. If the paragraph number is followed by 'n', the reference is to a footnote to that paragraph.

Make an accurate note of the reference, so that you can find it again easily in future, then locate the relevant main volume and paragraph.

4.2.1.2 Main volumes

The 'main volumes' give statements of the law of England and Wales, arranged by subject. Each self-contained subject is known as a 'title'.

Each volume has its own subject index at the back. This may be useful if your main volume was reissued after publication of the annual Consolidated Index, since reissue entails reordering of paragraph numbers.

4.2.1.3 Cumulative supplement

Over the years, the main volumes are reissued on a rolling programme. As time goes by, some information contained in older volumes will be superseded. Therefore, you must always check that the information in your main volume is up-to-date.

This updating process involves two stages. To begin with, consult the annual, two-volume 'Cumulative Supplement'. There will be a note in the front which gives you the date to which the content has been updated. Any developments affecting your area of law since publication of the main volume and the date of the Cumulative Supplement will be noted. Entries appear under the same volume and paragraph references as in the main volumes.

4.2.1.4 Noter-Up

Finally, check the 'Noter-Up' booklet. Replaced monthly, this will alert you to any very recent changes in the law. Once again, look under the volume and paragraph number of your original reference. If any developments are listed, short summaries will be found in the appropriate 'Monthly Review' booklet, which should be shelved alongside.

How to use *Halsbury's Laws of England*

| If you know the general subject of your research | If you are looking for a topic relating to a particular Act or case | If you are unsure of the subject of your research |

Turn to the *volume/title* which covers the general area – areas covered are listed on the spine of each volume

Turn to the *Consolidated Table of Statutes* or *Consolidated Table of Cases*, which will refer you to the relevant volume and paragraph(s)

Turn to the *Consolidated Index* volumes, which will refer you to the relevant volume and paragraph(s)

Turn to the table of contents at the front of the title, or the title index at the back of the volume, which will refer you to the relevant paragraph(s)

IS THE INFORMATION UP-TO-DATE?

Look in the annual hardback *Cumulative Supplement* for your volume and paragraph numbers. An entry means the law has changed between the publication date of the volume and the operative date of the *Cumulative Supplement*.

Then look in the Noter-Up booklet for your volume and paragraph numbers. An entry means the law has changed since the operative date of the *Cumulative Supplement*.

4.2.2 Using the online version

4.2.2.1 Scope

You can access the full text of *Halsbury's Laws of England* online via *LexisLibrary*. This also includes the updating material contained in the latest annual Cumulative Supplement and monthly Noter-Up. Content is updated weekly.

4.2.2.2 Searching

From the *LexisLibrary* home page, look in the *My Bookshelf* section for *Halsbury's Laws of England*. If it is not listed here, click the *Sources* link, then H, then *Browse* next to *Halsbury's Laws of England*.

There are two routes into the database: *Browse* and *Search*. In either case, the basic building blocks are numbered paragraphs. Each describes the law in a narrow area, and corresponds exactly to the numbered paragraphs in the equivalent printed volume of *Halsbury's Laws*.

Click on *Browse* to drill down to information on a topic, via a hierarchy of contents lists arranged by subject. Click on the + (plus) symbol next to headings in the list to see more specific entries. Click on the – (minus) symbol next to headings to see broader entries. A numbered heading without a + or – symbol corresponds to a paragraph.

PERSONAL INJURY CASE STUDY

For example, thinking again of our road traffic case study, if you are looking for an explanation of the law surrounding use of a mobile phone while driving, you would work through the following sequence:

Halsbury's Laws of England

    Road Traffic (volume 89 & 90 (2011))

        6. Use of Vehicles

            (8.) Avoidance of Danger

                427. Use of Mobile Telephones

Alternatively, use the *Search* option to search the whole encyclopedia. Enter search term(s) to retrieve a list of paragraphs where they occur. If you enter two or more search terms they will be treated as a phrase, unless you link them using Boolean connectors (see **3.5.3**). For example, to find out whether it is obligatory to wear seat belts in a car, you might search on **belt! and wear!**.

Browsing the contents list or searching will produce a list of numbered paragraphs. Click on the appropriate paragraph heading to view the full text. The screen will split. On the left is the text of the paragraph, and on the right the relevant footnotes. Any search terms are highlighted in yellow.

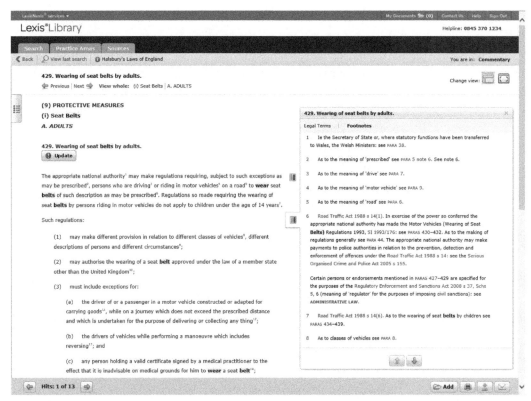

Reproduced with kind permission of LexisNexis

To jump to the previous or the next numbered paragraph of the encyclopedia, click on the arrow buttons labelled *previous/next*, to the left of the screen near the top.

The content of each paragraph online is exactly the same as the content of the corresponding printed volume of *Halsbury's Laws*. The printed volumes are reissued on a rolling programme, and so many are years old. Therefore, as we have seen, the printed encyclopedia includes an annual Cumulative Supplement and a monthly Noter-Up that function as updating tools. When using the online version, always check for an *Update* link. This merges the content of the Cumulative Supplement and the Noter-Up in the printed version. **It is essential to read both the paragraph and any update to establish the current state of the law.**

4.3 PRACTITIONER BOOKS

Solicitors seldom refer to student textbooks or other academic works. These are not primarily intended to assist a thorough and pragmatic assessment of the law relating to a particular issue in hand. Practitioner books are intended to fulfil this role.

Practitioner books are written for, and usually by, practising lawyers. They give detailed and comprehensive coverage of an area of the law, with special emphasis on practice and procedure. Often they reproduce selected primary sources as well.

Although many practitioner books have online versions, a printed edition (often in looseleaf format) remains the version of choice for many lawyers. So if you want to be a competent researcher, you should familiarise yourself with these texts.

4.3.1 Navigating practitioner works

The following guidelines will assist you to get the most from practitioner books:

(a)   Although the original author may be long dead, his or her authority is such that practitioner works often continue to be known by his or her name rather than the name of the current editor. For example, *Chitty on Contracts*, now in its 32nd edition and sometimes referred to as just *Chitty*, was originally written by Joseph Chitty (1796–1838).

(b)   Choose between a variety of access points, according to the nature of your research query:

- an overall table of contents: use this to plot the layout of the work as a whole
- tables of cases and legislation referred to (usually towards the front): use these to jump to discussion of particular court decisions, statutes or statutory instruments
- subject index (usually towards the back): use this to jump to discussion of particular topics
- subject sections may be labelled by coloured divider cards (each such section may also have its own table of contents)
- for their own quick reference, individuals often add umpteen coloured page-tabs to personal or shared copies

(c)   Keeping up-to-date is a challenge to publishers of practitioner works. Always take steps to establish how a source makes provision for currency:

- it may be replaced by a new edition every year (for example, *Archbold: Criminal Pleading, Evidence and Practice*)
- paperback supplements may appear during the lifetime of an edition; these accumulate updates to particular sections in the main work (for example, *Chitty on Contracts*)
- looseleaf format is another solution, as it allows individual pages to be replaced, so that changes to the law are integrated regularly into the text (for example, *Kemp and Kemp: Quantum of Damages*)
- titles in all these categories may be supplemented by a brief bulletin or newsletter, giving notes on recent cases or pieces of legislation

(d)   Always check near the beginning for a note of the cut-off date to which the publisher affirms that the law expressed is current, and make a record of this. Where they exist, online versions of practitioner works will be updated as frequently as the editors can manage. This may be daily, but it may be monthly or even quarterly. Do not assume that the content is current to today!

4.3.2 Precedent books

You should also be aware of precedent books. These assist practitioners in the drafting of documents by giving examples of structure and wording that may be adapted for use in a given matter. Annotations often explain the effect of particular wording and may cite relevant authorities. (See **Chapter 8**.)

4.4 WIDENING THE NET

All of the sources described in this chapter are secondary sources. In other words they state what a commentator believes the law to be. They offer valuable introductions and summaries, written by authors who are experts in their field and whose names may carry authority; but the statements of law they contain are nonetheless secondhand.

Primary sources, that is cases and legislation, are the raw materials of the law. These are the foundation of sound legal advice, and therefore the mainstay of sound legal research. Having established a preliminary overview of your topic, you must shift your focus to primary sources.

The following table, which deals mainly with primary sources, is intended to save your time and build your confidence in linking particular types of research query with particular sources. Each group of sources is listed in order of preference, on the basis of extent of coverage and ease of use.

How to:	Paper Route	Online Route
(1) Find where a case is reported using party names only.	(a) Start with the *Current Law Case Citators*. Check most recent citator volume first and, if the case is not listed, work backwards through all the volumes until you find the case. (Covers cases reported or cited from 1947 onwards. The latest *Current Law Monthly Digest* also contains a cumulative table of cases) (b) Secondly, try *The Digest*: Consolidated Table of Cases (c) Finally, try the table of cases in a practitioner work such as *Palmer's Company Law*, or *Hill and Redman's Law of Landlord and Tenant*	(a) *Westlaw: Cases* (b) *LexisLibrary: Cases* (c) *Lawtel: Cases* (1980–)
(2) Find summaries of cases	(a) Use the *Current Law Case Citators* to find where your case has been 'digested', ie summarised in the *Current Law Yearbooks* (1947–) (b) *The Digest* (good for older cases) (c) *Halsbury's Laws Annual Abridgement* volumes (and *Monthly Review* issues for recent coverage), if case is referred to elsewhere in *Halsbury's Laws*	(a) *Westlaw: Cases*: search for case, click *Case Analysis* (same summaries as *Current Law Year Books*) (b) *Lawtel: Cases* (1980–) (c) *LexisLibrary: Cases*: select *Case Overview* as source
(3) Find cases on a certain subject	(a) *The Digest*: Index (b) *Law Reports*: Consolidated Index (in 6 bound vols. 1951–2005, plus softback cumulations for recent years) (c) *Halsbury's Laws* (use footnotes) (d) *Current Law Year Books*: 1976, 1986, 1989 have cumulative subject indexes for the previous years. Then use the subject index in each succeeding volume	(a) *Westlaw: Cases*: search by *free text* OR *subject/ keyword* (b) *LexisLibrary*: search by terms in *Case Overview* (c) *LexisLibrary: Halsbury's Laws of England*; search for subject – important cases feature in footnotes (selective) (d) *Lawtel: Cases* (1980–)
(4) Find cases featuring a piece of legislation	(a) *Current Law Legislation Citators*: Start with the volume covering the year of the legislation and work forwards through all subsequent volumes, and for recent coverage check the Citator section in the looseleaf *Current Law Statutes* Service File (b) *Halsbury's Statutes*: Consolidated Table of Cases; lists cases citing sections of Acts that feature in annotations to those sections	(a) *Westlaw: Cases*: Advanced search: search under *legislation title* and *legislation provision no.* (b) *LexisLibrary*: search via *Legislation* and then select *Cases* in *Find out more* section (c) *Lawtel: Cases* (1980–)

How to:	Paper Route	Online Route
(5) Track the judicial treatment of a case in subsequent proceedings	(a) *Current Law Case Citators* volumes, cumulative table of cases in latest issue of *Current Law Monthly Digest*. Check most recent citator volume; work backwards if no reference found (b) *The Digest*: details of later judicial comment follow the summary	(a) *Westlaw: Cases:* search for case, click *Case analysis*; scroll down to *Key Cases citing* (b) *LexisLibrary: Case Overview: Cases referring to this case*
(6) Find where very old cases are reported	(a) *The Digest:* Consolidated Table of Cases (b) *English Reports:* Table of Cases (vols 177–178)	(a) *LexisLibrary: Cases* (b) *Westlaw: Cases*
(7) Find information about very recent cases	Prefer online sources, otherwise try (a) *Current Law Monthly Digests* (b) *Times Law Reports* (monthly cumulative indexes) (c) *Halsbury's Laws: Monthly Review*	(a) *Lawtel* (b) *LexisLibrary* (see *Judgments* source for transcripts – usually same day as decision handed down; see *All England Reporter* for summaries of recent cases) (c) *Westlaw*
(8) Find out the latest text of a Bill before Parliament, and what stage the Bill has reached	Prefer online sources	(a) Bills before Parliament (http:// services.parliament.uk/ bills): detailed coverage (b) Progress of public bills (www.parliament.uk/ business/bills-and-legislation/current-bills/ public-bill-list/)
(9) Find a statute in its latest amended form	*Halsbury's Statutes* (only if in force)	(a) *LexisLibrary: UK Parliament Acts* (only if in force) (b) *Westlaw: Legislation*
(10) Find out when a statute or sections of it came into force, and if any section has been repealed or amended by later legislation	(a) *Is it in Force?* for commencement of Acts passed since 1 January 1960. *Halsbury's Statutes Citator* for details of amendments and repeals (b) *Halsbury's Statutes* (use footnotes) (c) *Current Law Legislation Citators:* volumes, and for recent coverage the Citator section in the looseleaf *Current Law Statutes Service File*	(a) *LexisLibrary: Legislation UK Legislation Status Snapshots* (b) *Westlaw: Legislation: Legislation Analysis*

How to:	Paper Route	Online Route
(11) Identify which parts of a statute are later amendments	(a) *Halsbury's Statutes*: main volumes and Current Statutes Service binders: amended text appears enclosed by square brackets; footnotes give source of amendments (b) *Halsbury's Statutes* Cumulative Supplement and Noter-Up: list recent amendments not yet in main volumes	(a) *LexisLibrary: UK Parliament Acts*: amended text appears enclosed by square brackets; footnotes give source of amendments (b) *Westlaw: Legislation; Table of Amendments via Legislation Analysis*
(12) Find annotated versions of the original Act, with background: Parliamentary debates, etc	*Current Law Statutes* (1949–)	For debates in Parliament: Hansard (www.parliament.uk/business/publications/hansard)
(13) Find a statutory instrument by number, by title or by subject	(a) *Halsbury's Statutory Instruments*: all SIs in force are listed – some in summary, many in full text (b) Text of some statutory instruments is reproduced in practitioner works such as *Palmer's Company Law*	(a) www.legislation.gov.uk/uksi; full text (1987–) (b) *LexisLibrary: Legislation* (c) *Westlaw: Legislation*
(14) Find an account of the law on a particular topic, leading you to relevant legislation and cases	(a) *Halsbury's Laws* (use footnotes) (b) Looseleaf practitioner works (c) Textbooks (use footnotes and tables)	(a) *LexisLibrary: Halsbury's Laws of England* (b) *LexisLibrary: Glossary* on home page (c) *Westlaw: Insight*: online legal encyclopedia launched in 2012
(15) Find EU primary legislation: Treaties	*Blackstone's EU Treaties and Legislation* (selective full text; annual)	EUR-LEX (eur-lex.europa.eu/homepage.html)
(16) Find EU secondary legislation: Regulations, Directives, Decisions	(a) *European Current Law Year Books and Monthly Digests* (b) *Blackstone's EU Treaties and Legislation* (selective full text; annual)	EUR-LEX (eur-lex.europa.eu/homepage.html)
(17) Check whether an EU Directive has been implemented in the UK	*Halsbury's Statutory Instruments: EU Legislation Implementator*	(a) *Westlaw: EU*: search for Directive; look for link to *National Measures* (b) EUR-LEX (eur-lex.europa.eu/homepage.html); search for directive; click on title and then national transposition tab

How to:	Paper Route	Online Route
(18) Find EU cases (Court of Justice)	(a) *Current Law Case Citators and Monthly Digests* (b) *European Current Law*	EUR-LEX (eur-lex.europa.eu/homepage.html)
(19) Find European Court of Human Rights cases, citations, summaries, full text	(a) *Current Law Case Citators* (b) Emmerson, *Human Rights Practice* (looseleaf)	(a) European Court of Human Rights (www.echr.coe.int): Case-law – HUDOC database for full text of cases (b) *Westlaw: European Human Rights Reports* (c) *LexisLibrary*: European Court of Human Rights Cases (1960–)
(20) Find articles on topics in law, or case comment in periodicals	(a) *Current Law Year Books*: up to 1995, separate article index at back of volume; from 1996, references to articles under subject headings in main body of work (b) *Halsbury's Laws of England*: Monthly Review and Annual Abridgement volumes; arranged by subject	(a) *Westlaw: Journals*: search includes Legal Journals Index (comprehensive; 1986–) (b) *Lawtel*: Articles Index (selective; 1998–) (c) *LexisLibrary: Journals*: search across Journals Index which includes abstracts and full text articles
(21) Find out what abbreviations/citations stand for	(a) Raistrick, *Index to Legal Citations and Abbreviations*, 4th edn (2013) (b) *Current Law Year Books* and *Monthly Digests* list abbreviations at the front of each volume	*Cardiff Index to Legal Abbreviations* (www.legalabbrevs.cardiff.ac.uk/)

RESEARCHING CASE LAW

LEARNING OUTCOMES

After reading this chapter you will be able to:

- identify where you can find case reports
- understand how to cite cases
- explain which resources can be used to find case reports when you have incomplete information
- describe how to update a case and check whether it is still good law
- use online and printed sources to find cases on a particular subject.

5.1 HOW ARE CASES PUBLISHED?

Judgments delivered in court are published via a number of channels. You can access many online soon after the judgment is given. For example, the raw texts of judgments of the Supreme Court are published on the Court's free website on the day they are handed down (see www.supremecourt.gov.uk/decided-cases/). Another useful free site that gathers judgments from a variety of UK courts is *BAILII* (the British and Irish Legal Information Institute – see www.bailii.org). A large archive of transcripts of judgments can also be accessed via subscription databases such as *Lawtel*, *Westlaw* and *LexisLibrary*.

Over time commercial publishers select a small proportion of judgments as meriting 'reporting', usually because they break new legal ground. Their editors add value in various ways, such as provision of summaries ('headnotes') and tables of cases referred to. These series of reports should be your preferred source of case law. They are usually available in both paper and online formats.

Brief reports are published regularly in *The Times* newspaper. Case notes also appear in weekly practitioners' journals, such as the *New Law Journal* and the *Solicitors' Journal*. Some series of reports are intended to cover cases in specialist areas (eg, the *Road Traffic Reports* and the *Family Law Reports*). Finally, three general series feature the most significant cases across the law: the *All England Law Reports*, the *Weekly Law Reports* and the (confusingly named) *Law Reports*.

Cases that are not selected for inclusion in such publications are termed 'unreported'. This applies to more than 95% of the 200,000 or so cases decided by the UK courts each year. The Internet has facilitated widespread access to unreported decisions, in the form of case transcripts. However, they should be treated with caution as foundations for legal advice. The courts will permit an advocate to cite an unreported case only if it 'contains a relevant statement of legal principle not found in reported authority' (*Practice Direction (Citation of Authorities) (Senior Courts)* [2012] 1 WLR 780).

5.2   WHICH SOURCE OF CASES HAS THE MOST AUTHORITY?

The *Law Reports* are published by the Incorporated Council of Law Reporting for England and Wales (ICLR). They are the nearest to an official series of case reports for this jurisdiction (the Council is in fact a charity rather than a government body).

Uniquely, they include arguments presented by counsel and are checked by the presiding judge before publication. For these reasons, and by direction of the judiciary, an advocate citing a case before a court is required to use the version in the *Law Reports* in preference to any alternatives (see *Practice Direction (Citation of Authorities) (Senior Courts)* [2012] 1 WLR 780).

The *Law Reports* have been published continuously in various parallel series since 1865. The names of these series have changed frequently over the years, in line with the shifting structure of divisions of the courts. There are currently four separate series: Appeal Cases (abbreviated to AC); Chancery Division (Ch); Family Division (Fam); and Queen's Bench Division (QB). These reports are available in printed format and online via *Westlaw* and *LexisLibrary*. If a case is reported in the *Law Reports*, it will usually be the first citation listed (after any neutral citation – see **5.3.1**). On *Westlaw* it is easy to identify the *Law Reports* case report as an ICLR logo appears in the screen.

The *Weekly Law Reports* are also published by the Incorporated Council, appearing in three volumes annually. Judgments in volumes 2 and 3 are intended for revision and later republication in the *Law Reports*, so that the two series complement one another. Volume 1 contains less important cases, including cases likely to go to appeal. In each weekly issue, judgments are already earmarked for one of these three volumes.

5.3   HOW DO I CITE CASES?

In order to locate the report of a case, you often need to interpret its citation. Citations identify cases by notation, referring to a volume and page in a particular series of law reports. A typical citation for an English case is:

> *Jordan v Burgoyne* [1963] 2 QB 744

This tells you that the report of the case of *Jordan v Burgoyne* starts at p 744 of vol 2 of the Queen's Bench series of the *Law Reports* for 1963.

Certain conventions underpin the system of citation:

- Party names appear in italics.
- Year of publication appears in **[square]** or **(round)** brackets:
  - in the example above, the year appears in square brackets because it is essential for locating the case; volumes of the *Law Reports* are consecutively numbered within each year only, not from year to year;
  - by contrast, the case of *Bowker v Rose* is reported at (1977) 121 SJ 274; volumes of the *Solicitors' Journal* are consecutively numbered from year to year; therefore you can find this case simply by knowing that it is in volume 121; the year is strictly superfluous, so it appears in round brackets.
- The number of the volume in which the report appears comes before the (abbreviated) title of the series, and the number of the first page of the report comes after.
- References to different series of reports are ordered in a hierarchy: the neutral citation (if it exists – see below) comes first; then any reference to the *Law Reports*; the *Weekly Law Reports*; the *All England Law Reports*; other specialist series of law reports; newspaper law reports.

The convention of abbreviating titles of publications in the legal world is confusing. Most modern abbreviations are listed in *Current Law* (see the front of any *Monthly Digest* or *Year Book*) and at the front of volume 1 of *The Digest*. For a comprehensive list, see Raistrick, D, *Index to Legal Citations and Abbreviations* (3rd edn, 2008). A useful free to access, online source is the database of abbreviations maintained by the University of Cardiff (www.legalabbrevs.cardiff.ac.uk).

5.3.1 Neutral citation

In January 2001 a new system of neutral citation of judgments was introduced (see *Practice Note (Judgments: Neutral Citation)* [2001] 1 WLR 194). The system is 'neutral' as regards format and publisher. In other words, it identifies cases by a unique reference, independent of the series of reports in which they are reproduced and independent of whether they appear online or in print. The purpose is to enable reports of cases to be published and accessed more easily online.

All cases heard in the Supreme Court, the Court of Appeal and the High Court are now covered by these arrangements. A neutral citation is allocated by the court to every judgment. This is intended to feature in every subsequent publication of that judgment. It takes the form of year (in square brackets), abbreviation of the name of the court, and running serial number (the serial number reverts to 1 at the start of each calendar year). Here are some examples:

Supreme Court	[2017] UKSC 1, 2, 3, etc
Court of Appeal (Civil Division)	[2017] EWCA Civ 1, 2, 3, etc
Court of Appeal (Criminal Division)	[2017] EWCA Crim 1, 2, 3, etc
High Court (Administrative Division)	[2017] EWHC 1, 2, 3, etc (Admin)

Since 2001, judgments have also been set out in numbered paragraphs, which are easier to locate within electronic law reports than page references. The citation of the authority from a particular decision might thus be in the form: *Smith v Jones* [2001] EWCA Civ 10 at [59], ie, paragraph 59 in the judgment of *Smith v Jones*, the 10th judgment of the year 2001 in the Civil Division of the Court of Appeal of England and Wales.

5.4 HOW DO I FIND A CASE WITH AN INCOMPLETE CITATION?

Trainees are often asked to track down a case on the basis of incomplete information. For example, your supervisor may say something like 'I'm advising a client who's considering suing her bank for the return of unlawful charges. I saw an article that mentioned a successful case along the same lines, I think the name was Curtis or something. Can you dig out the case for me?'

If you have a citation to a series of law reports, this should be enough to locate a case, even if you do not know the names of the parties concerned. However, how do you locate a report if all that you know is the name of one or more of the parties?

You could type the party name into an online database in the hope that the case features there. The more common the surname, the less efficient this approach is likely to be. However, where the subject matter of the case is known, you could add this as a search term, or try checking the table of cases in a relevant practitioner book or student textbook. If this is unsuccessful, use the *Current Law Case Citator* if the case was decided since 1947 (or if you are unsure when the case was decided). Otherwise use *The Digest*.

5.4.1 Current Law Case Citator

The *Current Law Case Citator* is an index of cases by party. Coverage is comprehensive, beginning in 1947. It is published in paper form. The same content is available online via *Westlaw*.

The printed set comprises several volumes covering different date ranges (1947–1976; 1977–1997; 1998–2001; 2002–2004; annual supplements for recent years). Start with the most recent annual part and work backwards until you find the latest entry for your case. This will cumulate any earlier entries. For very recent cases, consult the 'cumulative table of cases' near the back of the latest issue of the *Monthly Digest* (no need to look in earlier issues for the same year!).

Here is an example of an entry in the *Current Law Case Citator*:

> *Slater v Lewisham LBC* [2006] EWCA Civ 394; [2006] 2 F.C.R. 90; [2006] H.L.R. 37; (2006) 150 S.J.L.B. 539; Times, May 3, 2006, CA (Civ Div)

Digested, 06/**2028**

Applied, 07/2140, 08/1850: Considered, 10/1693

With this in mind, consider the three important functions of entries in the *Current Law Case Citator*:

(1) Supply a full list of references, in descending order of authority, to enable you locate different reports of the case.

(2) Refer to a summary of the case in the relevant *Current Law Yearbook* (look for a reference beginning 'Digested', followed by the last two digits of the year/paragraph number, in **bold**). So, in the example above, a summary would be located in the *Current Law Yearbook 2006*, paragraph 2028.

(3) Enable you to update the case, by supplying references to later decisions where it has been the subject of judicial comment (look for references beginning 'Applied', etc; see **5.5** below for a fuller explanation)

Here is an example of a page from the *Citator* with another, more complex entry for the case of *Pepper v Hart*:

PEO   CASE CITATOR 2002-2004

People's Labour Party (HEP) *v.* Turkey see Yazar *v.* Turkey (22723/93)
Peoples Insurance Co of China (Hebei Branch) *v.* Vysanthi Shipping Co Ltd (The Joanna V) [2003] EWHC 1655; [2003] 2 Lloyd's Rep. 617, QBD (Comm) . . . .   *Digested,* 03/**206**
Pepper (Inspector of Taxes) *v.* Hart [1993] A.C. 593; [1992] 3 W.L.R. 1032; [1993] 1 All E.R. 42; [1992] S.T.C. 898; [1993] I.C.R. 291; [1993] I.R.L.R. 33; [1993] R.V.R. 127; (1993) 143 N.L.J. 17; [1992] N.P.C. 154; *Times,* November 30, 1992; *Independent,* November 26, 1992, HL; reversing [1991] Ch. 203; [1991] 2 W.L.R. 483; [1990] S.T.C. 786; [1991] I.C.R. 681; [1991] I.R.L.R. 125; (1990) 134 S.J. 1478; *Times,* November 15, 1990; *Financial Times,* November 16, 1990; *Guardian,* November 21, 1990; *Daily Telegraph,* November 19, 1990, CA (Civ Div); affirming [1990] 1 W.L.R. 204; [1990] S.T.C. 6; (1989) 86(46) L.S.G. 41, Ch D
. . . .   *Digested,* 93/**459**:
Applied, 93/3714, 94/2514, 98/321, 98/966, 01/4489, 03/3600:
Cited, 00/5239: *Considered,* 93/426, 93/1866, 93/2260, 93/3860, 94/968,
94/3413, 94/3900, 95/881, 96/1297, 96/1606, 96/3928, 01/5174, 04/628:
Distinguished, 94/125, 95/181, 95/2520, 97/4657, 00/2122, 01/4284:
Followed, 96/4190: *Not applied,* 01/4206: *Referred to,* 93/486, 94/353,
94/2723, 94/2729, 94/3445, 94/5459, 94/5899, 95/522, 95/861
Perathoner *v.* S Joseph Societe Free (formerly Proxad) [2003] E.C.D.R. 8, Trib Gde Inst (Paris)
Percy *v.* DPP; *sub nom* DPP *v.* Percy [2001] EWHC Admin 1125; (2002) 166 J.P. 93; [2002] Crim. L.R. 835; [2002] A.C.D. 24; (2002) 166 J.P.N. 111; *Times,* January 21, 2002, DC . . . .   *Digested,* 02/**825**:
Applied, 03/806
Peregrine Systems Ltd *v.* Steria Ltd A1/2004/0851 QBENF, CA (Civ Div); affirming [2004] EWHC 275; [2004] Masons C.L.R. 20, QBD (TCC)
Perera *v.* Sri Lanka (1091/2002) (2004) 11 I.H.R.R. 67, UN HRC
Perera *v.* Zambia (828/1998) see Francis Silva *v.* Zambia (825/1998)
Perez de Rada Cavanilles *v.* Spain (2000) 29 E.H.R.R. 109; [1998] H.R.C.D. 981, ECHR   *Digested,* 00/**3237**:
Applied, 02/3727

Reproduced with kind permission of Sweet & Maxwell

(The case of *Pepper v Hart* is particularly significant in relation to the process of legal research; see **6.3.2** below for more information.)

To search for the same information about a case using *Westlaw*, go to the home page and click on *Cases* at the top of the screen. A search template will appear. Enter one or more names in the *Party Names* box and click *Search*. A list of results, with citations (*Where Reported*), will appear. To view the *Current Law* abstract of a particular case, click *Case Analysis*. A list of citations features again near the top of the summary. If the full text of the case is available to view on *Westlaw*, one or more of these citations will appear in colour and underlined, as a link.

Here is the beginning of the *case analysis* document on *Westlaw* for *Pepper v Hart*:

Reproduced with kind permission of Westlaw UK

5.4.2 The Digest

The Digest is a multi-volume encyclopedia. It indexes and summarises over 500,000 cases in an alphabetical subject arrangement. Irish, Scottish, Commonwealth and EU cases are covered, as well as English cases. It is especially useful for tracing older cases (although its coverage extends to the present). Follow these steps to trace a named case using *The Digest*:

> Look up the first party in the *Consolidated Table of Cases* volumes at the end of the set; *an entry here will refer you to a main volume*

> Look up the party name again in the 'table of cases' at the front of the main volume; *an entry here will refer you to a paragraph in the same volume*

> Look up the paragraph number for a summary of the case, a list of citations to full reports of the case, and references to judicial comment in later cases ('Annotations')

5.4.3 Case Overview

Case Overview is a case citator that is available in online form only, via *LexisLibrary*.

To access from the home page of *LexisLibrary* click *Cases*, then click on *Case Overview* in the left-hand column.

Type the name of one or both parties in the box labelled *case name*. The full citation for your case will appear at the top of the results screen. This includes references to a wide range of publications where the case is reported, including (if it features in full on *LexisLibrary*) links to the full text.

5.5 HOW DO I UPDATE A CASE?

Once you have found your case, you must **always** check if it is still good law. You can do so using printed or online resources.

5.5.1 Online resources

If you have access to a subscription legal database, such as *Westlaw* or *LexisLibrary*, checking for developments to a case is relatively straightforward. In *Westlaw*, from the home page, click on *Cases* at the top of the screen. Enter one or more names in the *Party Names* box and click *Search*. Then click *Case Analysis* beneath the appropriate entry in the list of results that appears. At the top of the screen you will see a status icon indicating the type of subsequent judicial treatment the case has received. For example, a no entry icon signifies negative judicial treatment and warns that at least one point of law in the case has been overruled or reversed. Scroll down to the *Appellate History & Status* section to track the progress of the case. To check later judicial treatment in other cases, scroll further down to the section headed *Key Cases Citing*.

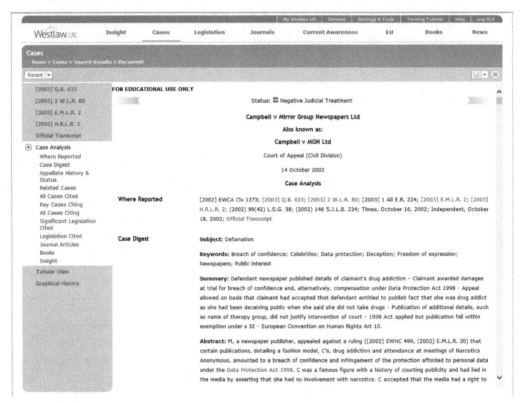

Reproduced with kind permission of Westlaw UK

Case Overview (part of *LexisLibrary*) is an alternative online citator for researching subsequent judicial consideration. Access it via *Cases*, select *Case Overview* as your source and then carry out your search. The result will give you access to the *Case History* and cases referring to this case. You will also see status icons: green for positive treatment in subsequent cases; red for negative; yellow for mixed or cautionary; and blue for neutral.

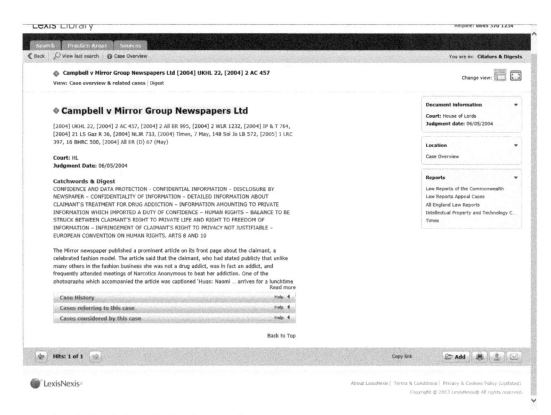

Reproduced with kind permission of LexisNexis

Both *Case Overview* and *Westlaw* use a variety of symbols to flag the standing of individual judgments. (*Westlaw* also features symbols in connection with legislation.) It is important to understand the significance of these, especially because, unfortunately, the two publishers do not use the same symbols.

Within *Case Overview*, you will come across the following in the Help section:

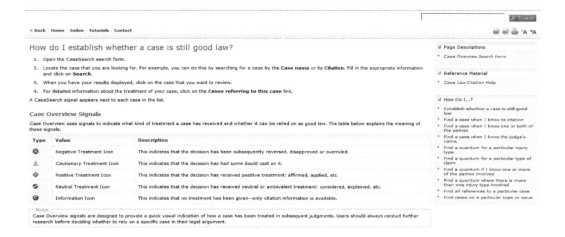

Reproduced with kind permission of LexisNexis

Within *Westlaw* search results, you will come across the following:

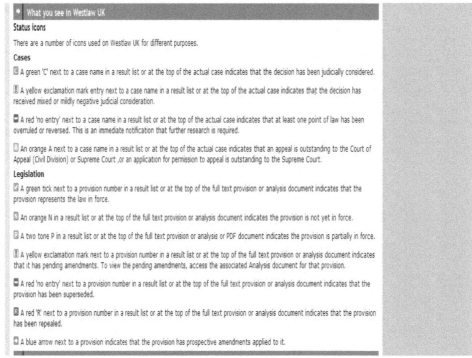

Reproduced with kind permission of Westlaw UK

5.5.2 Printed resources

The Digest does this job of reporting developments by the 'annotations' section of each case summary. However, the best source for the subsequent judicial treatment of a case is a citator, such as the *Current Law Case Citator*. (If the case pre-dates 1947 it is still worth checking here, since consideration in a post-1947 judgment qualifies an older case for inclusion.)

Using the printed version, the procedure is to find the latest reference to the case in an annual volume (entries in these volumes are cumulative), so work backwards from the most recent citator until you find a reference to your case. Then check the case lists in the latest issue of the *Monthly Digest* for any recent developments. Here is an example of an entry in the 1977–88 citator:

> R *v Blackburn (James)* (1979) 1 Cr App R (S) 205, CA Digested, 81/**525**: Considered, 87/1035:
> Cited, 89/1071: Referred to, 84/880: Distinguished, 88/977

The case of R *v Blackburn* is summarised, or 'digested', in the *Current Law Year Book* of 1981 at para 525. It has been commented upon in various ways in subsequent decisions that are also summarised. The references 'considered, 87/1035', etc are to summaries of these other cases in later year books.

Certain conventional terms denote the effect of later decisions on the status of earlier decisions: terms such as 'applied', 'distinguished' and 'followed'. For definitions, see the section entitled 'Meaning of terms used in classifying annotating cases' at the beginning of each volume of *The Digest*.

5.6 HOW DO I FIND CASES ON A SUBJECT?

Cases on a particular topic may be traced using a general source, such as *Halsbury's Laws of England* or a relevant practitioner book (see **Chapter 4**). Another useful printed source is *The Digest*.

Online databases are very useful for subject searching, since they offer the facility to search for occurrences of keywords anywhere in the text of documents. However, beware of information overload! You may find that you generate large numbers of results, many of which are irrelevant to your purpose. If this does happen, try using the 'sort by relevance' option, if available, to bring the most meaningful results to the top of your results list.

5.6.1 Using The Digest to find cases on a subject

The Digest is arranged alphabetically by subject. It is therefore very useful for identifying cases that deal with a particular topic.

Follow these steps to trace cases on a subject using The Digest:

> Look up the topic in the paperback Index volumes at the end of the set; entries here will refer you to volume, subject heading and paragraph numbers where summaries of cases on the topic can be found

> Follow the references and read the summaries to identify cases that meet your research needs; update these cases by following up any references to 'Annotations'

> Developments may have affected the status of these cases since the publication date of the main volume; to check for these, look up the same reference in the annual Cumulative Supplement; further cases on the same topic may also appear here

> Finally, check for developments since the publication of the Cumulative Supplement by looking up the same reference in successive issues of the Quarterly Survey

5.6.2 Using Current Law to find cases on a subject

Each Current Law Year Book (and Monthly Digest) includes a subject index. In theory, it is therefore possible to track cases on a subject, including summaries, by consulting each volume consecutively from 1947 onwards. This is clearly laborious, and not recommended! However, all of this content may be searched for the same purpose in one go using Westlaw.

At the home page, click Cases at the top of the screen. Enter one or more keywords in the Free Text box and click Search. Try to be as specific as possible. If you generate too many results using Free Text, try the Subject/Keyword search. A list of judgments whose summaries contain your keyword(s) will appear. Click Case Analysis beneath the entry of any case that looks promising. Go to Case Digest — Abstract to make sure that the case concerns the area of law in which you are interested (as you may retrieve some cases where your keywords feature only incidentally). If you then wish to read a full report of the case, look to see whether any of the citations in the Where Reported section are in colour and underlined. If they are, the full report is available on Westlaw itself – just click the link. If they are not, make a note of the citation and look for the report elsewhere, either within another database or on the library shelves.

5.6.3 Using full text databases to find cases on a subject

Most online versions of single series of law reports, such as All England Law Reports on LexisLibrary or Weekly Law Reports on Westlaw, permit free text subject searching using keywords. This is a thorough and powerful search facility.

However, it is important to understand the coverage of the database that you are using (for example, if you choose to narrow your case search on *LexisLibrary* to *All England Law Reports*, you will of course retrieve references to that single series only, when in fact the database features many other series in addition, including the authoritative *Law Reports*).

You may prefer to search across all case reports on a particular database. However, if you do this and use a general search term, you might generate a large volume of results, not all of which may be particularly relevant. Therefore, look for ways to make your results list more meaningful. For example, in *Westlaw*, select *Cases*, then click on the *Advanced Search* option. This will give you more search fields and enable you to restrict your search by limiting the date, or court or even cases heard by a particular judge. Consider searching by *Subject/Keyword*. These keywords are applied by the database editors, and if you use this field you will get fewer, more relevant results than if you use the same term in the *Free Text* field. If you are unsure of the appropriate keyword, either look at the *List of Terms* provided by *Westlaw* or, when you find a relevant case, look at the keywords applied to it and then re-run your search using that term. The *Cases* search screen in *LexisLibrary* also offers similar search options.

Another way of finding the most relevant cases from a large list of results is to use the *Sort by Relevance* option offered by both *LexisLibrary* and *Westlaw*. This works by reordering your results so that those cases with the most mentions of your search term are listed first.

5.6.4   Chart of specialist law reports

The following selective chart identifies the leading series of law reports across a range of practice areas:

Subject	Title	Abbreviation	Online Access
Business and Company	British Company Cases	BCC	Westlaw
	Business Law Reports	Bus LR	Westlaw
	Butterworths Company Law Cases	BCLC	LexisLibrary
Commercial	All England Law Reports. Commercial Cases	All ER (Comm)	LexisLibrary
	Commercial Law Cases	CLC	Westlaw
	Lloyd's Law Reports	Lloyd's Rep	i-Law (Informa)
Consumer	Goode: Consumer Credit Reports	GCCR	LexisLibrary
Competition	Common Market Law Reports. Antitrust	CMLR	Westlaw
Crime	Criminal Appeal Reports	Cr App R	Westlaw
	Criminal Appeal Reports (Sentencing)	Cr App R (S)	Westlaw
	Justice of the Peace Law Reports	JP	LexisLibrary
Employment	Industrial Cases Reports	ICR	Westlaw
	Industrial Relations Law Reports	IRLR	LexisLibrary
EU	All England Law Reports. European Cases	All ER (EC)	LexisLibrary
	European Court Reports	ECR	EUR-Lex / LexisLibrary / Westlaw
	Common Market Law Reports	CMLR	Westlaw
Environment	Environmental Law Reports	Env LR	Westlaw

Subject	Title	Abbreviation	Online Access
Family	Family Court Reports	FCR	LexisLibrary
	Family Law Reports	FLR	Family Law Online
Housing	Housing Law Reports	HLR	Westlaw
	Landlord and Tenant Reports	L&TR	Westlaw
Human Rights	European Human Rights Reports	EHRR	Westlaw
Immigration	Immigration Appeal Reports	Imm AR	BAILII
Insurance	Lloyd's Law Reports: Insurance and Reinsurance	Lloyd's Rep IR	i-Law (Informa)
Intellectual Property	Fleet Street Reports	FSR	Westlaw
Local Government	Butterworths Local Government Reports	LGR	LexisLibrary
Media	Entertainment and Media Law Reports	EMLR	Westlaw
Personal Injury	Butterworths Medico-Legal Reports	BMLR	LexisLibrary
	Personal Injuries and Quantum Reports	PIQR	Westlaw
Professional Negligence	Professional Negligence and Liability Reports	PNLR	Westlaw
Property	Estates Gazette. Law Reports	EGLR	EGi (Estates Gazette Interactive)/LexisLibrary
	Property, Planning and Compensation Reports	P&CR	Westlaw
Revenue	Simon's Tax Cases	STC	LexisLibrary
	HMSO Tax Cases	TC	LexisLibrary
Road Traffic	Road Traffic Reports	RTR	Westlaw
Wills and Probate	Wills and Trusts Law Reports	WTLR	None

RESEARCHING LEGISLATION

LEARNING OUTCOMES

After reading this chapter you will be able to:

- explain how to cite legislation
- understand how to find legislation using printed and online resources
- describe how to establish whether legislation is in force
- identify the means of updating legislation.

6.1 INTRODUCTION

There are two major classes of legislation in the UK:

(a) *Primary legislation* is passed by Parliament in the form of Acts (also known as statutes); the number of Acts passed each year varies – over the last decade, the average annual figure is 36.

(b) *Secondary legislation* is made under powers delegated by Parliament, usually to government ministers; it almost always takes the form of statutory instruments (also known as regulations or orders); around 3,000 are created each year.

It is vital to check that the version of any legislation that you refer to is in force. Some provisions do not come into force for some time after they have been passed by Parliament. Many are then amended over time, or even repealed altogether.

There are many different sources of legislation, in paper and online form. The first question to ask before you choose a source is this: do I need the original version of this provision, or do I need the version of the provision that is in force now? If, as is commonly the case in legal practice, you need the version in force now (ie, incorporating any subsequent amendments and repeals), the best printed sources are *Halsbury's Statutes of England* (see **6.3.4**) and *Halsbury's Statutory Instruments* (see **6.5.2**). Online alternatives for legislation in force are *Westlaw* (see **6.7**) and *UK Parliament Acts* on *LexisLibrary* (see **6.6**).

6.2 HOW DO I CITE LEGISLATION?

A statute is generally cited by its 'short title' (which should include the year it was passed), eg, 'Human Rights Act 1998'. You may also come across citations by 'chapter number' (the first statute passed in a given year is chapter 1, and so on). Thus the Human Rights Act 1998 may be cited as 'c 42 1998' (because it was the 42nd Act to be passed in 1998).

The present system of citing statutes by their calendar year and chapter number began in 1963. Prior to that, statutes were referred to by the year of the monarch's reign or the 'regnal year' (where each regnal year began with the anniversary of the sovereign's accession to the throne) and the running chapter number. The short titles by which many of these surviving pre-1963 Acts are informally known were invented subsequently for convenience. So, for example, the Act that lawyers refer to as the Criminal Libel Act 1819 is formally cited as: '60 Geo 3 & 1 Geo 4 c. 8'. That is, the eighth Act to be passed during the parliamentary session that spanned the sixtieth (and last) year of the reign of George III and the first year of the reign of George IV. See any of the guides listed in the Bibliography for a full explanation of this complicated system.

The body of a statute is divided into numbered sections, each containing a different rule of law. When you refer to a rule of law contained in a statute, you should identify where it can be found. It is usual to abbreviate 'section' to 's', so that 's 1' refers to section 1. Sections are sub-divided into subsections, eg s 1(1); paragraphs, eg s 1(2)(a); and even sub-paragraphs. In larger statutes, sections may be grouped together into different parts, each dealing with a separate area of law.

Some statutes have one or more schedules at the end. The content of schedules varies: for example, some may contain detailed provisions which are not found in the main body of the Act, or they may expand or define phrases in the Act or contain detailed amendments of earlier legislation. The last schedule will normally say which earlier statutes the present Act repeals. References to schedules are often abbreviated as 'sched' or 'sch' and the divisions are known as 'paragraphs', often abbreviated to 'para'.

A statutory instrument is cited by its title and also by the form 'SI [year]/[serial number]', eg, SI 1998/3132, which was the first published form of the Civil Procedure Rules 1998. The serial numbering reverts to '1' at the start of each calendar year.

The body of a statutory instrument is divided. The names of these divisions depend on the form of the title. If it is called an 'Order', the divisions are known as articles. If it is entitled 'Regulations', the divisions are also known as regulations. If it is entitled 'Rules', the divisions are also known as rules. A subdivision is always known as a paragraph.

The following table summarises the conventions for citing divisions and sub-divisions of the various categories of legislation:

Category	First division (numbered 1, 2, 3 etc)	Second division (numbered (1), (2), (3) etc)	Third division (lettered (a), (b), (c) etc)
Primary Legislation:			
Act	section	subsection	paragraph
Bill	*clause*	*subsection*	*paragraph*
Secondary Legislation:			
Order	article	paragraph	sub-paragraph
Regulations	regulation	paragraph	sub-paragraph
Rules	rule	paragraph	sub-paragraph
Schedules:			
Schedule	paragraph	sub-paragraph	paragraph

6.3 WHERE CAN I FIND ACTS?

6.3.1 Official versions of Acts of Parliament

6.3.1.1 Chronological

Upon receiving Royal Assent, the official version of an Act is published by Her Majesty's Stationery Office (HMSO). It appears in paper form and also, within a chronological sequence, on the website www.legislation.gov.uk. The paper versions are republished each year as a series of hardback volumes entitled *Public General Acts and Measures*.

6.3.1.2 Consolidated

The legislation.gov.uk website also makes freely available official consolidated versions of Acts on the Internet (that is, versions that incorporate subsequent repeals and amendments). However, for the practising lawyer, there is a significant caveat:

- Around half of all Acts do not yet incorporate changes applied by subsequent Acts that were passed from 2003 onwards (the database calls such changes 'effects'). Updating gaps are flagged in two ways. A 'Changes to Legislation' message appears above the Table of Contents to each Act, stating either that there are no known outstanding changes, or that outstanding changes remain to be applied by the Editorial Team. In addition, any changes waiting to be applied are also listed at the top of each provision.

The legislation.gov.uk website is continually being enhanced and it is a useful free source. However, for the lawyer engaged in legal research, it is not yet a viable alternative to commercial databases of legislation, such as *LexisLibrary* (see **6.6**) or *Westlaw* (see **6.7**).

6.3.2 *Current Law Statutes*

Current Law Statutes publishes statutes chronologically. They first appear as looseleaf booklets. These are later republished as several hardback volumes each year. This original version of the statute is then 'frozen' permanently: subsequent amendments and repeals are not incorporated.

The editorial annotations to *Current Law Statutes* are especially helpful in carrying out so-called 'Pepper v Hart' research. The decision of the House of Lords in *Pepper v Hart* [1993] AC 593 opened the way for the courts to consider what was said in Parliament during consideration of a Bill in circumstances where perceived ambiguity creates a need to clarify the intentions of the legislature. *Hansard* is the verbatim official record of proceedings in Parliament (the full text is available at www.parliament.uk/business/publications/hansard). The preface to each Act in *Current Law Statutes* gives *Hansard* references to all debates in Parliament, as well as further background information on the events that prompted legislative proposals.

> **PROFESSIONAL CONDUCT POINT**
>
> The decision in *Pepper v Hart* creates a professional responsibility to take into account *Hansard* as a primary source of research to assist legislative interpretation, especially in areas of the law that are heavily statute-based (for example, tax).

6.3.3 *Law Reports. Statutes* series

Current Law Statutes first appeared in 1949. If you need to consult an older Act as it was originally passed by Parliament, you may need to refer to the (confusingly titled) *Law Reports. Statutes* series (1865–). Once again, the original version of the statute is 'frozen' in this source: any subsequent amendments and repeals are omitted.

6.3.4   Halsbury's Statutes of England

Halsbury's Statutes of England contains an annotated version of all statutes in force in England and Wales. Amendments are incorporated; repealed provisions are excluded. The arrangement is alphabetical by subject. It is the best printed source for consulting up-to-date versions of statutes.

To find out the law using the paper version of *Halsbury's Statutes of England*, you must take four steps:

- index;
- main volumes;
- Cumulative Supplement; and
- Noter-Up.

6.3.4.1   Consolidated index

This paperback volume contains an *alphabetical list of statutes*, a *chronological list of statutes*, and a subject index (called the *consolidated index*). The subject index should be used if you are uncertain of the provision that you need. Think of subject terms that identify the problem you are researching. The subject index will refer you from these keywords to relevant statutes in a main volume:

disorderly conduct

licensed premises, on, **13** [703]

The number in **bold** is the number of the volume in which the relevant statute appears. The following number in light type and square brackets is the paragraph number. If the second number is not enclosed in square brackets then it refers to a page number in the main volume. If the volume reference is followed by **(S)**, the provision is a recent one and will be found in one of the *Current Statutes Service* looseleaf binders. The volume and subject arrangements of these are the same as the main set.

6.3.4.2   Main volumes

The 52 'main volumes' feature statutes in force in England and Wales, arranged alphabetically by subject. Volume 1 begins with agriculture. Volume 52 ends with water. In addition, these are supplemented by *Current Statutes Service* binders A–F. Each binder is clearly labelled to show the volume numbers that it supplements.

If a statute covers several subject areas, it may be split over several different volumes. The text is up to date to the year of publication of the volume (printed on the spine). Amended text appears in square brackets; text that has been repealed appears as "...."; text that will be amended or repealed at a future date appears in *italics*. Detailed footnotes provide useful commentary in relation to: parliamentary debates; amendments and repeals; derivation of older provisions in the case of consolidating legislation; commencement details; cross-references to other related provisions; judicial interpretation; linked subordinate legislation; and references to words defined elsewhere in the Act.

6.3.4.3   Cumulative Supplement

Over the years, main volumes are reissued on a rolling programme. Therefore you must always check whether the information in any main volume has changed since the volume was published.

This updating process involves two stages. To begin with, consult the annual hardback *Cumulative Supplement*. Check the first couple of pages for a note confirming the date to which the legislation has been updated. Any developments affecting your statute between the publication of individual main volumes and the cut-off date of the *Cumulative Supplement* will be noted. The *Cumulative Supplement* is arranged by subject. Look up the subject covered by the main volume, eg Employment, and then entries are listed alphabetically, so look up the name of the Act.

6.3.4.4 Noter-Up

Lastly, check the looseleaf *Noter-Up* binder. This is updated monthly and will alert you to any very recent changes in the law. Here you should look for the subject area covered by the main volume, eg Employment. Then Acts are arranged chronologically, starting with the earliest statute in that area which is still in force.

How to use *Halsbury's Statutes*

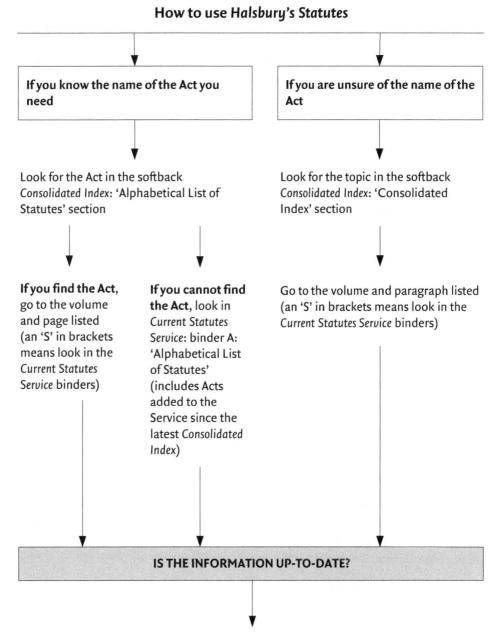

If you know the name of the Act you need

If you are unsure of the name of the Act

Look for the Act in the softback *Consolidated Index*: 'Alphabetical List of Statutes' section

Look for the topic in the softback *Consolidated Index*: 'Consolidated Index' section

If you find the Act, go to the volume and page listed (an 'S' in brackets means look in the *Current Statutes Service* binders)

If you cannot find the Act, look in *Current Statutes Service*: binder A: 'Alphabetical List of Statutes' (includes Acts added to the Service since the latest *Consolidated Index*)

Go to the volume and paragraph listed (an 'S' in brackets means look in the *Current Statutes Service* binders)

IS THE INFORMATION UP-TO-DATE?

Look in the annual hardback *Cumulative Supplement* for your Act (arranged by subject alphabetically). An entry means the law has changed between the publication date of the volume and the operative date of the *Cumulative Supplement*.

Then look in the *Noter-Up* binder using the subject area of the main volume. Acts are arranged chronologically. An entry means the law has changed since the operative date of the *Cumulative Supplement*.

Always check both the *Cumulative Supplement* and Noter-Up to update.

6.4   HOW DO I ESTABLISH WHETHER AN ACT HAS COME INTO FORCE?

A statute that has passed all its parliamentary stages and received Royal Assent may not necessarily come into effect straight away. To complicate matters further, often some sections of statutes enter into force before others. Sometimes sections are brought partially into effect, for a limited purpose and period, before entering fully into force later. And just occasionally a statute is repealed before it enters into force at all (eg, the Antarctic Minerals Act 1989).

The last section of a statute usually deals with arrangements for its own commencement. A specific date may be given; a specific period after the date of Royal Assent may be stipulated; or the commencement may be delayed until such time as the Secretary of State makes a commencement order (usually by way of a statutory instrument).

If no commencement statement is made within the text of a statute (sometimes the case with older statutes), you may assume that it came into force on the date of Royal Assent.

6.4.1   Is it in Force?

The paperback volume, *Is it in Force?*, is reissued twice yearly as part of *Halsbury's Statutes of England*. It lists statutes passed since 1 January 1960, with commencement details. Arrangement is by year, then alphabetical by title of statute, then by section. A supplement dealing with the current year appears in the looseleaf *Noter-Up* binder of *Halsbury's Statutes of England*. The same content is also available on *LexisLibrary* (choose *Sources: H: Halsbury's Is It In Force?*).

Note: The title '*Is it in Force?*' is misleading. A more accurate title might be '*Has it Come into Force YET?*', in the sense that this publication deals with commencement information only; it does not deal exhaustively with amendments and repeals that may affect the status of your statute since its date(s) of commencement. For sources of information on amendments and repeals, see **6.8**.

If your statute was passed by Parliament before 1960, you will need to consult the text of the provision itself for information about commencement. Alternatively, a practitioner book may give useful guidance.

6.5   WHERE CAN I FIND STATUTORY INSTRUMENTS?

6.5.1   Official versions of statutory instruments

The official version of a statutory instrument is published by Her Majesty's Stationery Office (HMSO). It appears in paper form and also on the website www.legislation.gov.uk. These texts are not subsequently amended to show the effects of later legislation. The paper versions are republished each year as a series of hardback volumes entitled *Statutory Instruments*.

6.5.2   *Halsbury's Statutory Instruments*

Halsbury's Statutory Instruments collects all statutory instruments in force in England and Wales. Those instruments that the editors judge to be most valuable to practising lawyers are reprinted in full; the remainder appear in summary. The arrangement is alphabetical by subject, and so this is the best hard copy source for discovering what relevant secondary legislation exists on a given topic.

To find out the law using the paper version of *Halsbury's Statutory Instruments*, you must take three steps:

- index;
- main volumes; and
- service binder.

6.5.2.1 Index

The annual paperback *Consolidated Index* contains a subject index and an alphabetical list of instruments by title. If you are uncertain of the title of the provision that you need, think of subject terms that identify the problem you are researching. The subject index will refer you from these 'keywords' to a main volume and a page.

If the reference in an index appears as '(S)' followed by a citation, the provision is a recent one and will be dealt with in the *Service* looseleaf binder.

6.5.2.2 Main volumes

The 22 main volumes feature statutory instruments in force in England and Wales, arranged by subject. Volume 1 begins with agriculture. Volume 22 ends with water. Each subject opens with a chronological contents list and a list of relevant instruments no longer in force. The text is up-to-date to the year of publication of the volume (printed on the spine). Footnotes provide detailed commentary.

6.5.2.3 Service binders

The looseleaf *Service* binder contains a variety of indexing and updating tools. These include a *chronological list of instruments*, covering the whole publication and allowing you to find a provision where you only know its citation.

The largest section, the *Monthly Update*, lists changes to the statement of law given in the main volumes. Over the years, main volumes are reissued on a rolling programme. Therefore you must always check whether the information in any main volume has changed since the volume's year of publication. Entries appear under the same volume and subject heading as in the main volumes. Check for any new provisions using the *Chronological List of Instruments*. Then check for any changes to the effect of existing provisions using the *List of Changes*.

How to use Halsbury's Statutory Instruments

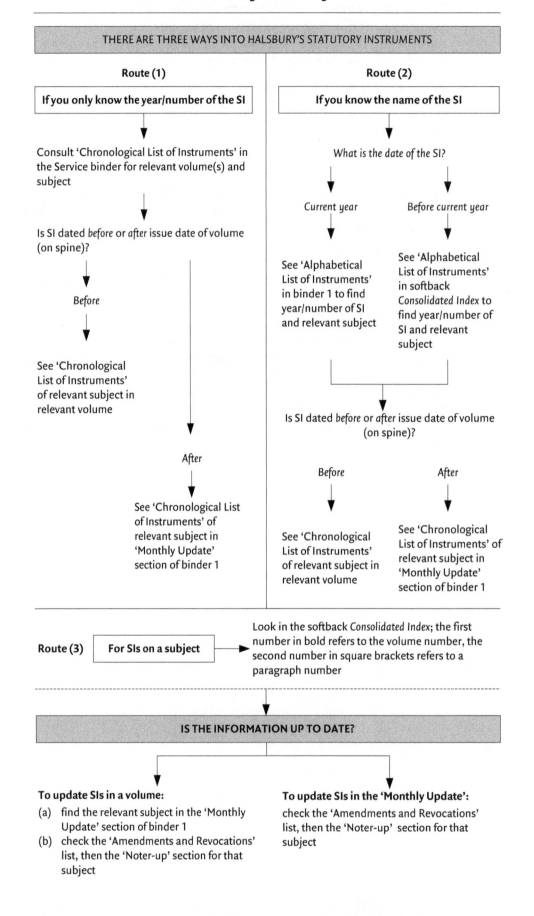

THERE ARE THREE WAYS INTO HALSBURY'S STATUTORY INSTRUMENTS

Route (1)

If you only know the year/number of the SI

Consult 'Chronological List of Instruments' in the Service binder for relevant volume(s) and subject

Is SI dated *before* or *after* issue date of volume (on spine)?

Before

See 'Chronological List of Instruments' of relevant subject in relevant volume

After

See 'Chronological List of Instruments' of relevant subject in 'Monthly Update' section of binder 1

Route (2)

If you know the name of the SI

What is the date of the SI?

Current year

See 'Alphabetical List of Instruments' in binder 1 to find year/number of SI and relevant subject

Before current year

See 'Alphabetical List of Instruments' in softback *Consolidated Index* to find year/number of SI and relevant subject

Is SI dated *before* or *after* issue date of volume (on spine)?

Before

See 'Chronological List of Instruments' of relevant subject in relevant volume

After

See 'Chronological List of Instruments' of relevant subject in 'Monthly Update' section of binder 1

Route (3)   For SIs on a subject

Look in the softback *Consolidated Index*; the first number in bold refers to the volume number, the second number in square brackets refers to a paragraph number

IS THE INFORMATION UP TO DATE?

To update SIs in a volume:
(a) find the relevant subject in the 'Monthly Update' section of binder 1
(b) check the 'Amendments and Revocations' list, then the 'Noter-up' section for that subject

To update SIs in the 'Monthly Update':
check the 'Amendments and Revocations' list, then the 'Noter-up' section for that subject

6.6 LEGISLATION ON LEXISLIBRARY

6.6.1 Scope

LexisLibrary contains the full, amended text of UK primary and secondary legislation in force. Legislation that has been recently enacted but is not yet in force is also included. Most of this material is split between two databases: *UK Parliament Acts*, comprising all Public General Acts, and *UK Parliament SIs*, comprising all statutory instruments of general application.

6.6.2 Searching

Within *LexisLibrary*, select *UK Parliament Acts* or *UK Parliament SIs* as appropriate. Look for these options either in the *My Bookshelf* section of the home page; or by clicking *Legislation* and using the drop-down arrow in the *Sources* field to select your preferred source; or by clicking the *Sources* tab, then *Choose: . . . U.*

To search for a named piece of legislation, enter search terms in the box labelled *Title*. You can also specify a *Year* and a particular *Provision* (section or schedule number).

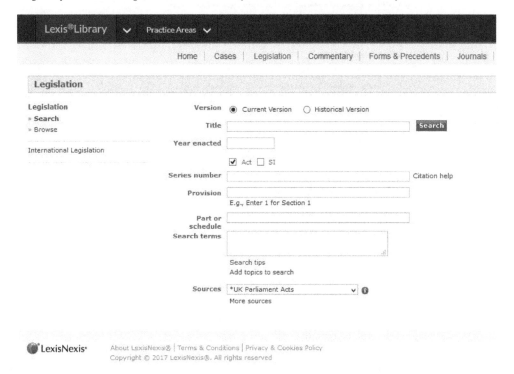

Reproduced with kind permission of LexisNexis

To search for legislation on a topic, enter keyword(s) in the box labelled *Search terms*. Click the red *Search* button to retrieve a list of sections of legislation where these occur. If you enter two or more search terms they will be treated as a phrase, unless you link them using Boolean connectors (see **3.5.3**). If you get too many results, try sorting them by relevance or use the *search within results* option, entering another keyword.

> **PERSONAL INJURY CASE STUDY**
>
> For example, our road traffic case study involves a car whose driver was alleged to be on the telephone at the time of a collision. Searching *UK Parliament Acts* with the terms **"mobile telephone" and driving** retrieves s 26 of the Road Safety Act 2006, which creates an offence of driving while using a hand-held mobile phone.

From the list of search results, click on the appropriate heading to view the full text. Amended text appears in square brackets; text that has been repealed appears as '...'; text that will be amended or repealed at a future date appears in *italics*. Footnotes provide brief details about commencement and sources of amending legislation. Blue arrows at the top of the screen enable you to move to the previous or next section of the legislation. Click on the grey tab on the left to see a Table of Contents of the Act. If a *Stop press* icon appears, it is alerting you to recent changes to the legislation which may not have been incorporated into the text on the screen. Click the icon for more information and assistance.

On the right of the screen you can link to older versions of the legislation. Under *Find out more* you can access information about commencement, repeals and amendments via a source called *Status Snapshot*. This merges the content of *Is it in Force?* (see **6.4.1** above) and *Halsbury's Statutes Citator* (see **6.8.2** below). Note also the option to link to *Annotations*; this links to commentary drawn from *Halsbury's Statutes* (see **6.3.4.2**). The *Find Out More* section also allows you to link to commentary, cases or journal articles relating to the section on the screen.

Reproduced with kind permission of LexisNexis

6.7   LEGISLATION ON WESTLAW

Westlaw is a good alternative to *LexisLibrary* for researching legislation.

On the home page, click *Legislation*. The *Basic Search* screen permits either browsing or searching of the text of UK Acts and SIs, as amended. It is possible to search either by *Title* and *Provision Number* or, to find material about a topic, by *Free Text* or *Subject/Keyword*. A useful extra *Statutory Definition* search option offers the facility to find definitions of a word or phrase within the text of different pieces of legislation.

Remember that when searching *Westlaw* for a phrase, you must enclose the phrase within double inverted commas. If you do not, this particular database will assume that you wish to combine the two terms with a Boolean **and** between them (see **3.5.3** above if you need to remind yourself about Boolean connectors). This is likely to produce a different set of results.

Each Act or SI that matches your search will be displayed along with a link to the *arrangement* of that Act or SI. This is like a table of contents. Section numbers within the table link to full text, and each features an icon that signifies legal status:

•   A green tick indicates that the provision is in force in full.

- An orange and green 'P' icon appears if the provision is only partially in force.
- An orange 'N' appears if the provision is not yet in force.
- A red 'R' appears if the provision has been repealed.
- A yellow '!' indicates amendment(s) pending.

When viewing a particular provision, a menu to the left of the full text gives access to further *Legislation Analysis*. This brings together a wide range of information about the provision, such as: a table of amendments (historical and pending); commencement details; details of jurisdictional extent; a list of any SIs made under the provision; details of related legislation; and lists of cases and journal articles that cite the provision.

Reproduced with kind permission of Westlaw UK

The *Advanced Search* screen adds options to search for *Historic Law* and *Prospective Law*, as well as the *Law in Force* today. This permits you to travel through time in your research, to read versions in force at a particular date in the past or future. If you do elect to include historic and/or prospective versions, your search results will carry their own set of icons to denote legal status:

- A green tick indicates that the provision is in force in full.
- A blue arrow indicates that the provision is prospective, and so the text displayed will incorporate amendments that are currently pending.
- A yellow exclamation mark indicates that the provision is liable to amendments that are currently pending.
- A red 'no entry' sign indicates that the provision has been superseded.

6.8 HOW DO I UPDATE LEGISLATION?

It is vital to check for changes to the legal status of legislation that you use in the course of your research.

Legislative updates take two principal forms: later amending legislation, and statements of interpretation by judges in subsequent cases.

The issue of amending legislation is especially critical if the source you have consulted is one that publishes measures chronologically as enacted (for example, *Current Law Statutes*). You can rely on the consolidated versions in *Halsbury's Statutes* and *Halsbury's Statutory Instruments* in paper format being current to within a month or so, provided all the updating steps have been followed through properly.

6.8.1   Online resources

Legislation on commercial databases such as *Westlaw* and *LexisLibrary* is generally updated daily, in the sense that the editors add new material every day. However, it does not follow that the content is current to today. Incorporating all the effects of new legislation is a complex and time-consuming task, and it makes it difficult for publishers of databases to state exactly how current the text of amended legislation can be relied upon to be. Within *UK Parliament Acts* on *LexisLibrary*, for example, the publisher states: 'Source Currency: This source is updated on a regular basis.'

Furthermore, where recent legislation materially changes earlier legislation, but the editors have not yet incorporated these changes, each affected section will feature a red warning symbol along with the words *Stop press!* Click these words for more information about the likely changes.

6.8.2   Halsbury's Statutes Citator

Halsbury's Statutes Citator is a quick reference tool for tracing changes to Acts. This paperback volume is published twice yearly as part of *Halsbury's Statutes*. It will list amendments or repeals to individual sections or entire Acts. The arrangement is by year, then alphabetical by title.

The text of *Halsbury's Statutes Citator* appears on *LexisLibrary* both as a free-standing source, and also merged within *UK Legislation Status Snapshots* (see **6.6.2** above).

6.8.3   Current Law Legislation Citator

The *Current Law Legislation Citator* gives references to subsequent legislation and cases that have changed the legal status of a statute or a statutory instrument.

The printed version of the *Current Law Legislation Citator* comprises a series of hardback volumes, each covering a series of years, starting in 1947. These are supplemented by paperback volumes dealing with the most recent years. Recent months are covered by sections in the looseleaf *Current Awareness Service File*.

Each volume is arranged chronologically by year, then provision number (chapter number for statutes or serial number for statutory instruments), then section number. The procedure is to find the earliest reference to your provision, then methodically to check the lists in subsequent volumes for later developments. The material is also available on *Westlaw* if you use the *Legislation Analysis* link when looking at a particular piece of legislation.

RESEARCHING EUROPEAN UNION LAW

LEARNING OUTCOMES

After reading this chapter you will be able to:

- identify which resources to use to research European Union (EU) law
- find EU legislation on the *Europa* and *EUR-Lex* websites
- explain how to check if an EU directive has been implemented in the UK
- understand which sources to use to find EU case law.

7.1 INTRODUCTION

Following the result of the referendum on the UK's membership of the European Union on 23 June 2016, you might think there is no longer a need for your research to include reference to EU law. However, this is not the case. The UK remains part of the EU and subject to EU law until such time as the terms of the exit have been agreed under Article 50 of the Treaty on European Union. EU law and its application will remain relevant for many years to come. Therefore, it is still important to consider the possible impact of European law on the area you are researching.

Researching the law of the European Union (EU) requires skill and tenacity. The structure of the material is complex. The volume of new legislation and cases is large. Publication of some documents is delayed by translation. There is often a significant further time lag before developments filter into practitioner sources covering the state of UK law. Researchers who specialise in EU law become adept at using a variety of methods in their hunt for authority that may affect clients' business decisions. For example, telephoning an official department may yield significant information that no standard source can offer.

This brief introduction to researching EU law will familiarise you with the key information sources. With some practice, you will be able to track down references to EU legislation and cases. You will also develop a feel for spotting possible 'Europoints' in a file, even if no such point seems to be in issue at first sight.

The *Official Journal of the European Union* (OJ) is the official compendium of EU legislation (L series) and other official documents of the EU institutions, bodies and agencies (C series and its supplements). From 1 July 2013, the electronic version of the OJ is authentic (has legal force) – see Regulation (EU) No 216/2013. Generally, the paper version no longer has any legal value (http://eur-lex.europa.eu/content/oj/e-oj.html).

The European Union itself also publishes a vast amount of information, including primary legal materials, on the Internet. The major sites are *Europa* (http://europa.eu) and *EUR-Lex* (http://eur-lex.europa.eu/homepage.html). However, unfortunately they are not always the easiest sites to navigate. There is a help section which includes tutorials on using *EUR-Lex* (http://eur-lex.europa.eu/content/guided-tour/home-guided-tour.html), or try using *Google* for searching instead (see www.google.co.uk): type keyword(s) into the search box as usual, followed by 'site:europa.eu'. Alternatively, if you have access to a subscription database such as *Westlaw*, *LexisLibrary* or *Lawtel*, you may find it easier to use it to find EU information.

If you have access to the *Practical Law* database, there is a comprehensive section dealing with all aspects of Brexit, which contains an extremely useful guide on researching EU law. From the home page, select Brexit: the legal implications, then click on the EU law tab and then select EU Survival Kit; the Online research tools section is particularly helpful.

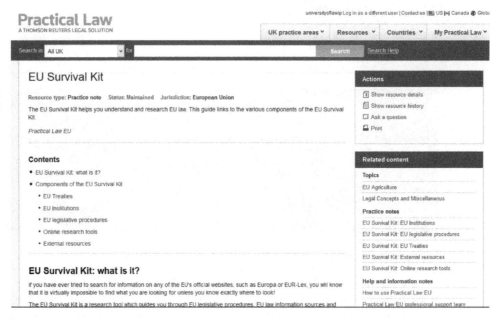

© Thomson Reuters

7.2   GENERAL SOURCES

7.2.1   EUR-Lex

Notwithstanding the caveat about the difficulties of searching for material on *EUR-Lex*, you should familiarise yourself with it, especially as you may not have access to EU materials via the legal databases.

EUR-Lex is the legal portal within the *Europa* website. It offers free access to EU law, including the *Official Journal of the European Union* L-series (Legislation) and C-series (Information and Notices), treaties, legislation, international agreements, preparatory acts and parliamentary questions. Case-law coverage includes judgments of the Court of Justice and the General Court of the European Union. Also available are the Commission documents (the 'COM' series), a collection of consolidated legislation, and the texts of treaties. There are further links to summaries of EU legislation and a link to a publication called *The ABC of European Union Law*, which sets out to examine the roots of the European project and its development as a legal order.

In this chapter we shall examine how to search *EUR-Lex*. There are three options for searching from the home page. First, *Quick* search gives you the ability to search by *free text*, *CELEX number* (a unique identifier of a document on *EUR-Lex*) or keywords. As the text option would search across the entire database, yielding a large number of results, and you are unlikely to have the *CELEX number*, you may not find this option particularly useful.

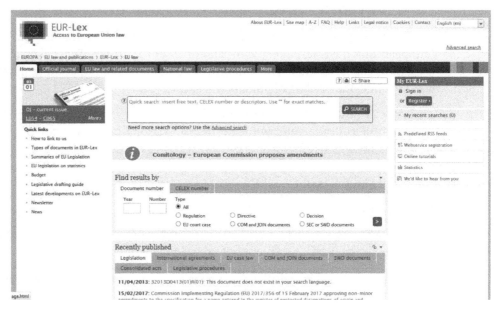

© European Union

The second option, which you may find more useful, is to search by *document number*. Select the document type (eg, *Regulation*, *Directive*, or *EU court case*), enter the year and the number and click *Search*. This is a relatively straightforward process provided you know the year and number of the legislation or case you are looking for.

The third option, if you do not have the document reference number, is to select the *Advanced search* facility available under the Quick search box. This allows you to carry out a more focused free text search. You can limit your search to a particular collection on the database (eg, *EU case law*), search for words that only appear in the title of a document, select a date range, etc.

© European Union

7.2.2   European Current Law

The printed publication *European Current Law* allows you to trace developments over time. Monthly parts summarise legislation and case law. They include tables and indexes that accumulate throughout the year. All material is subsequently republished as a bound 'year book'.

7.3 PRIMARY LEGISLATION

The primary legislation of the EU comprises the founding treaties that established the three European Communities, along with later amending treaties. These documents lay out the aspirations and objectives of the Union. The accession treaties that admit new Member States also fall under the heading of primary legislation.

The official text of the treaties may be freely accessed via *EUR-Lex* (see http://eur-lex.europa.eu/collection/eu-law/treaties.html). Various paper sources reprint the treaties, including the annual textbook, *Blackstone's EU Treaties and Legislation*.

7.4 SECONDARY LEGISLATION

7.4.1 Introduction

The secondary legislation of the EU sets out how the objectives expressed in the treaties are to be accomplished. Various categories of provision fall under this heading:

Category	Description	Example, as published in the *Official Journal*
Regulations	Directly applicable to Member States: no need for national legislation	Commission Regulation (EC) No 2/2009 of 5 January 2009 establishing the standard import values for determining the entry price of certain fruit and vegetables
Directives	Member States must legislate to implement within a fixed period	Directive 2008/122/EC of the European Parliament and of the Council of 14 January 2009 on the protection of consumers in respect of certain aspects of timeshare, long-term holiday product, resale and exchange contracts
Decisions	Addressed to particular Member States, companies or individuals	Commission Decision of 23 January 2009 establishing the Committee of European Securities Regulators (2009/78/EC)
Recommendations and opinions	Non-binding suggestions for action	Commission Recommendation of 11 February 2009 on the implementation of a nuclear material accountancy and control system by operators of nuclear installations

In practice, you will mainly encounter regulations and directives. From 1 January 2015 the numbering of EU legislation changed. Previously, a regulation was cited by running number then year (ie, Regulation 1/99 was the first regulation of 1999); a directive was cited by year then running number (ie, Directive 99/1 was the first directive of 1999). The new method aims to harmonise and simplify the numbering system so the type of provision is always followed by the year and sequential number. For example, Regulation (EU) 2015/1, Directive (EU) 2015/2, Council Decision (EU) 2015/3. For more information, see http://eur-lex.europa.eu/content/tools/elaw/OA0614022END.pdf.

Informal nicknames are often given to pieces of European legislation. For example, the Directive on Cocoa and Chocolate Products (Directive 2000/35) is commonly known as the 'Chocolate Directive'. This is a problem if you are trying to find the piece of legislation and all you know about it is its nickname. *Lawtel EU* features a useful list of legislation nicknames, with links to the full titles and full text. To access this from the *Lawtel UK* home page, click *Specialist Areas*, select *EU*, *Practice Tools*, *Glossaries* and then *Legislation Nicknames*. You can also find a useful EU glossary here.

7.4.2   Sources of EU secondary legislation

7.4.2.1   EUR-Lex

EUR-Lex provides access to secondary legislation.

If you know the year and number of the Regulation, Directive or Decision, you can use the search *By document number* option from the home page.

Alternatively, from the *EU law and related documents* tab, you can click *EU Legislation* and search from there.

© European Union

If you select the *Search in Legislation* option, you can carry out a free text search. The *Directory of European Union Legislation* allows you to see all legislation on a particular subject, such as *Freedom of movement for workers*. The *Recently published* (legislation from the last 14 days) option is likely to be less useful.

The official text of all EU legislation is the text printed in the *Official Journal*. As with UK legislation, this is subject to amendment and repeal over time. A project to consolidate the vast body of EU legislation for free publication on the Internet is ongoing. To access this material, go to the *EUR-Lex* home page and select *Consolidated legislation* from the *EU law and related documents* tab. The project aims to collect legislation, with amendments, into 'families' of documents for ease of use.

© European Union

Selecting the *Directory of European Union consolidated legislation* option will then allow you to browse by subject to find the latest amended version of legislation. However, use with caution as, at the time of writing, it does include the significant caveat: '*This directory is still in an experimental phase. Some references may be missing, especially for amendments published after the last consolidated version.*'

© European Union

From this page you can also link (from the left-hand column) to *Legislation in Force* (see **7.4.3** below) and *Legislation in Preparation*.

7.4.2.2   *Blackstone's EU Treaties and Legislation*

The annual text *Blackstone's EU Treaties and Legislation*, edited by Foster, reprints a convenient selection of the most useful and frequently consulted secondary legislation.

7.4.3   How to check if EU legislation is in force

European Union secondary legislation is subject to later amendments and repeals. Besides the collection of legislation in force on *EUR-Lex*, there are several ways of tracing the current status of a given provision.

The most straightforward option is to select the Advanced search option from the home page (http://eur-lex.europa.eu/homepage.html), select Legislation as the collection to search and tick the box to limit to legislation in force.

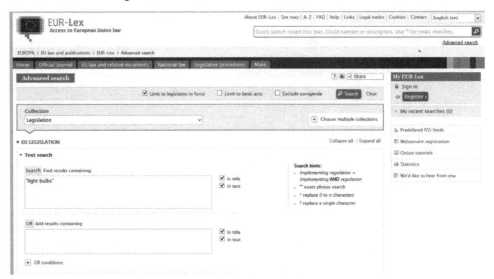

© European Union

Another option is to browse the Directory of European Union Legislation by subject (http://eur-lex.europa.eu/browse/directories/legislation.html).

© European Union

However, be aware that browsing until you find what you need can be time-consuming.

If you are unsure whether a piece of EU legislation is in force, check whether the proposal has been adopted and published in the *Official Journal*. EU legislation does not have legal force until it has been published in the *Official Journal*.

7.4.4 How to check if an EU directive has been implemented in the UK

A handy source is the paperback *EU Legislation Implementator*. This is reissued annually as a supplement to *Halsbury's Statutory Instruments* and is updated by the looseleaf 'Service' issues to that encyclopedia. It is divided into three parts:

- Part 1 – *Chronological Table of Directives*: chronological list of all directives, with the latest date for implementation (*Transposition Deadline*) and a reference to the UK implementing legislation alongside. So, for example, if you wanted to know whether Directive 99/103 has been implemented in the UK, this book would tell you that the target date for implementation was 8 February 2001 and that the relevant UK legislation includes the Units of Measurement Regulations 2001 (SI 2001/55) and the Weights and Measures (Metrication Amendment) Regulations 2001 (SI 2001/85). You would then need to refer to a suitable UK law source for the text of those UK Regulations.

- Part 2 – *Table of Directives by Subject Area*: contains the same information as Part 1 but presented in subject order to aid the user where the directive number is not known, so Directive 99/103 would be found in the section on 'Weights'.

- Part 3 – *Table of Statutory Instruments*: chronological list of UK statutory instruments linking them to the directives they implement.

EUR-Lex includes details of national implementing measures in relation to EU directives. Click on the *National law* tab (http://eur-lex.europa.eu/collection/n-law.html) and then *National transposition measures*. However, be aware that developments can take a long time to filter through to this source. Another option, if you have access, is to find the directive within *Westlaw* which also has links to *National Measures*.

7.4.5 Proposed legislation

It is important to be alert to proposed legislation when researching the European dimension of a problem. However, draft EU legislation is notoriously difficult to trace. It can take several years to agree the final version of a measure. Final drafts are generally published as COM documents (also known as 'COM docs'), this being the title of a range of working documents of the European Commission. They are cited in the form: COM (*year*) *running number* final. Final drafts also appear in the *Official Journal*, C-series (Information and Notices). These can be accessed by clicking *EU Preparatory Acts* from the *EU law and related documents* tab on the *EUR-Lex* home page (http://eur-lex.europa.eu/collection/eu-law/pre-acts.html). Several commercial current awareness services are intended to alert subscribers to proposed EU legislation, such as the 'EU Daily Update' service from the subscription database, *Lawtel*.

As a last resort, advice may be obtained by contacting the offices of the European Commission Representation in the UK (see http://ec.europa.eu/unitedkingdom/about_us/index_en.htm for details).

7.5 CASE LAW

7.5.1 Introduction

European Union cases are heard before either the Court of Justice or the General Court. Before implementation of the Lisbon Treaty on 1 December 2009, these were known as the European Court of Justice and the Court of First Instance respectively.

The term 'Court of Justice of the European Union' refers collectively to the Court of Justice, the General Court and any specialist Judicial Panels created (such as the EU Civil Service Panel).

The UK practitioner will be unaccustomed to certain aspects of the procedure of EU courts:

(a)   Judgments are preceded by an 'opinion' of the Advocate General; this is not necessarily binding on the court, but its reasoning is usually followed.

(b)   Applications to the court that concern the same area of law may be joined together.

(c)   The names of parties are often very long; some leading cases are therefore referred to by nicknames, which may or may not appear in electronic databases or indexes to paper sources.

(d)   The court delivers one judgment only; there are no dissenting opinions.

Be careful to differentiate EU case law from the case law of the European Court of Human Rights (www.echr.coe.int/ECHR). This court belongs to a separate institution altogether, the Council of Europe. It hears complaints concerning alleged violations by Nation States of the European Convention on Human Rights.

7.5.2 Citation

The case number is an important feature of citations for EU cases. A full citation gives the case number first, followed by the parties, then the citation of the authoritative report in the paper version of the *European Court Reports*. For example:

C-295/95 *Farrell v Long* [1997] ECR I-1683

The case number comprises a running serial number followed by the year of application or reference to the Court (note that application and judgment may be separated by several years). Since the creation of the Court of First Instance in 1989, all cases are prefixed by 'C-' (Court of Justice, or '*Cour*' in French) or 'T-' (General Court, or '*Tribunal*' in French).

7.5.3 Sources of EU cases

All judgments of the Court of Justice and the General Court are freely available on the *Curia* website within *Europa* (http://curia.europa.eu/). Click *En* to access information in English, then click *Case-law* in the left-hand column to produce a choice of search options.

If you know the case number, searching is straightforward: select *Numerical access*, select the Court and date range, scan down the chronological list and click the appropriate reference. For judgments up to and including 1997, this will automatically link to the authoritative version on *EUR-Lex* that was published in the *European Court Reports*. For later cases, this will link to the transcript of the judgment on the *Curia* website itself.

For access by party or by topic, select *Search form*. This permits free text searching (*Text*). It also allows you to confine your search to material classed under one of 50 or so broad subject headings, via the *Subject-matter* drop-down menu.

© European Union

After some delay, judgments are translated into all EU languages and then published in the *European Court Reports*.

The paper version of the *European Court Reports* is the authoritative source for EU case law. Electronic versions are available via *EUR-Lex*. If you know the year and number of the case, you can search from the home page, *By document number*, select *EU court case* and enter the year and case number.

Alternatively, select the *Advanced search* option, choose *EU case law* as the collection and fill in the search form with what details you have (date, court, subject or party names should be typed in the *text search* boxes).

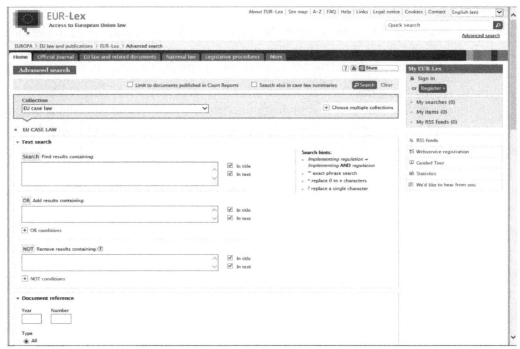

© European Union

Westlaw and *LexisLibrary* also feature the full text of the *European Court Reports*, and you may find the search engines on these databases easier to use than the *Curia* or *EUR-Lex* websites.

The *Common Market Law Reports* is a more timely (but unofficial) alternative to the *European Court Reports*. All significant EU cases are included, as well as selected decisions of Member State national courts. The paper version appears in five volumes each year (vols 4 and 5 deal with antitrust matters). It is indexed by subject, by case party and by case number. The full text is also available via *Westlaw*.

Another useful source is the *All England Law Reports European Cases*, which reports cases from the Court of Justice and the General Court and opinions of the Advocates General. The online version is available via *LexisLibrary*.

Finally, *The Digest* may be used to trace the full citation of leading EU cases, and to search for cases on a subject.

RESEARCHING FORMS AND PRECEDENTS

LEARNING OUTCOMES

After reading this chapter you will be able to:

- explain how forms and precedents are used in practice
- understand how to use *Atkin's Court Forms* and the *Encyclopaedia of Forms and Precedents* in printed and online versions.

8.1 INTRODUCTION

Collections of forms and precedents provide specimens of the documents which lawyers need to draft. They can save much time and effort by avoiding reinventing the wheel, although as we have already learned, they should not be used uncritically (see **1.3.4** above).

Many firms hold their own bank of know-how and precedents for future use in similar transactions. These may exist in the form of paper records, or they may be accessed via the firm's intranet (so searchable from the lawyer's desktop).

A variety of commercial publications reproduce versions of prescribed or common documents. Some are limited in scope and aim to assist the specialist practitioner, such as M Waterworth, *Parker's Will Precedents* (8th edn, 2014). Others are more general in scope, such as J Kelly, *Kelly's Draftsman* (21st edn, 2014) which gathers into one book the most frequently needed precedents in general practice (and is also available online via *Kelly's Legal Precedents* on LexisLibrary).

Two complementary publications give comprehensive coverage: *Atkin's Court Forms* and the *Encyclopaedia of Forms and Precedents*. Both of these substantial encyclopedias are published by LexisNexis and are available online via *LexisLibrary*. The online texts may be accessed individually (as described below) or searched in combination (via the *Forms and Precedents* search form).

In recent years, a variety of online publishers have developed clusters of precedents and other know-how that may be accessed upon payment of a subscription. Practical Law Company (PLC) is prominent in this field, with know-how services across a wide variety of practice areas. Each service combines a bank of standard documents with commentary and analysis, email updates, and practice notes and checklists. From the PLC home page, select a practice area, eg Employment, then select a subject, eg unfair dismissal, then choose Standard Documents and Clauses to access a list of precedents in that area.

LexisNexis has also developed another database, *LexisPSL*. This is intended to be a more pratice-based service, and in each practice area you can access a wide range of precedents for legal transactions and procedures.

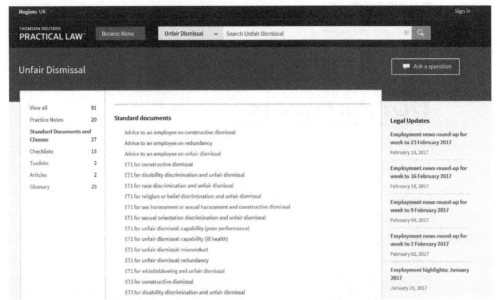

© Thomson Reuters

8.2   ATKIN'S COURT FORMS

Atkin's Court Forms is a comprehensive encyclopedia of forms, precedents and procedural advice connected with civil litigation. It reproduces the main documents required to transact civil proceedings before the courts and judicial tribunals of England and Wales. Arrangement is broadly by subject, or 'title', with each group of forms introduced by commentary on the relevant substantive and procedural law, including step-by-step guidance and checklists. Footnotes refer to useful related information, such as practice directions, case law, legislation and court rules. The value added by commentary and footnotes should not be underestimated: this is more than merely a compendium of forms.

8.2.1   Using the printed version of *Atkin's Court Forms*

To use the printed version of *Atkin's Court Forms*, follow these steps:

Note that the Civil Procedure Rules and the Family Procedure Rules each have their own separate volume.

8.2.2 Using the online version of Atkin's Court Forms

To research the online version within *LexisLibrary*, follow these steps:

- from the home page, click the Forms and Precedents link;
- from Sources – click the drop-down arrow and select *Atkin's Court Forms*;
- if searching, either elect to *Search within: All*, or limit your search to *Form or Precedent*, or *Commentary*;
- if you know the title or number of the form, use those fields; if not, use the *Search terms* field;
- or click *Browse*, to drill down to a particular volume, or enter *Search terms* where indicated.

Note that it is also possible to search across all forms and precedents content available on LexisLibrary, including but not limited to *Atkin's*. To do so, click the *Search* tab then select *Forms & Precedents* on the bar below. Note that the box labelled *Sources* defaults to: *All Subscribed Forms and Precedents Sources*. To review and amend coverage, click the down arrow next to the *Sources* box. You will see that the list which appears includes *Butterworths Civil Court Precedents*, for example.

8.3 ENCYCLOPAEDIA OF FORMS AND PRECEDENTS

The *Encyclopaedia of Forms and Precedents* (or EFP) is a comprehensive source of precedents for non-contentious civil transactions. It contains around 15,000 complete precedents (including those for sale of land, commercial law, family, wills and trusts). Arrangement is broadly by subject, or 'title', with each group of documents introduced by useful commentary on the relevant law and practice. In addition, annotations to the precedents offer practical drafting guidance and references to other helpful information, such as cases and legislation. As with *Atkin's Court Forms*, the value contained in the commentary and footnotes should not be overlooked.

How to use the printed version of the Encyclopaedia of
Forms and Precedents

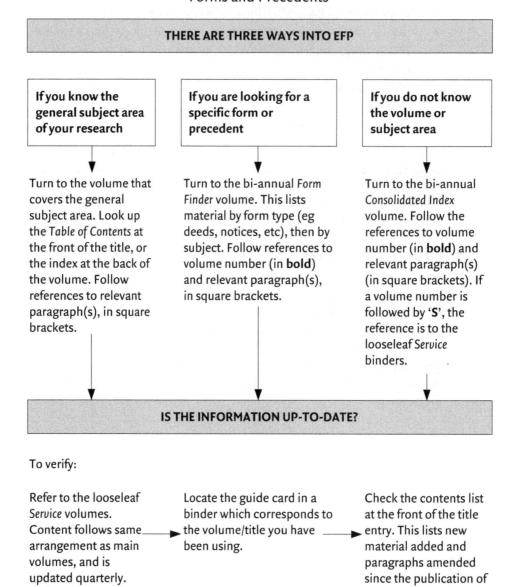

THERE ARE THREE WAYS INTO EFP

| **If you know the general subject area of your research** | **If you are looking for a specific form or precedent** | **If you do not know the volume or subject area** |

Turn to the volume that covers the general subject area. Look up the *Table of Contents* at the front of the title, or the index at the back of the volume. Follow references to relevant paragraph(s), in square brackets.

Turn to the bi-annual *Form Finder* volume. This lists material by form type (eg deeds, notices, etc), then by subject. Follow references to volume number (in **bold**) and relevant paragraph(s), in square brackets.

Turn to the bi-annual *Consolidated Index* volume. Follow the references to volume number (in **bold**) and relevant paragraph(s) (in square brackets). If a volume number is followed by '**S**', the reference is to the looseleaf *Service* binders.

IS THE INFORMATION UP-TO-DATE?

To verify:

Refer to the looseleaf *Service* volumes. Content follows same arrangement as main volumes, and is updated quarterly.

Locate the guide card in a binder which corresponds to the volume/title you have been using.

Check the contents list at the front of the title entry. This lists new material added and paragraphs amended since the publication of

8.3.1   Using the online version of EFP

The online version of EFP has two parts, either of which may be searched separately. One component is the full text of the encyclopedia itself. The other is an index that merges the subject approach of the printed *Consolidated Index*, and the *Form Finder* (for locating a specific known precedent). Note that many indivdual forms can be filled in on-screen. A piece of software called 'Hotdocs' may need to be installed in order to edit these documents.

The online version is available via *LexisLibrary*. It is accessible via both the *Forms and Precedents* and *Sources* links.

It is usually best to start searching with the *Index* component. This links easily to the full text of documents, and is likely to pin down the material you need in the least time. Follow these steps:

- click the *Sources* tab;
- click E in the alphabetical list that appears;

- tick the box next to *Encyclopaedia of Forms and Precedents Index*, then click the red *OK – continue* button;
- enter *Search terms* where indicated, eg divorce and pension;
- from the results list, click on the one that looks most relevant;
- if you get a large number of results, you can select the sort by relevance option;
- click any volume and paragraph reference to access the full text of the appropriate precedent.

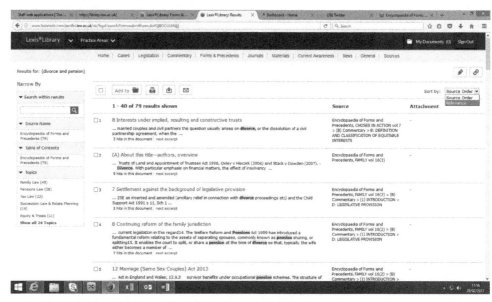

Reproduced with kind permission of LexisNexis

As previously mentioned in relation to *Atkin's*, note that it is also possible to search across all forms and precedents content available on *LexisLibrary*, including but not limited to the *Encyclopaedia of Forms and Precedents*. As a reminder, access this wide pool of material by clicking the *Search* tab, then select *Forms & Precedents* on the bar below. The default option is to search *All Subscribed Forms and Precedents Sources*. You can review and amend coverage by clicking the down arrow next to the box labelled *Sources*.

THE RESULT OF LEGAL RESEARCH

> **LEARNING OUTCOMES**
>
> After reading this chapter you will be able to:
>
> - explain the importance of recording your research
> - understand how to report your research effectively.

9.1 RECORDING RESEARCH

It may be tempting to jump straight into researching your problem and rely on memory rather than stopping to make notes at each stage. However, this is not an efficient approach. It may be only at the end of a research trail that the value of a particular piece of information becomes clear: accurate references will then save time. And what if your supervisor questions the answer? Or if he or she asks you to check back on something, or enquires about the steps you took to reach your answer?

At each stage of your research, as well as recording the information you discover, make a note of what you do and when you do it. Your record should include:

(a) the date your research was carried out (especially important with Internet sources, where content may change daily);

(b) full citations for legislation, case law and other primary sources consulted;

(c) for books: the author, title, edition, year and publisher;

(d) for journal articles: the title of the journal, title of the article, author, year and volume number;

(e) for databases: the name of the database, and the name of the section of the database (for example, *UK Parliament Acts* on *LexisLibrary*);

(f) keywords used during searches;

(g) page references or website addresses for key pieces of information;

(h) dates of publication (including the date of the latest release for a looseleaf source);

(i) any dates to which the law as stated is claimed to be up-to-date by the publisher.

Here is an example of a good research trail for a simple research query:

Topic	What are the penalties for importing cocaine into the UK?
Date of research	24 February 2017
Source used	*Halsbury's Laws of England*
Keywords used	Controlled drug – offences – import and export (*Consolidated Index*)

Result	Directed to paragraph 491 of volume 75 (5th edition) for a summary of the penalties upon conviction for import of a Class A drug (including cocaine)
How updated	Checked 2016 Cumulative Supplement and Noter-Up (February 2017) – lists amendments in SI 2013/625, SI 2014/1275, SI 2014/3277, SI 2015/891 and SI 2015/664

9.2 REPORTING RESEARCH

If your research is carried out at the request of your supervisor, it is important that you communicate the results clearly. In any event, it is as well to make a clear record of the legal basis for advice.

Reports in practice will take different forms, depending on the purpose and importance of the research, and whether the researcher understands the client's position fully. As a trainee, you are likely to begin with relatively simple tasks, so that a relatively simple form of report will suffice. Suggestions for the content of more elaborate forms of reports, together with useful advice on style and layout, can be found in **Chapter 1**.

The following general points should be borne in mind:

(a)   The main aims of the report are to answer the question clearly, including enough detail of the research for sources to be traced and for conclusions to be checked easily.

(b)   Begin by restating the objective; if you have a different view of the issue from your supervisor, you are unlikely to produce a satisfactory answer.

(c)   Include a brief summary of your conclusions near the beginning of the report, separate from any reasoning or source references, so that the main message is quickly apparent.

(d)   If your problem is complex, involving several linked issues, list the issues and report on each one separately.

(e)   Consider the recipient of the research in making choices about style and layout. Is it appropriate to report results in note form? Is it reasonable to assume knowledge of the legal background? Will technical language be easily understood?

(f)   If the factual context is known, the results should be applied to the facts, and brief notes should be made of obvious practical implications.

(g)   Give full source references: include the title and citation of primary sources and the page/paragraph numbers of the publications where they were found.

(h)   Consider attaching photocopies or print-outs of the most relevant sources.

(i)   State what steps were taken to update: give the date of the latest sources used, and also give (where possible) the date to which the law as stated is claimed to be up to date by the publisher.

(j)   State the date that the research was carried out. Record the time spent on research. Your supervisor will need this information for billing purposes.

(k)   State the date that the report was compiled.

9.3 CITE IT RIGHT

Various guides exist to set standards for the form of citation of legal authorities. It is good practice to follow a standard approach to citation when recording and reporting a piece of research, for the sake of consistency and to avoid ambiguity. However, unfortunately, different organisations have developed different sets of standards. For example, most legal publishers will follow their own in-house rules of citation. There are also differences in approach between countries (which may be significant for solicitors working in the UK offices of US firms, for example).

One set of rules is now rising to prominence in academia in the UK, and also serves as a reliable and comprehensive style guide for researchers in practice. It is *OSCOLA* (*The Oxford Standard for Citation of Legal Authorities*, 4th edn, 2012). The text of *OSCOLA* is available for free on the Internet (see www.law.ox.ac.uk/publications/oscola.php). Detailed guidance and examples cover references to a wide range of UK and European primary sources, and commentary. A separate guide is available covering references to international law.

PART III

ORAL COMMUNICATION SKILLS

INTRODUCTION TO ORAL COMMUNICATION SKILLS

LEARNING OUTCOMES

After reading this chapter you will be able to:

- appreciate the importance of good communication skills in practice
- demonstrate passive and active listening skills
- explain the difference between open and closed questions
- recognise the impact of 'body language' on effective communication.

10.1 THE IMPORTANCE OF ORAL COMMUNICATION SKILLS

One-third of what is said is not heard

One-third is heard but not understood

One-third is understood – but may not be accepted

(adapted from a passage in *The Skills of Negotiating* by Bill Scott)

All solicitors need to possess good oral communication skills in order to defeat the 'one-third rule', quoted above, and to become effective interviewers, negotiators or advocates.

During the working day a solicitor will communicate with a wide variety of individuals. The most obvious occasions when oral communication skills are important are when interviewing clients or presenting a case to a court, but a solicitor will also need to communicate with other professionals, such as accountants, surveyors, estate agents and police officers, and with members of the public, such as witnesses, and, of course, with colleagues in his or her own office.

In research carried out by Avrom Sherr (1991) it was estimated that solicitors spent, in total, an average of 30% of their time interviewing clients, in discussions with other lawyers, negotiating, acting as an advocate, interviewing witnesses and spending time with counsel. All of these activities involve oral communication skills.

PERSONAL INJURY CASE STUDY

Consider the facts of this case study. If you are acting for Caroline Marsh, how many different people would you expect to communicate with as you prepare to launch her claim?

At the very least you will need to discuss the case with the client, witnesses, solicitors acting for the other parties, police officers who attended the scene, the client's GP and any other expert medical witness involved in her ongoing care, and her insurance company and/or its solicitors.

TRANSACTION CASE STUDY

Consider the facts of this case study. If you are acting for the sellers of Toast & Tea, think about the range of people you would expect to be involved in the transaction and with whom you would need to be able to communicate.

Clearly you would need to be able to communicate with your clients, and you may possibly need to obtain information from their employees. You would need to be involved in discussions with the clients' accountants on issues relating to the accounts, valuation of the business and possible taxation advice. Sale of the business may involve the transfer of leasehold and/or freehold premises and therefore contact with surveyors, landlords and/or their agents and banks (if there are mortgages on the properties). There may also be contact with official bodies, such as HM Revenue and Customs in relation to taxation issues and licensing authorities in relation to any licences held by the business which may need assigning to the purchaser.

10.1.1 Communication with clients

PROFESSIONAL CONDUCT POINT

In establishing a range of measures to help solicitors achieve better standards in client care and complaints handling, The Law Society and the Legal Services Complaints Commissioner (4 March 2009) stated that '[e]xcellence in client care, from initial contact through to handling complaints, is an important part of demonstrating your professionalism as a solicitor'.

The Law Society periodically updates its guidance on the management of complaints, the most recent version being the Handling Complaints Practice Note (13 August 2013). Interestingly, in the previous version of this guidance, the Complaints Management Practice Note (1 February 2013), The Law Society observes that '[g]ood communication is essential to ... high quality client care ... Poor communication will result in clients feeling that they have not been understood, taken seriously or valued ... Effective communication can help to resolve disputes quickly and build greater client loyalty.'

Employing appropriate skills when communicating with clients is an inherent part of a solicitor's duties under Chapter 1 of the SRA Code of Conduct 2011, which sets out minimum standards of client care which solicitors should provide.

Proper communication with clients will promote satisfaction with the solicitor's service. There will be fewer complaints relating to the standard of service, which in turn allows the solicitor more time to concentrate on generating more business for the firm. Fewer complaints should also lead to a reduction in his or her professional indemnity premiums.

A happy client will be a loyal client, who will be ready to recommend the solicitor to others. In 'A guide to good complaints handling', the Legal Ombudsman reports that:

> [a] recent survey into the use of legal services found that 82% of consumers would choose a lawyer based on personal experience or recommendations from friends, relatives and work colleagues. Satisfied customers will be loyal ... [and] spread the word; they'll tell other people how much they like your business and value the service you offer.

> **TRANSACTION CASE STUDY**
>
> If, when acting for the purchaser, you provided a good service and kept the client well informed and happy then further instructions are very likely to follow. The client will no doubt have many employees, properties and contracts with suppliers and customers, all of which will, at some point in the future, generate the need for further legal advice.

In its Practice Note of 1 February 2013, The Law Society suggests that a 'satisfied client can recommend up to five new clients, but a dissatisfied client can lose the practice up to 23 new clients'. The impact of better communication in turn leads to a more successful and profitable business for the solicitor with fewer complaints made about the quality of his or her service.

Looking at it from a wider perspective than just the solicitor's own firm, in the long term The Law Society believes that better communication techniques will lead to an overall improvement in levels of client satisfaction which may reduce the number of complaints and formal claims against solicitors and thereby enhance the public's overall perception of the legal profession.

So, from a personal, professional and business perspective, the solicitor should be very keen to ensure that he or she establishes a good line of communication with his or her clients.

10.1.2 Communicating with those who are not clients

Solicitors also need to establish and maintain good working relationships with their colleagues in the office (whether professional or administrative); a solicitor who acts in a professional manner and is polite, clear when giving instructions and who is prepared to listen will promote a better atmosphere in the office. People who have a happy and professional working environment are generally more productive and provide a better service.

Consulting or instructing members of other professions, representatives of official bodies (eg, court staff) and interviewing members of the general public are all a regular part of a solicitor's daily workload. Clear, concise, polite and appropriate communications should minimise any delay in getting a response and reduce possible confusion in their interpretation of the solicitor's request, instructions or questions. It is clear to see that using appropriate communication skills will also enhance the solicitor's reputation in the community and amongst the professionals with whom he or she deals. This will promote more referrals of clients to the solicitor's firm.

Employing appropriate communication skills with people inside and outside the solicitor's own office will improve the service that a client receives and, as explained at **10.1.1**, this has a beneficial impact on the solicitor's reputation and his or her business.

10.1.3 Developing communication skills

Although oral communication skills are largely based on common sense, people's ability to use them varies enormously. Some people are naturally better than others at communicating, but everyone is capable of improvement. Like any other skill (driving a car, playing a musical instrument, playing a sport), performance can be improved by learning specific skills and techniques, and then practising them.

At first, practising new techniques can feel artificial ('It's just not me'), but after a while the technique usually becomes second nature (like changing gear in a car). However, skills training should not be allowed to suppress natural ability, and it is possible to be a competent interviewer, negotiator or advocate without necessarily having to perform every technique by the book. It is a question of balance; but success comes through practising sound techniques. Brilliant mavericks are rare.

When communicating with anyone, it is important to recognise any difficulties they may have in hearing and understanding the conversation. Individuals may have physical or mental disabilities, or there may be issues relating to culture or language. It is therefore necessary to take these difficulties into account when preparing for such a meeting, for example by employing an interpreter.

This chapter introduces those aspects of oral communication skills which are common to interviewing, negotiation and advocacy. **Chapters 11–13** explain and illustrate with examples how the skills apply to each of these activities.

10.2 LISTENING

In order to advise a client, or to persuade an opponent or the court, solicitors have first to *demonstrate* that they have both heard and understood what the other has said. In its Practice Note of 1 February 2013, The Law Society recommends that you should 'genuinely listen to the client and seek to understand the situation from their point of view'. This will lead to clients feeling 'more confident that they are being taken seriously'.

This involves listening carefully to what is being said. Listening is an underrated skill which requires considerable concentration. Listening as a solicitor is very different from listening in the context of ordinary social discourse, where interchanges are shorter and more fluid and where there is less need to pick up every nuance or recall precisely what was said.

Listening as a solicitor is also different from listening to lectures, where students do not necessarily have to interrelate with the lecturer and may be able to copy up notes from elsewhere later. Nevertheless, students who are good listeners in lectures will find that this skill will help them enormously in practice.

Most authorities on oral communication skills make a distinction between 'passive listening' and 'active listening'.

10.2.1 Passive listening

Passive listening involves using silences and other unobtrusive signals to encourage the speaker to continue. For example, when interviewing, negotiating or conducting advocacy, the solicitor might want to induce the speaker to carry on speaking and thereby perhaps volunteer a crucial piece of information.

Silences can be embarrassing in normal social situations, so many people learn during their upbringing to avoid them. Yet silence is one of the most powerful techniques available to a solicitor. It may require a conscious effort to remain silent for longer than normal in the hope that the speaker will fill the void with more information.

Other non-obtrusive signals a solicitor may give the speaker to encourage him or her to continue include:

- eye contact;
- posture;
- nodding;
- acknowledgements ('Uh, huh');
- express invitations ('Go on').

10.2.2 Active listening

Active listening, as the phrase suggests, involves more obtrusive techniques which demonstrate to the other person that the solicitor has both heard and understood.

The most common form of active listening is summarising (ie, giving a short, clear precis of what the speaker has just said). Like silence, the technique is not regularly employed in social conversations and so requires a conscious effort.

Summarising is also used by solicitors to check the effectiveness of communication in the reverse direction (ie, that the other person has heard and understood the solicitor).

10.3 QUESTIONING

Questioning skills are well-known tools of the solicitor's trade. Questions may be classified according to the breadth of the response they allow (ie, as open or closed questions).

10.3.1 Open questions

Open questions give maximum freedom to the person being questioned, they encourage expansion and they do not seek to influence the content of the reply:

> 'So what happened next?'
> 'What were your reactions to that?'
> 'How did you respond to the offer?'
> 'Why did you do that?'
> 'Tell me about your relationship with the managing director.'
> 'Tell me more about ...'

Open questions do not necessarily have to be worded as questions: 'Tell me ...' is a phrase which can be used to invite an open response.

10.3.2 Closed questions

Closed questions invite a narrow answer, from a few words or a sentence to a 'Yes'/'No' reply (sometimes called 'Yes/No questions'):

> 'Were you also carrying a knife?'
> 'Did you accept the offer?'

One particular form of closed question is the leading question. For example, the questioner might deliberately seek to influence the content of the reply by asking a question which encourages a particular answer: 'So you must have been drunk, mustn't you?'

10.4 NON-VERBAL COMMUNICATION

Non-verbal communication includes eye contact, posture and gestures, and is often called 'body language'.

Careful observation of the body language of other people can provide clues as to how they are feeling, or how they are responding to advice or to an argument, and may therefore be influential in deciding how to proceed. However, tread cautiously, because the clue might not be conclusive: the interpretation of body language is controversial, and is subject to cultural variations. Avoiding eye contact may be regarded as an indication of evasiveness and even a lack of truthfulness in some cultures. In others it may be a sign of politeness and sincerity. Be aware of non-verbal communication, but do not allow it to distract you from everything else.

Similarly, awareness of how your own body language affects both yourself and others can help in deciding how to convey your message more effectively. Although it is sometimes said that one cannot (or should not) 'fake' body language, cause and effect are often interrelated. Sitting with your arms tightly folded and your legs crossed, or nervously drumming your fingers or tapping your foot, can affect your own feelings as well as influencing others' perceptions of you. Sitting or standing in a physically relaxed manner can help you feel more relaxed and convey the impression of confidence to an observer.

10.5 CONCLUSION

This chapter introduces the oral communication skills which will serve as useful tools for a solicitor, whether he or she is conducting an interview or a negotiation or acting as an advocate. Reference should be made to **Chapters 11–13** for further discussion and illustration of how these skills may be employed in each of these three contexts.

INTERVIEWING AND ADVISING

LEARNING OUTCOMES

After reading this chapter you will be able to:

- appreciate the importance of interviewing skills in practice
- recognise the range of skills you will need to develop to be a good interviewer
- understand the steps that need to be taken when preparing for a client interview
- plan a structured approach to a client interview
- recognise the purpose of each stage of a structured interview
- identify the skills which are appropriate for each stage of a structured interview
- use appropriate listening and questioning techniques
- integrate relevant aspects of the SRA Code of Conduct 2011 into a client interview.

11.1 WHY IS IT IMPORTANT FOR A SOLICITOR TO BE A GOOD INTERVIEWER?

Chapter 10 explored the general importance of good communication skills to a solicitor's standard of service to his or her clients, and to his or her own and the firm's reputation and business interests. This chapter will illustrate how those skills are employed when conducting an initial interview with a client.

So, why is it important for a solicitor to be a good interviewer?

11.1.1 Building good relationships and reputations

A significant proportion of a solicitor's working life is spent interviewing clients and witnesses. In research carried out in 1991 on behalf of The Law Society, Avrom Sherr found that on average a solicitor spends around 15% of his or her time interviewing clients and around 3% of his or her time interviewing witnesses.

The initial interview is usually the first time the solicitor and client meet. As the old saying goes, you never get a second chance to make a first impression. Making a good first impression is crucial if you want the client to feel comfortable enough and confident enough to instruct you to act for him or her.

This meeting will therefore be the basis upon which you will start to build a rapport with the client.

The information obtained during the interview will influence the direction that the client's case will follow, so good use of listening, questioning and analytical skills will ensure you establish as full a picture as possible. It is also the time to establish the terms and conditions of your retainer so that each of you understands the work that you will undertake on the client's behalf.

Remember, a happy client is a loyal client who will recommend your firm to others. More importantly, failure to communicate effectively with your client may lead to a dissatisfied client, poor or even negligent advice, and the possibility of complaints, disputes and damage to the firm's reputation.

11.1.2 Law Society guidance

As noted at **10.1.1**, The Law Society believes that good communication skills provide the foundations to building long-term relationships with clients, a good personal reputation and a publically respected profession. In order to promote excellence in both communication skills and professional attitudes to client care, The Law Society has published a number of practice notes which outline the Society's guidance on good professional practice. Whilst having no legal force, firms with robust practice procedures which follow the spirit of the guidance are less likely to find themselves subject to complaints from their clients and more likely to be able to provide a good account of their actions should any such complaints be brought against them.

The following practice notes provide guidance that is of particular relevance to the skills and practice procedures discussed in this chapter:

- 'Initial interviews', issued 6 October 2011
- 'Use of interpreters in criminal cases', issued 20 October 2015
- 'Client care information', issued 5 September 2016
- 'Police interviews involving sign language interpreters', issued 21 December 2015
- 'Providing services to D/deaf and hard of hearing people', issued 12 July 2012

(These practice notes will be referred to in the following form in this chapter: 'Practice Note of 20 October 2015', etc.)

When studying the on the Legal Practice Course, a student must meet the Solicitors Regulation Authority's learning outcomes for Interviewing and Advising. The guidance given in this chapter encompasses those outcomes.

11.2 OBJECTIVES OF A SOLICITOR/CLIENT INTERVIEW

As mentioned at **11.1**, this chapter concentrates on the skills needed during the first interview with a client.

There are five main objectives:

- to establish good *rapport* between the solicitor and the client;
- to obtain relevant *information* from the client;
- to help the client reach appropriate *decisions*;
- to plan future *action*;
- to deal with client care and costs information issues.

Other legal interviews (eg, with witnesses or other professionals) usually serve more limited purposes.

11.3 COMMON FAILINGS

There are many reasons why a solicitor may fail to achieve the above objectives.

For example, the solicitor may:

- fail to listen properly;
- talk too much;
- make a premature diagnosis;
- restrict the areas in which the client feels free to talk;
- be over-directive in suggesting what further action is necessary;
- be over-technical when giving advice.

The skills referred to later in this chapter will reduce the likelihood of any of these failings occurring.

11.4 TWO INGREDIENTS FOR SUCCESS – SKILLS AND STRUCTURE

11.4.1 Skills

In order to achieve the objectives referred to at **11.2**, you need to make effective use of a wide range of skills.

The principal skills involved are:

- listening;
- questioning;
- analysing;
- explaining;
- note-taking.

These will be considered in more detail at **11.5**.

11.4.2 Structure

The objectives at **11.2** are easier to achieve if you prepare for and conduct the interview in a logical and coherent manner.

Structure and management involve:

- creating a *suitable environment* for the interview;
- *preparing adequately* for the interview;
- using an *appropriate* '*model*' for the interview itself.

A 'model' is merely a predetermined structure, under which the interview is divided into a logical sequence of stages. Each stage involves the performance of essential tasks and requires the use of different combinations of the skills referred to above.

The model used in this book is:

GREETING

(1) PRELIMINARIES

(2) OBTAINING THE FACTS

(3) FILLING IN THE DETAIL

(4) ADVISING

(5) CLOSING

PARTING

The model is easy to follow and may be used in any legal context, although the length of time spent on each stage will usually vary depending on whether the interview is litigation or transaction based.

A detailed explanation of these stages will be given at **11.8**, but a brief overview of the three central stages will help your understanding of what follows at **11.5** about the relevant skills.

11.4.2.1   Obtaining the facts

This involves the client giving an account of the matter with as little interruption from the solicitor as possible. It is therefore characterised by the client talking and the solicitor *listening*, observing the client's body language and encouraging the client to continue.

11.4.2.2   Filling in the detail

This involves a more active role by the solicitor to ensure that a complete and accurate picture is obtained and recorded. This stage is therefore characterised by the solicitor *questioning* the client and *taking notes* of what the client says.

11.4.2.3   Advising

This involves supplying the information which the client needs in order to make necessary decisions and to give the solicitor instructions for any further action. This stage therefore usually takes the form of the solicitor *analysing* and *explaining* the client's position, explaining the range of options open to the client and then *engaging in a dialogue* to make necessary decisions and to agree a plan of action.

11.5   THE SKILLS

11.5.1   Listening – an undervalued skill

Encouraging a client to explain why he or she has come to see you is generally a more effective way of gathering information than attempting to do so by a series of closed questions (see **10.3.2**). You should therefore avoid asking closed questions until you have a reasonably full version of the case.

If the client is verbose, you may need to adopt a more forceful braking role, but this should occur only when absolutely necessary.

Listening is an undervalued skill which involves a range of techniques to sustain information giving.

11.5.1.1   Silence

In everyday conversation, periods of silence can sometimes seem awkward and even cause embarrassment.

In an interview, these periods give the client time to recall facts and to organise his or her thoughts so that he or she is better able to tell the story as he or she remembers it and to express the feelings it creates.

You must therefore learn to control the natural urge to fill silences.

11.5.1.2   Body language

Consider how your body language may help or hinder building good rapport with the client. For example:

- eye contact: a friendly, but not prolonged stare;
- posture: leaning slightly towards the client;
- head-nodding: but not too much;
- avoiding irritating/distracting mannerisms, eg, pen-tapping, foot-drumming, reading while the client is speaking, looking at your watch, etc.

11.5.1.3 Acknowledgements

These are brief indications (without interrupting) showing attention, interest, and understanding, such as:

> 'Yes, I see'
>
> '... in Brussels?'
>
> 'Mhmmmm'.

11.5.1.4 Invitations to continue/elaborate

Examples are:

> 'Go on'
>
> 'What happened?'
>
> 'Tell me more about that'.

11.5.1.5 Reflecting feeling

This involves making it clear that you understand how the client feels, for example, 'I can quite see why you feel so angry about this' or (in relation to bereavement) 'I'm sorry to hear that'.

It involves expressing empathy with the client's feelings; not being judgmental about them.

The technique is useful in building rapport and is particularly important where the client's emotions will be a major factor in the case, for example in matrimonial cases or where the client has recently been bereaved.

However, reflecting feeling may also be appropriate in interviews which may appear to be less personal, for example when a commercial client has anxieties about losing face within the company if a transaction fails to reach a satisfactory conclusion.

You can gain valuable insights into the client's feelings by observing and correctly interpreting the client's body language, not merely from listening to the client's words and tone of voice.

11.5.2 Questioning

In an initial interview, a solicitor needs to obtain information on:

- the nature of the client's problem or proposed transaction;
- the relevant background facts;
- the client's feelings and objectives.

Whilst much of this may be obtained through use of the listening techniques discussed above, it will usually be necessary to clarify and probe further by questioning.

For an initial interview, particularly in the early stages, open questions usually have more advantages than closed questions and failure to recognise this leads many interviews into an interviewer-dominated style. It is important to avoid asking more than one question at a time.

11.5.2.1 Open questions

The advantages of open questions are that they:

(a) allow the client to select the subject matter;

(b) allow the client to select the information the client believes to be relevant;

(c) allow the client to start with information about which the client feels comfortable;

(d) enable the client to get things 'off his or her chest';

(e) give the client freedom to reflect and to feel more actively involved in the interview;

(f) encourage memory by association, which may produce information which would be overlooked if the client were asked only closed questions.

> **TRANSACTION CASE STUDY**
>
> Assume you are acting for the sellers. What aspects of the transaction will you encourage the clients to discuss to help you get an overview of the deal through the use of open questions? The clients are most likely to start their explanation with a description of the deal. You would probably need to use open questions to build a picture of the following topics:
>
> (a)   the stage that negotiations have reached;
>
> (b)   the nature of the business;
>
> (c)   who the owners are and the value attributed to the business (some idea of the assets and liabilities);
>
> (d)   the plans for employees;
>
> (e)   the clients' proposed time frame for the deal and any deadlines that you would be expected to meet (for example the deal must be completed before the end of the current tax year).

The use of open questions should allow a solicitor to get a great deal of information relatively quickly and so form an overview of the situation. However, on their own, open questions are unlikely to be sufficient due to the following disadvantages:

(a)   they may initially produce insufficient information;

(b)   they may encourage the client to verbosity and/or irrelevance;

(c)   they may inhibit a reticent client.

11.5.2.2   Closed questions

Once you have an overview of the case, you can then start to focus on the aspects where you need more detail. The advantages of closed questions are that they:

(a)   are a good method of obtaining precise details;

(b)   may guide a client less stressfully through a sensitive area;

(c)   may give confidence to an initially reticent or anxious client;

(d)   may help to prompt memory;

(e)   help to clarify and probe areas of ambiguity or uncertainty;

(f)   may quieten a verbose client.

The disadvantages are that they:

(a)   may lead to an over-clinical or 'processing' style of interview;

(b)   may deprive the client of the opportunity to state the case in his or her own words;

(c)   may inhibit rapport;

(d)   reduce the opportunity to listen to and observe the client, and to understand his or her needs;

(e)   may lead the solicitor to miss important areas of information because the client is not allowed to associate ideas freely;

(f)   may even result in the solicitor directing the interview down a totally irrelevant path;

(g)   if overused, may result in the client feeling interrogated.

11.5.2.3   The 'T-funnel'

As noted at **11.5.2.1** and **11.5.2.2**, the use of just open questions or just closed questions does not elicit the range of information that the solicitor needs. By combining the two techniques, the solicitor can achieve a thorough exploration of the information.

The use of open questions followed by closed questions is sometimes known as the T-funnel sequence of questioning:

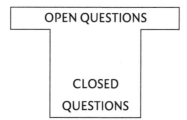

The solicitor introduces a particular topic with a series of open questions. Only after the open questions cease to be productive are they narrowed into closed questions.

Premature use of closed questions may distort the response or lead to important details being omitted.

PERSONAL INJURY CASE STUDY

Assume you are acting for Caroline Marsh. What general areas would you need to encourage the client to explain by using open questions?

You will need to know:

(a)   when, where and how the accident happened;

(b)   a description of the personal injury, damage to property and any financial loss the client has suffered;

(c)   the consequences of the accident on her personal and working life;

(d)   insurance details of the client and the other parties.

The client is likely to be very ready to explain what happened from her point of view, to give her view as to who was at fault, to mention if the emergency services attended and if the police plan to take any action. She is unlikely to have described the scene in sufficient detail for you to be able to give advice. You need to be sure that she has covered the following details:

(a)   the direction in which she was travelling;

(b)   the speed at which she was travelling;

(c)   the weather conditions;

(d)   the time of day;

(e)   a precise description of the junction (for example if there were traffic lights, road markings, road works);

(f)   whether she had any passengers;

(g)   whether there were any independent witnesses;

(h)   exactly what happened after the collision and what was said by whom to whom;

(i)   contact details for all parties and for any police officer who attended;

(j)   details of her insurance, including any excess.

In using the T-funnel approach, you can use open questions to establish an overview of the accident based on the client's immediate memory. You can then review what the client has told you, if necessary imposing a logical structure to the order of events as you clarify your understanding. The use of closed questions at this stage should enable you to get all relevant facts before you move on to giving advice.

(Open questions)	
Solicitor	'What happened after the collision?'
Client	'I was really shaken and it took me a few minutes to compose myself. I turned off my radio because the noise was getting to me.'
Solicitor	'What happened next?'
Client	'I got out of my car.'
Solicitor	'Yes ...?'
Client	'Well, I went over to where he'd parked his car and spoke to him.'
(Closed questions)	
Solicitor	'Could you tell me exactly where you were both standing?'
Client	'Yes, he was standing by the offside front wing of his car and as I approached him I am afraid I told him what I thought of him.'
Solicitor	'Can you remember the words you actually used?'
Client	'I said "You fool, why the hell didn't you indicate?"'
Solicitor	'Did he reply?'
Client	'Yes, he said "I'm sorry – I didn't realise they'd changed the lane markings".'
Solicitor	'Anything else?'
Client	'No.'
Solicitor	'Was anyone else present?'
Client	'Yes – his work mate was standing right next to him.'

11.5.2.4 Further clarification and probing

It will often be necessary to probe further:

- to resolve remaining areas of ambiguity;
- to jog the client's memory;
- to clarify the client's needs and reaction to the consequences of the action;
- to discover how the client will respond to the legal process (in litigation) or to a counter-argument or proposal (negotiating a transaction).

The following are some techniques to achieve these objectives.

Going back one stage

This involves taking the client back one stage in the narrative and inviting him or her to relive the sequence of events in order to jog the memory:

> 'Take me through that again but starting from before you were approaching the road junction.'

This technique is useful, as it encourages the client to fill in any gaps in the narrative.

Leading questions

Leading questions may be a useful way of helping clients to convey something which they may have difficulty articulating in their own words:

> 'So you've had disagreements with the managing director before?'
>
> 'So sexual intercourse did take place on that occasion?'

Prefacing a question with an explanation

This can counteract the client perceiving your question as irrelevant, or allay the client's anxiety in a sensitive area. For example:

'I know you're very confident of being acquitted, but if you are convicted, the magistrates will sentence you immediately. For that reason I now need to ask you some questions about your financial circumstances.'

There is, however, a danger that the explanation may influence (and therefore distort) the client's reply.

Cross-checking

This is often necessary where the information given by the client reveals gaps or contradictions which require explanation. For example:

'Are you quite sure about that because according to the police report you said you'd drunk three pints?'

Devil's advocate

To play devil's advocate is to suggest to the client a different and adverse interpretation of his or her story. For example:

'If you're so sure that the accident wasn't your fault, why did you say to the other motorist: "I'm sorry – I just didn't see you coming"?'

It is generally advisable to explain why you are doing this because, otherwise, your apparent hostility is likely to damage rapport. For example:

'I'm sorry to ask you so bluntly but it's a question you are bound to be asked in court if this gets to trial.'

11.5.2.5 Summarising

This is an extremely important and useful technique.

Its purpose is to double-check that your understanding of the facts and of your client's feelings and concerns is correct.

A summary of the key facts should be given at the end of the filling in the detail stage and before moving into the advising stage:

'Now before we talk about what needs to be done let me just check with you that I have got a correct and complete list of all your relevant assets.'

Apart from giving the client an opportunity to correct errors and supply additional facts, summarising reassures the client that you have heard and understood what you have been told. It also gives you a useful breathing space to think about the matter and the advice that needs to be given. It may also identify some areas on which further questioning is needed before you can safely advise.

Remember that summarising your understanding of the client's feelings and objectives is just as important as summarising factual information:

'So let me see whether I've correctly understood what you are hoping to achieve out of all this ...'

'So would it be fair to say that you would only be prepared to go to court if Janice's name could be kept out of it?'

Summarising helps you to identify if further questions need to be asked and to formulate the advice to give.

11.5.3 Analysing

As the facts and the client's goals are being identified, the solicitor must (at least mentally) analyse which facts and legal principles are relevant, how the law applies to those facts and so reach a conclusion about the client's position and the range of available courses of action.

This process is familiar even to an inexperienced solicitor because it involves essentially the same techniques needed to answer traditional problem-solving questions in law examinations.

One obvious difference is that in real life the solicitor has to elicit the relevant information rather than having it spoon-fed in the form of a given scenario. Another difference is that the solicitor has little or no time for quiet reflection before being expected to offer at least a tentative view of the position.

What tends to happen in most interviews is that, at quite an early stage, the solicitor starts to form a provisional theory about the likely end position.

PERSONAL INJURY CASE STUDY

Consider what legal principles spring to mind if, whilst interviewing Caroline Marsh, she discloses the following information:

'The van driver was not wearing a seat belt.'

'The fog was really heavy; why did the van driver not have his lights on?'

'I was using my mobile phone at the time of the crash.'

'As a result of the injuries I was unable to go on a pre-booked holiday. I did not have any holiday insurance.'

With each piece of information you will be analysing it and starting to frame advice. Thoughts of contributory negligence, criminal offences and remoteness of damage will begin to take shape. These initial thoughts will help you identify further questions you need to ask, and these ideas will inevitably have to be reviewed and modified as additional information emerges. You must be careful to avoid reaching a conclusion until all the facts have been obtained.

Like all skills, this process becomes easier with experience, practice and greater familiarity with the law in question.

Listening, questioning, note-taking and trying to formulate advice cannot be tackled simultaneously – just one reason why it is helpful to build in periods of 'thinking time' as discussed at **11.5.2.5** above.

11.5.4 Explaining

Once you have analysed the client's position, a number of matters will usually have to be explained before the client can be expected to make decisions and give instructions.

When advising a client, you should ensure that the client understands his or her legal position and the legal process that will be necessary to achieve the desired outcome.

11.5.4.1 Explaining the legal position

Explaining the relevant law frequently involves explaining concepts which will be second nature to you and which you would normally express in legal terminology (such as 'consideration' or 'implied conditions/warranties', etc).

It is therefore easy to overlook the simple fact that concepts and terminology which seem quite straightforward and normal to you can be totally bewildering and meaningless to a lay client.

Clarity is vital, and legal jargon should therefore be avoided at all costs. You must bear in mind that *accurate and faultlessly reasoned advice is utterly useless to a client who cannot understand it.*

> **TRANSACTION CASE STUDY**
>
> Assume that you have informed the clients that they face a significant capital gains tax bill on the sale of their business. The clients had hoped to reinvest the money in a new business venture and wish to know if there is any way of mitigating their liability to capital gains tax. Consider the clients' reaction to the following explanation:
>
> > 'If the consideration which a person carrying on a trade obtains for the disposal of his interest in qualifying business assets used for the purposes of the trade throughout the entire period of ownership is applied by him, within a specified period, in acquiring other qualifying business assets which are taken into use in a trade then, that person on making a claim, may be treated for the purposes of CGT as if the consideration for the disposal was such that it creates neither a gain nor a loss.'
>
> Whilst wholly correct in law, it is highly unlikely that even a quite sophisticated business client will follow and understand this long sentence, or appreciate the practical consequences of the statement. The use of such complex language will not only inhibit the clients' understanding, but it will also impact on rapport as the clients may well be intimidated, become irritated or even angry at the prospect of paying for advice that they do not understand.
>
> The advice should be couched in clear, simple English with short sentences to facilitate understanding. The following advice covers the same legal point in a much more accessible way:
>
> > 'There is a possibility of claiming a tax relief. This relief applies if you use the money you receive from the sale of Toast & Tea to purchase things such as land and buildings for use in your new venture. The benefit of the relief is that you will not have to pay the tax bill when you sell Toast & Tea. The tax will be deferred. You will still have to pay tax on the profit but not until you come to sell your new business assets in the future.'
>
> With advice given in these terms, the clients will be better able to understand it and be in a position to discuss the implications with you.

It is true to say that, with practice and experience, you will learn your own way of expressing legal concepts in ways that clients will understand.

11.5.4.2 Outlining the relevant procedure

The client's understanding of his or her legal position is one thing, but appreciating the legal procedures which must be followed is quite another. The client should be made aware of the steps that need to be followed to achieve his or her desired outcome. It is also wise to flag up the possibility of potential problems, which may mean that the process takes longer than expected or may lead to you having to follow a different course.

Managing your client's expectations in this way should ensure that the client feels more closely involved with the matter, and less likely to believe that things are going wrong or that you have made a mistake in your handling of the case.

You should also bear in mind that, even when you have explained matters clearly, it is often unrealistic to expect the client to remember everything once the interview is over. For this reason, it is desirable in most cases to send a follow-up letter to the client summarising the advice which you have given (see **11.8.10**).

It is often helpful to ask the client whether what you have said has been understood and to offer to repeat the advice. If overdone, this technique may appear patronising. If used appropriately, even the most self-confident client will appreciate your concern, and a more timid client, who may be reluctant to ask directly, will welcome a genuine offer of clarification.

11.5.5   Note-taking

Note-taking is an important and difficult skill.

No solicitor can memorise every piece of information on all his or her files, and there may be occasions when some other member of the firm will need to take over the file permanently or temporarily.

The file must therefore contain a complete, accurate and legible record of the interview. You must make sure your attendance note records the relevant facts, the advice given, the decisions made by the client and any follow-up steps which you and/or the client will be taking.

This is best achieved by taking manuscript notes during the interview itself and, if necessary, by having a fuller and/or clearer version typed afterwards.

Failing to take notes during the interview, intending to dictate everything immediately after the interview, is fraught with danger because you may unavoidably become involved in other distractions and be unable to do this before memory has faded. The longhand notes must, at minimum, be sufficient to operate as an *aide memoire* of the vital facts, names, dates, assets, etc from which a fuller record can later be prepared.

Difficulties can arise if you try to take detailed notes too early in the interview, while the client is trying to explain why he or she has come to see you. If you write while the client is actually talking, this can damage rapport for two reasons. First, it is very difficult to follow the meaning of what the client is saying if you are frantically trying to translate it into a written note. Secondly, it is impossible to write at length without losing eye contact with the client. Few things are more off-putting for a client than trying to relate a story to the top of someone's head. On the other hand, it can be equally off-putting if you interrupt the flow of the client's narrative by requesting time to write everything down.

The solution is simple: *do not attempt to take notes during the obtaining the facts stage*; instead, concentrate on listening to the client's version of events and defer taking notes until the 'filling in the detail' stage. This may mean that you have to ask the client to repeat some matters, but this is likely to be less time consuming in the long run. Alternatively, restrict note-taking to very brief jottings which do not destroy eye contact but which will serve at a later stage as a reminder of topics which need to be expanded.

Even when fuller note-taking starts, try to develop a concise style and be selective about what you write down. Headings can be used effectively to give a structure to your notes. Ensure that key names, addresses, figures, dates and verbatim accounts of conversations are accurately worded. Never be embarrassed to ask the client for the correct spellings if names are unfamiliar.

11.6   CLIENT CARE AND COSTS INFORMATION

> **PROFESSIONAL CONDUCT POINT**
> Chapter 1 of the SRA Code of Conduct 2011 sets out the general requirements a solicitor must comply with in relation to client care and the provision of information as to costs. The question here is how many of these numerous matters need to be dealt with during the first interview.

In its Practice Notes of 6 October 2011 and 5 September 2016, The Law Society issued guidance on the SRA Code of Conduct which makes it clear that, as a matter of client care and good practice, it is generally appropriate for some matters to be dealt with expressly during the interview, whilst other matters can properly be left to a follow-up or client care/ costs information letter.

As to costs information, Outcome 1.13 of the SRA Code of Conduct 2011 requires that:

'clients receive the best possible information, both at the time of engagement and when appropriate as their matter progresses, about the likely overall cost of their matter.'

Chapter 1 outlines a number of issues to be addressed. Most complaints made about solicitors are related to the issue of cost, so the information on costs must be given in plain English and be accurate and not misleading.

It is sensible to give a 'simple overview' of the costs during the interview and, following the interview, if you are retained by the client, to give full information in writing to the client.

There are three separate occasions during the interview which present logical opportunities to discuss different aspects of the costs:

(a)   during the preliminary stage of the interview when it is essential to discuss at least the cost of the interview;

(b)   during the advising stage of the interview, when discussing the possible options it will be necessary to discuss the potential costs of each option and whether the possible benefit justifies the associated risks (including, where relevant, any risk of the client becoming liable for an opponent's costs);

(c)   during the closing stage when, having a complete picture of the client's current situation and the proposed course of action, it is possible to explain the likely overall costs of the matter.

11.7   AN OVERVIEW OF THE STRUCTURE OF THE INTERVIEW

Having a clear idea of how you plan to structure and manage the interview is the key to retaining control and ensuring that all necessary matters are properly addressed. The following checklist provides you with a handy overview of the stages of the interview. It is a useful guide to keep in front of you to help you maintain your structure. A detailed explanation of each stage of the interview is given at **11.8**.

1. **Plan for the interview**
   (a) Organise an appropriate room for the interview
   (b) Carry out a conflict check
   (c) Ensure the client has been warned to bring proof of identity for an identity check
   (d) Research and prepare a checklist (if appropriate)
   (e) Consider if there is any need for an interpreter
   (f) Prepare two copies of the client care information sheet
   (g) Ensure no interruptions

2. **Greeting**
   Meet, greet and seat the client appropriately, confirm your status within the firm and establish good rapport

3. **Preliminaries**
   (a) Check the reason for the client's visit by way of a closed question
   (b) Discuss any time constraints and the proposed structure of interview
   (c) Explain the cost of the interview, reassure the client that you will deal with costs more fully later in the interview and check that the client accepts the charges outlined

4. **Obtain facts**
   Let the client explain the reason for his or her visit; use open questions and listening techniques (and avoid note-taking)

5. **Fill in detail**
   (a) Clarify and fill gaps in the facts using the T-funnel approach
   (b) Identify and explore the client's concerns
   (c) Summarise (a) and (b)

6. **Advising**
   (a) Outline relevant law and procedure clearly, accurately and comprehensively, taking into account all relevant factual, practical and legal issues
   (b) Explain available options, both legal and non-legal
   (c) Discuss with the client the advantages/disadvantages of the options (including a discussion on the associated risks/benefits) to assist the client in reaching a decision
   (d) Outline further steps to be taken to implement any proposed course of action

7. **Closing**
   (a) Ask client whether there is anything else he or she wishes to discuss
   (b) Confirm the follow-up tasks of both solicitor and client
   (c) Give the name of an alternative contact within firm
   (d) Estimate the time frame for the matter
   (e) Give the best information possible relating to the costs of the matter
   (f) Discuss next contact including whether a further meeting is necessary and, if one is needed, when is it likely to be and who is responsible for arranging it

8. **Parting**

9. **General matters**
   (a) Maintain rapport throughout, seeking to establish a professional relationship
   (b) Structure the interview appropriately
   (c) Take appropriate notes
   (d) Manage the client's expectations in terms of your service and the likely outcomes

11.8 STRUCTURE AND MANAGEMENT OF THE INITIAL INTERVIEW

11.8.1 Before the interview

11.8.1.1 The environment

It is important that the interview takes place in an environment which will help rather than hinder effective communication. The aim should be to create an atmosphere in which the client will feel calm and relaxed, and which will give a favourable impression of you and your firm.

PROFESSIONAL CONDUCT POINT

Principle 9 of the SRA Code of Conduct requires you to conduct business in a manner that recognises the need for 'equal opportunity and respect for diversity'. The environment in which the interview takes place should take into account any specific needs of the client, for example the need for wheelchair access or difficulties arising from being hard of hearing.

You should therefore ensure:

(a)   that the client will be physically comfortable;

(b)   that the interview will be free from unnecessary interruptions (with a minimum of background noise if the client is hard of hearing);

(c)   that the office surroundings convey a sense of well-organised professionalism without being austere and/or impersonal.

Seating arrangements may also help or hinder effective communication. Views on this topic differ, and an arrangement which seems friendly and welcoming to one client may strike another as over-familiar or even invasive.

However, as far as possible, the arrangement should be one in which:

(a)   the solicitor and client can see and hear each other clearly (this is especially important in the case of clients who are deaf/hard of hearing and may be reliant on lip reading or sign language);

(b)   the client does not feel kept at a distance at one extreme or invaded at the other;

(c)   the solicitor and (if necessary) the client can make written notes in comfort.

The traditional arrangement in which the solicitor and client face each other from opposite sides of the solicitor's desk will usually satisfy the above criteria, provided the desk is not piled high with files and papers. It is also the arrangement which most clients will be expecting.

However, depending on the personality of the client and the nature of the matter, you may decide that a less formal arrangement, perhaps without the intervening desk, would be more relaxing for the client and therefore more conducive to communication.

Furthermore, there may be occasions (eg, where the client needs to explain a plan, diagram or map to the solicitor) when sitting alongside the client is the only effective arrangement.

You should therefore consider the possibility of other arrangements and adopt them whenever appropriate.

The above comments presuppose that the interview will take place in an environment over which you have some degree of control, but the interview may, for a variety of reasons, take place in surroundings (eg, hospital ward, prison cell, crowded court corridor, etc) over which you will have little or no control.

11.8.1.2 Preparing for the interview

There are a number of matters to address in advance of your first interview with a client.

Conflict check

PROFESSIONAL CONDUCT POINT

Chapter 3 of the SRA Code of Conduct 2011 says that, generally, a solicitor must not act for a client if there is a conflict of interest, or potential conflict of interest, with a current client.

No matter who in the office makes an appointment for a new client to see a solicitor, it is important that they know that they must obtain some basic information from the client. The client should be asked for the following information:

(a)   his or her name, address and telephone number;

(b)   basic information about the subject matter he or she wishes to discuss (for example, a personal injury claim resulting from a car accident or the sale of a business);

(c)   the name of any other person involved in the case.

This information will enable the firm to do a conflict check to ensure that there will be no risk of a conflict of interest arising if the firm accepts instructions from this client.

If the client does not book an appointment in advance then this information should still be obtained and a conflict check carried out before the interview proceeds.

PERSONAL INJURY CASE STUDY

When Caroline Marsh rings to make an appointment to discuss her position following a car accident, she will be asked for the names of the other parties involved in the accident. She will, of course, give the names of Adam Worcik and Paul Chester. This information will allow the firm to carry out a check in the firm's client database. If the firm already acts for Mr Worcik or Mr Chester then it must not act for Caroline Marsh. The arranged interview would have to be cancelled.

TRANSACTION CASE STUDY

This case study has an additional complication. The conflict check still needs to be carried out to ensure that, for example, your firm does not already act for Robert Grove Ltd, the proposed purchaser of Toast & Tea. In addition, consideration must be given as to whether you can properly act for all three sellers. It is usually the case that, as long as they are all in agreement as to the general terms of the sale, their interests in selling the business do not conflict and that you are safe to take initial instructions from all three of them, although of course this must be checked at the start of the interview. However, care must be taken to ensure that, even if this is the case at the start, it continues to be so throughout the transaction as further complexities arise. It may well be that, in relation to certain aspects of the sale and purchase agreement, you will need to recommend that they each take independent advice later on. This may happen, for example, if the partners plan to work for Robert Grove Ltd after the sale. They will each need to negotiate their own employment contracts and so will need to take independent advice on this aspect of the deal.

Identity checks

In cases where the Money Laundering Regulations 2007 apply, a new client should be warned when booking the appointment that the firm will need evidence of his or her identity. He or she should be asked to bring proof of his or her identity to the interview. Generally speaking, a solicitor must not accept instructions from a new client involved in regulated activities until he or she has confirmation of the client's identity.

Research

In the case of a client who has instructed the firm before, it will facilitate good rapport and promote the efficient use of both your and the client's time if, as far as possible, you familiarise yourself with the client. Research the client's case history and talk to colleagues who have dealt with the client before.

In the case of a new client, where possible obtain background information on the client (and, where relevant, the client's business).

Where relevant and possible, you may decide it would be useful to request documents in advance from the client.

From the information provided by the client you may have some idea as to the law that is likely to be relevant to the case. You may wish to carry out some legal research on that area of law in advance of the interview.

> **PERSONAL INJURY CASE STUDY**
>
> Assume you have been instructed by Adam Worcik. He mentioned to your secretary when booking the appointment that the car driver would not have been so badly hurt if she had been wearing a seat belt at the time of the accident. You may therefore need to check the up-to-date position on the details of the relevant criminal offence and remind yourself of the principles of contributory negligence.

However, in anticipating what may be relevant, be careful not to pre-judge the issues or 'pigeon-hole' the client.

Checklists

Some interviews lend themselves to the use of checklists. As discussed in the previous paragraph, once you know why a client is coming to see you, it is possible to anticipate the topics that may be relevant to his or her case. Therefore, through careful planning you could draw up a checklist to use during the interview as an *aide memoire*.

Used appropriately, a checklist has the obvious advantage that essential information is unlikely to be overlooked. A checklist also provides you with a concise and convenient source of information for speedy future reference.

However, interviewing a client simply by running through a checklist, particularly at the beginning of the interview, may inhibit effective communication. You may appear to be merely 'processing a case' rather than listening to the client's unique personal problem.

Using a checklist in such a manner may damage rapport. The client may get a feeling of not being listened to if your questions jump from one topic to another rather than follow up on the client's current train of thought. Indeed, premature use of a checklist (ie, before a correct diagnosis of the problem has been made) can waste valuable time while a mass of irrelevant information is accumulated. In other words, make quite sure that your chosen checklist is appropriate before using it.

Interpreters

Give some thought to the use of a language or sign language interpreter, for example if the client does not speak the same language as you or if he or she has a hearing impairment. In its Practice Note of 12 July 2012, The Law Society recommends that in preparing for a meeting with a client, it is essential to establish whether she or he has any specific needs relating to his or her ability to communicate. If, for example, an interpreter is needed, it is possible the client will bring a member of her or his family or a friend along to the interview to provide such support. If not, or in cases where it is preferable to have an independent professional interpreter, you will need to organise for this support to be provided. If possible, you should try to brief the interpreter before the interview as to his or her role and the confidential nature of the interview.

> **PROFESSIONAL CONDUCT POINT**
>
> If you are involved in criminal proceedings, you should refer to the Practice Note of 20 October 2015. This Practice Note explains the importance of the role of an interpreter and gives guidance on identifying the need for an interpreter. There is also guidance on the allocation of responsibility for arranging for and paying interpreters for defendants, prosecution witnesses and defence witnesses. The Practice Note includes useful information as to how to contact and select an appropriate interpreter and the role of the interpreter in the proceedings.
>
> Further, in its Practice Note of 21 December 2015, The Law Society sets out its guidance relating to ensuring that an accurate record is kept of interviews at police stations involving sign language interpreters. If the interviewee requires use of a sign language interpreter then a solicitor should insist that a video record of both the interpreter and the interviewee be made.

Client care information sheet

> **PROFESSIONAL CONDUCT POINT**
>
> Some information has to be given to a client 'at the outset' of a matter.
>
> - The firm must make clear how it is regulated and how this affects the protection available to the client (Outcome 1.7).
> - The firm must inform clients of their right to complain and how to complain (Outcome 1.9) and of their right to complain to the Legal Ombudsman, the time frame for doing so, and full details of how to contact the Legal Ombudsman.
> - Outcome 1.12 of the SRA Code of Conduct 2011 requires that clients are in a position to make informed decisions about the services they need, how their matter will be handled and the options available to them. Such decisions will include decisions about the level of seniority of the person advising them. Indicative Behaviour 1.3 suggests that clients are told, in writing, the name and status of the person dealing with the matter and the status of the person responsible for its overall supervision. In its Practice Note of 6 October 2011, The Law Society recommends that this is explained during the first interview.
> - Outcome 1.13 requires the client to receive the best possible information on costs (see **11.6**).
>
> Therefore, during or before the first interview, The Law Society recommends that the firm should give the client an information sheet which the solicitor can explain to the client during the interview. The information would include:
>
> (a)   the name and status of the solicitor or other person conducting the interview, and of the person supervising;
>
> (b)   information on the costs of the interview;
>
> (c)   details of the client's right to complain and of how to complain;
>
> (d)   details of the right to complain to the Legal Ombudsman and how to make contact;
>
> (e)   information confirming how your services are regulated.

It may be sensible to prepare two copies of this note and, during the interview, ask the client to sign and date both copies. One copy should be handed to the client for his or her records, and the other should be retained on the solicitor's file.

PROFESSIONAL CONDUCT POINT

This information should still be supplied in writing, if possible, when conducting an interview over the telephone. Use should be made of e-mail and fax facilities, where available. Alternatively, the information should be covered orally during the interview, and the solicitor should be careful to note that it was discussed.

Ensure no interruptions

You should ensure that the interview will be free from interruptions, so ensure your telephone is put on silent or, more preferably, that it will divert calls.

11.8.2 The interview – a model

GREETING

(1) PRELIMINARIES

(2) OBTAINING THE FACTS

(3) FILLING IN THE DETAIL

(4) ADVISING

(5) CLOSING

PARTING

What now follows is a step-by-step account of each successive stage in the model (see **11.4.2**), indicating the purpose of each stage and which skills need to be employed. The checklist at **11.7** provides a useful overview of this structure.

11.8.3 Greeting

The importance of a warm and friendly greeting cannot be over-emphasised.

When you are ready to see the client, either go yourself to the reception area and escort the client to where the interview will take place, or make sure that some other member of staff does so. A client who is left to find his or her own way to your office through a bewildering maze of corridors is unlikely to arrive feeling welcome.

The client will form an impression of you as soon as you meet. You should therefore do everything possible to ensure that this impression is favourable and that the client is made to feel welcome, comfortable and relaxed.

Greet the client by making eye contact and addressing the client by name. You should also introduce yourself by name and explain your status within the firm (eg, trainee solicitor, solicitor, partner, etc).

PERSONAL INJURY CASE STUDY

Imagine you are instructed by Paul Chester and are meeting him for the first time. How will you greet him?

> 'Good morning Mr Chester. My name is Alex Ireland and I am a trainee solicitor with the firm. Please take a seat.'

In most cases the greeting will also involve *shaking hands*. This may not always be appropriate, for example if the client is a child.

Be aware of any cultural differences which may make eye contact or shaking hands inappropriate. If relevant, consider telling the client that you are not familiar with his or her culture and do not wish to cause offence.

Friendly conversation about such things as the weather, the client's journey or difficulties in parking his or her car may help put the client at ease.

The above points are simply common courtesy and may seem obvious, but they are extremely important.

After greeting, it is a matter of judgement how quickly you proceed to the business at hand, but most clients will have been rehearsing what they wish to say and will be ready to begin at once.

11.8.4   Preliminaries

As mentioned at **11.8.1.2**, the client will have given some indication of the general nature of the problem and the reason for seeking advice when arranging the appointment for the interview.

Nevertheless, ambiguities may still arise. 'I want to see a solicitor about a will' may not necessarily mean that the client wishes to make a will; he or she may want to challenge the validity of a will. It is therefore sensible to *ask the client to confirm your understanding of the reason for the visit before encouraging the client to launch into a lengthy account of the facts.* This should be a quick check by way of a closed question to avoid the client thinking he or she is being invited to fully explain the reason for his or her visit.

Once this confirmation has been obtained, there are two matters which should be dealt with before the interview proceeds further.

11.8.4.1   How will the interview be conducted?

It makes sense to start by letting the client know how long you have available for the interview *and to find out whether the client is under any time constraints.* If you are using an interpreter during the interview, allow twice as long as normal because everything will need to be repeated.

It is also helpful to say a little about how you propose to conduct the interview:

> First, I'll ask you to explain why you have come to see me. Then I will need to ask you some questions and make some notes. Finally, when I have got the complete picture, I shall explain what your legal position is and what options I think are open to you. Between us, we can then try to decide which course of action would best suit your needs.

11.8.4.2   The cost of the interview

> **PROFESSIONAL CONDUCT POINT**
>
> Outcome 1.13 of the SRA Code of Conduct 2011 requires that clients are given the best information possible, both at the time of engagement and as the matter progresses, about the likely overall cost of their matter.

Clients naturally tend to be concerned about the cost of the interview and, indeed, of the whole matter. Until the complete picture has been obtained, it is usually difficult to say anything meaningful about the latter, and this must therefore be postponed until later stages of the interview (see **11.8.8.2**).

However, now is a good time to ascertain whether the client will be paying the costs or if there is an external source of funding. If the client is a company, its parent company, directors or shareholders may be providing support towards the costs. An employee may be supported by a trade union. It is crucial to establish from the start if the client is eligible for Legal Aid, or if he or she has the benefit of any legal expenses insurance (if not you should consider whether to advise the client to seek 'after the event insurance').

You must provide full information about the costs to the client even if he or she is not going to be paying for the charges himself or herself. If you have any fee-sharing arrangements with relevant third parties then you must make this clear to the client.

Whilst a full discussion of the costs of the matter will need to be delayed until later in the interview, now is a good stage to clarify the cost of the interview. In referring the client to the client care information sheet (see **11.8.1.2**), you should explain to the client what your charging rate is or, if such be the case, that the firm's policy is to charge a fixed fee, for example for an initial half-hour interview. If the firm's policy is to provide the initial interview free of charge, then it will be reassuring for the client if this is confirmed by the solicitor early on in the interview. Once the initial costs have been explained clearly to the client, *you should check whether the client is genuinely content to accept this arrangement.* You may like to mention that you will return to the matter of costs at the end of the interview when you have a better idea of the client's situation.

TRANSACTION CASE STUDY

Imagine you are instructed by the sellers. How will you explain the cost of the interview based on the fact your charge-out rate is £150 per hour plus VAT? In addition, how will you manage your client's expectations as to how long the interview will last? You anticipate that this is going to be a complex interview; you have not arranged any further appointments this afternoon.

Solicitor: 'I realise that there is a lot for us to get through this afternoon. I have no other commitments this afternoon, do you need to leave at any particular time?'

Client: 'No, I really want to sort out as much as possible today so that we can get the deal moving.'

Solicitor: 'Well, now is probably a good time to mention my firm's charges for this interview. You will see from the information sheet that I have prepared for you that the firm charges my time out at £150 per hour plus VAT. Are you happy to proceed on this basis?'

Client: 'Yes.'

Solicitor: 'Good. I will, of course, return to the matter of costs at the end of the interview when I have a better idea of the work that is likely to be involved in dealing with the sale of your business.'

11.8.4.3 Keeping control

If during the preliminaries stage you need to ask questions, it is important to use only closed questions. In order to keep control of the interview, the client should not perceive any question as an invitation to launch into his or her reason for making the appointment until you are ready for him or her to do so.

11.8.4.4 Skills summary

(1) Explaining.

(2) Closed questions.

11.8.5 Obtaining the facts

The objective is to obtain the client's account of the facts or of the proposed transaction. Remember that in some cultures it is not usual to discuss personal matters with strangers, even for professional reasons. You may need to allow time for trust to build, perhaps even over several meetings. It may help to explain why you need the information and what it is to be used for. Such clients may find it easier to talk to someone else in your presence, rather than directly to you.

Encourage the client to give an account of the matter in his or her own words. This should be with as little interruption from you as possible.

Consider the impact on the client of the following choice of words and expressions:

'So, where shall we start?' (Does not inspire confidence)

'What's the problem, then?' (There may not be a 'problem')

'Thank you for sending me the documentation ... It seems to me ...' (Over-directional – premature diagnosis)

'Things don't look too good, do they?' (Prematurely pessimistic – provokes anxiety)

'Don't worry, we'll sort this out for you.' (Prematurely optimistic – raises expectations)

'Funny, this is the sixth one we've had in like this in the last month.' (Treating client as a 'case' to be processed – not a human being)

'This is the one, I think. Now then, where are we? ... Let me see ... dah dah dah dah ... Oh yes that's right, this is a GBH case, isn't it?' (Disorganised – unprepared – confusing use of jargon)

Clearly, therefore, you must give very careful thought to the form of words which you use to invite the client to begin this process.

If you are interviewing a client about a road accident it may be perfectly sensible to say, 'Perhaps you could start by telling me exactly what happened on the day of the accident'.

On the other hand, if the client wishes to make a will, saying 'Could you now give me some general background information?' or 'Just tell me the story in your own words' is too vague to indicate what sort of information you require. A more focused form of words would be, 'It's a good idea to make a will. Is there any particular reason that has prompted you to do so now?', or 'Perhaps you could start by explaining what you would like your will to deal with'.

Whatever form of opening words you decide upon, it can also be helpful if, during this part of the interview, you also ask questions along the lines of, 'It would be helpful if you could let me know any particular concerns which you have' and 'Do you foresee any problems?' *Remember to avoid asking more than one question at once.*

You should concentrate on using the various listening techniques discussed at **10.2** and **11.4.1** and confine questions to open questions which will encourage the client to continue the narrative.

As the client begins to build up a picture of the reason why he or she has come to see you, it is important that your questions try to follow his or her train of thought. Your open questions should encourage the client to expand on a particular topic or, as appropriate, to move on to a different aspect. You should avoid jumping around topics and asking questions as they occur to you, irrespective of the particular train of thought that a client is focussing on. You should also avoid just following a random list of questions you prepared earlier. Jumping around topics will hinder your ability to build up a clear picture and is more likely to cause the client to omit facts from his or her explanation. A good questioning technique should be logical and should facilitate the client's recall and thought processes.

There will be ample opportunity in the next stage of the interview ('Filling in the detail') to clarify matters. You should therefore resist any temptation to do so at this stage, because a series of closed questions can easily destroy the client's concentration.

For the same reason, making written notes should, if possible, be restricted to what can be written without interrupting the client's narrative flow (see **11.5.5**).

This comparatively passive role can be a difficult one to master if you are a naturally talkative person. It does, however, enable you to maintain eye contact with the client and to observe the client's general demeanour and manner of delivery. This is very helpful in building rapport with the client and in picking up body language signals about the client's feelings.

If you employ an interpreter during the interview, it is important to remember that the client is the focus for your attention. The solicitor/client relationship is still central to the interview and there should be no independent discussion of the interpreter's views. This becomes more difficult if the interpreter is a friend or relation of the client. There is more chance that side conversations will take place. You should always ask for a translation of any such discussions. In addition, you should be wary of any sign that the interpreter is adding his or her own view to the translation.

11.8.5.1   Skills summary

   (1)   Listening.

   (2)   Open questions.

   (3)   Brief (if any) note-taking.

11.8.6   Filling in the detail

The objective is to ensure that you obtain a full and accurate understanding and record of the relevant facts and of the client's wishes and objectives.

You will not usually be able to give the client effective advice immediately after the client has completed his or her account of the matter in the 'Obtaining the facts' stage.

In most cases, it will be necessary to ask the client to fill gaps or explain discrepancies in the narrative or to supply information which the client had not considered to be relevant.

You will also need to take written notes (see **11.5.5**) and check that you have correctly understood what the client has said.

It may also be necessary to examine documents. You should not try reading a document at the same time as the client is speaking. Not only might this hinder rapport, but it is very difficult to read and listen at the same time. Explain to the client that you need a few moments to read the document so that there is a 'comfortable' silence while you are reading.

This is the stage of the interview during which you assume a more active and directive role.

Questioning skills become more important although, even at this stage, it is generally best to use the T-funnel approach (discussed at **11.5.2.3**). In other words, see what information can be elicited in response to open questions before pinning down the client with more specific closed questions.

It may be necessary to use some of the clarifying and probing techniques (see **11.5.2.4**) to jog the client's memory or to explore discrepancies or weaknesses in the client's version of events.

Before completing this stage of the interview and moving on to give advice, *it is important to summarise what the client has said* in order to double-check that you have correctly understood the position (see **11.5.2.5**).

11.8.6.1   Skills summary

   (1)   Questioning – the T-funnel approach.

   (2)   Note-taking.

   (3)   Clarifying and probing.

   (4)   Examining documents.

   (5)   Summarising.

11.8.7   Advising

> **PROFESSIONAL CONDUCT POINT**
>
> You will want to give the client a clear explanation of the issues involved and the options available to the client. You should explain:
>
> (a)   the relevant issues, the different ways in which the matter could progress and any likely complications;
>
> (b)   the available options;
>
> (c)   whether the possible outcomes merit the risk and expense;
>
> (d)   your role and responsibilities and the services your firm can or cannot provide.

In essence you will usually need to:

(a)   explain the current legal position of the client;

(b)   discuss with the client the main options (both legal and non-legal) if is or her legal position is not to his or her liking;

(c)   help the client to reach a decision/give instructions;

(d)   agree a plan of action.

11.8.7.1   Explaining the client's legal position

> **PROFESSIONAL CONDUCT POINT**
>
> Principle 4 of the SRA Code of Conduct 2011 requires those regulated by the SRA to act in the best interests of each client, and Principle 5 requires them to provide a good standard of service. In addition, it is essential to observe the rules governing solicitors who are conducting financial services activities and to avoid such work unless authorised to conduct it.

This is the first interview. Therefore, if:

(a)   the matter is not routine; or

(b)   you do not have experience in the particular area of law; or

(c)   the client does not insist on preliminary 'off the cuff' advice; or

(d)   the matter is not urgent,

it is quite proper to postpone advising until you have had an opportunity to carry out research, or, if a trainee solictor, to take advice from your supervising solicitor.

Clients do not always need or expect to be given immediate advice. If you are in a position to give advice then it is essential to package it in a way that allows the client to follow your line of reasoning and understand it. The client's legal position should be explained in simple and comprehensible language. You should therefore avoid jargon. Furthermore, you should be aware that the amount of information which a client can absorb is limited (see **11.5.4**).

Every time you are preparing to conduct an interview, you should give conscious thought to the best way of explaining the likely relevant issues to a lay client, for example the fiduciary duties of directors or the dissolution of a partnership at will under the Partnership Act 1890. You should try to work out a jargon free way of explaining, for example, the difference between an off-the-shelf company and a tailor-made company or the difference between the roles of shareholders and directors. There is no need to use statute names, section numbers or case names; in fact such details are undesirable because, rather than impressing a client, they will only serve to confuse or overload a client with unnecessary details.

Clarity of advice also involves trying to structure your advice so that it is given to the client in an order that is easy to follow. For example, in a criminal case it would probably make more sense to explain first what the prosecution has to establish before moving on to explain the availability of particular defences.

In its Practice Note of 6 October 2011, The Law Society recommends that, when advising, 'you should include information on: likely complications which commonly arise ... [and] the different ways a particular matter could progress'. The aim is to ensure that the client appreciates that his or her case involves a complex matter, and it reduces the risk that, at a later date, the client concludes that 'you did not handle the matter properly'.

11.8.7.2   Discussing the main options

Whilst needing to understand the current legal position, the client is generally less interested in being given a detailed resumé of the law than in being told what courses of action are available. However, some explanation of the law is necessary in order to set the available options in context.

Clients need to be given a clear explanation of what realistic options are open to them in order to achieve their desired objectives. Managing the client's expectations now can reduce the risk of dissatisfaction and complaint later on in your relationship. This explanation must be supported by thorough discussion with the client of the relative merits of each option.

Clearly, the strength of the legal aspects of the case will influence this discussion, but you must also remember that there are other factors which will have an impact on the client's decision. In particular, the client's decision as to which option to pursue may be influenced by the possible timeframe involved, the level of costs, the commercial risks and personal factors such as emotion, health, family relationships, professional embarrassment, employee relations and possible adverse publicity.

PROFESSIONAL CONDUCT POINT

Indicative Behaviour 1.13 of the SRA Code of Conduct 2011 suggests that to meet the Chapter 1 Outcomes you should discuss with the client whether the potential outcomes justify the expense or risk and, in particular, any risk that the client may have to cover his or her opponent's costs. It is sensible to make a record of the risk assessment and the risk should be kept under review, with the client being updated as to any changes, as the matter progresses.

TRANSACTION CASE STUDY

Assume that you are acting for the purchaser who tells you that, for tax reasons, this deal must take place within the next 10 days. Your advice may well have been that the purchaser should carry out a very extensive investigation into the assets and liabilities of Toast & Tea (so-called 'due diligence'). This process should discover any problems that exist, for example with the physical state and legal title of the properties or the contractual relationships with suppliers. However, such a process will be time-consuming and expensive. If time is short then due diligence should perhaps focus on the property or contractual relationships which are of greatest interest to the client. If due diligence is to be limited, the client will need to weigh up the risk of buying assets with 'hidden problems', which may give rise to expense in the future, against the risk of losing the deal or losing the tax advantage by not completing in the next 10 days.

The discussion should take account of these non-legal factors. For example, litigation is not only emotionally stressful, costly and time consuming, it can be severely disruptive to a business if employees, partners or directors have to spend days at court waiting to give evidence. It may make commercial sense for a client to do nothing about a particular issue because, despite any injustice, it is not economically worthwhile. It may be that cash flow will prevent the taking or defending of an action. Equally, it may be commercially necessary to defend an action, despite the costs, to preserve a good name, trade mark, goodwill or a position in the market.

You should try to involve the client in the discussion so that you can jointly weigh the advantages and disadvantages of each option. Clients cannot be expected to choose between available options unless the solicitor has clearly explained the pros and cons of each option and the action required to implement each option. This will help the client to reach a decision, as will *entering into a dialogue* with the client to ensure that the client is making the right decision for the right reasons. Even a client who comes to the interview with a clear idea of how he or she wants the matter to progress will be interested in the options. At least then his or her decision is an informed one.

11.8.7.3   Helping the client to reach a decision

All major decisions concerning the case or transaction are for the client to make. It is the client's case, not the solicitor's. However, opinion is divided on how far the solicitor may recommend a course of action for the client.

There are two schools of thought.

(a)   The non-directive school suggests that a solicitor should only present the options and leave it entirely to the client to decide which to follow. The advice is characterised by the preamble, 'On the one hand X, but on the other hand Y. However, it is for you to decide'. This approach may avoid a charge of negligence if the route followed by the client proves to be the wrong option. However, it is not particularly helpful to the client. Given the status, experience and cost of solicitors, clients often expect a recommendation.

(b)   The directive school involves the solicitor in taking greater control of the decision-making process.

A combination of each approach is appropriate in most cases. It is important to explain the realistic options to the client and to explore the positive and negative consequences of each. Provided the client actively participates in this explorative discussion and you actively seek the client's views and preferences, the decision will often be clear.

Furthermore, if the matter is non-urgent, difficult or complex, the client may need time to reach a considered decision.

11.8.7.4   Agreeing a future plan of action

Once key decisions have been taken, it will usually be necessary to agree a more detailed plan of campaign, ie, to decide what is the best way of carrying out the course of action which has been agreed. This presents a useful opportunity for you to explain your role and the services your firm can offer.

For example, if your client has decided to try to settle a matter by agreement rather than go to court, you will still need to decide:

(a)   whether to approach the other side immediately or await their next move;

(b)   whether any first approach should be made by you or the client, and if so:

   (i)   whether it should be by letter, telephone or in person;

   (ii)   what (if any) opening offer should be made and how far the client is prepared to go in order to settle.

As before, you should explain clearly the range of options and try to engage the client as fully as possible in the decision-making process.

In bringing this discussion to a close, you should ensure that everything has been discussed to the client's satisfaction. A form of wording could be as follows: 'Can I just check whether you clearly understand your position or if there is anything you would like me to clarify.'

11.8.7.5   Skills summary

(1)   Summarising.

(2)   Explaining.

(3)   Listening.

(4)   Note-taking.

11.8.8   Closing

Once the issues have been discussed with the client, and the client has decided what needs to be done or has decided to go away and consider his or her options more carefully, there are still a number of matters to deal with before you conclude the interview.

11.8.8.1   Client care and costs information

PROFESSIONAL CONDUCT POINT

At the closing stage you should ensure that the client has as clear a picture as possible of what will happen next and the costs that he or she is likely to incur.

The outstanding client care issues to be covered and costs information to be imparted are as follows:

(a)   providing the name of an alternative contact in case of complaint;

(b)   explaining the possible time frame for completion of the matter;

(c)   giving the best information possible as to the costs of the matter, including any disbursements;

(d)   establishing when your next contact with the client will occur;

(e)   confirming the advice given in the interview in a follow-up letter and maintaining a proper record of the interview.

A guide to the issues to be dealt with during the closing stages is set out at **11.8.8.2**. This guidance encompasses these outstanding matters and includes further recommendations which, as a matter of good practice, should be considered at this stage of the interview.

11.8.8.2   A professional closing

There are a number of matters to be addressed in closing the interview and in ensuring that both you and your client are clear as to what will happen next, how quickly the matter will be resolved and what it will all cost. Whilst most of these matters can be dealt with in any convenient order, it is recommended that asking if the client has anything further to discuss should be dealt with first.

Is there anything else?

You should always make sure that the client has had an opportunity to discuss all matters and concerns.

Make a specific point of asking the client if there is anything else he or she wants to discuss. This forms a bridge between the advising stage and the performance of the other closing tasks. Its purpose is to ensure that there are no other matters which the client wishes to discuss before the solicitor starts to close the interview. This should not be treated as a meaningless ritual, and the client should be made to feel free to respond affirmatively.

This may be characterised as follows, 'Before I start to round off this meeting, can I just check that there is nothing else that you want to bring up or ask me about?'. Two further points need to be emphasised:

(a)   This should sound to the client like a sincere and genuine enquiry, not a formality, as in the familiar, 'well if there is nothing else then...'.

(b)   The question, 'Is there anything else?' can perform the function described above, but it should not be repeatedly posed throughout the interview as a substitute for asking sensible questions to elicit information.

This question should be asked before dealing with all the other closing tasks. If it is left until the end of the closing then, if the client does have something else to talk about, the closing tasks may change. This means the interview will have to be closed again, possibly with different follow-up tasks, different cost implications and a different time frame. Asking, 'Is there anything else?' at an appropriate stage allows the solicitor to keep better control of the structure at the end of the interview. It avoids any misunderstanding or confusion that could arise from effectively closing the interview twice.

Next steps/follow-up tasks by solicitor

During the interview, it is essential to establish exactly what, if anything, the client is instructing you to do (see **11.8.7.4**). If you are dealing with a new client, especially one who is not used to consulting solicitors, you should explain your role and the services your firm provides. You may already have covered these matters when discussing a plan of action with the client (see **11.8.7.4**)

In the closing stages of the interview, it is helpful to summarise what steps you have agreed to take and when you will take them. The steps will vary from case to case but might involve taking a statement from a witness, obtaining a police or medical report, writing a letter before action, carrying out a company search, preparing a draft will or partnership agreement, or drafting a divorce petition.

In most cases, it will be appropriate to write a follow-up letter (see **11.8.10**) to the client summarising what has been discussed and agreed. Telling the client that you intend to do this is obviously reassuring.

If you have not already done so, now is a good time to check that you have an accurate note of the client's address and telephone number. Check also to which address the client wishes correspondence to be sent. This may be relevant if, for example, the matter involves a partnership dispute when the client may prefer correspondence to be sent to his or her home address rather than business address. Equally, in a divorce case, the client may prefer correspondence to be sent to him or her care of a friend or family member.

Next steps/follow-up tasks by client

You should also remind the client of any action that he or she has agreed to take. This might include supplying information or documents which were not available during the interview or thinking about the advice or discussing his or her options with others and contacting you once a decision has been reached. If there is nothing you need the client to do at this stage, it is useful to state this clearly.

Alternative contact

Giving the name and status of the person handling the case is something which should have been explained when you introduced yourself as part of the greeting or preliminaries stages of the interview.

When closing the interview, it may be useful to remind the client of your name and status. It will not always be necessary to give the name of the person with overall supervision of the matter during the interview itself; this can be left to the follow-up letter. However, in some cases this may be appropriate. For example, if you have introduced yourself as a trainee solicitor, it can be reassuring to the client to be told that your work is supervised.

In all cases you should provide the client with an alternative point of contact in the firm. This is the name of a person he or she can speak to if, when the client contacts the office, you are not available, or if the client has any complaint. Reference can also be made here to the client care information sheet you prepared in advance (see **11.8.1.2**).

A form of wording which covers all these aspects could be as follows:

> 'As I mentioned at the start of the interview, my name is Joseph Adkin and I am a trainee solicitor with the firm. My work is supervised by Alice White who will be familiar with your case. If, when you contact the office, I am not available, please feel free to speak to Mrs White. Mrs White's contact details are on the information sheet I gave you at the start of the interview.'

Time frame for the matter

The client should be given some indication of how long the *matter* will take to complete, remembering to take into account any deadlines to which the client needs you to work (for example, the matter must be completed by the end of the tax year). This should help manage the client's expectations and minimise the risk of complaints about delays in situations where the outcome is likely to take some time to attain. Sometimes an estimate is quite easy to give:

> 'As the agreed terms are quite straightforward, I shall be able to send you and Simon a draft of the partnership agreement by the end of the week. Then, if you're both happy with it, it should be possible to sign the final document sometime during next week.'

In other cases, particularly where court proceedings are a possibility, it may be impossible to do more than give a very broad estimate because future developments will to a large extent be unpredictable and outside your control. Even in these situations, you should try to give some indication of time frame, even if it is only to indicate that the matter could potentially take years rather than months.

Estimating the costs of the matter/method of charging

Costs will already have been discussed during the course of the interview. As stated at **11.8.4.2**, it will usually be possible to explain early in the interview how the interview itself is to be paid for, but it is seldom possible at that stage to discuss the likely cost of the matter itself. When discussing the client's options (see **11.8.7.2**) there should have been an analysis of whether the benefits of any proposed course of action outweigh potential risks as to costs, and you may have considered the possibility of offering the client a conditional fee arrangement.

In closing the interview, a summary of the position as to costs ensures the client understands clearly the potential cost implications he or she is facing. Information on costs, together with details of possible disbursements (charges or fees that will be incurred by the solicitor in carrying out the legal work which are not included in the firm's charging rate, such as the charge for a company search or payment of stamp duty land tax), should be summarised as part of the closing stage of the interview.

Costs should be discussed in a business-like way. You are providing a service to the client, and you should not therefore appear to be embarrassed at having to discuss money.

PROFESSIONAL CONDUCT POINT

Outcome 1.13 of the SRA Code of Conduct 2011 requires you to give your client the best possible information on the likely overall costs of the matter.

It is sensible to outline your standard billing arrangements and discuss any requirements for receiving funds on account.

Deciding just what information you can reliably give the client will involve consideration of a range of possible ways of handling this particularly tricky aspect of client care.

An agreed fee

In some cases, commonly domestic conveyancing and simple will drafting, the firm may agree a fixed fee for handling the client's matter. The agreed fee should have been mentioned at the opening stage of the interview (see **11.8.4.2**). During the closing stage of the interview, having received detailed instructions and not having found any unforeseen complications, it is appropriate to confirm the agreed fee. You should also confirm when the agreed fee is to be paid and whether there are any disbursements (including how much they are likely to be and when they will need to be paid).

Estimating the likely costs

As most firms calculate their bill by using an hourly charging rate, the likely costs of the matter will involve the solicitor estimating how much time will be involved in handling the matter. While, as a bare minimum, the client should be told the firm's hourly charging rate (and, if relevant, whether the rate may change during the retainer), this information is not in itself helpful if the client has no idea of how many hours' work will be involved. The rate should be coupled with a realistic estimate of the time to be charged.

In non-contentious matters, such as setting up a simple company or drafting a partnership agreement, an estimate of the overall cost is usually possible. For example, in a matter where you are instructed to draft a partnership agreement where the individuals have already agreed the terms that they wish the contract to cover, you may be happy to advise the client as follows:

> 'As I mentioned at the start of the interview, my firm charges my time at £100 plus VAT per hour. In my experience, drafting the sort of partnership agreement which you and your partners will need is likely to cost in the region of £400–£500 plus VAT.'

However, in many cases, it will be necessary to make it clear to the client that only a rough estimate of the total cost can be given (or perhaps a range of possible costs) because of the uncertainty as to how much work may need to be undertaken and the time it may take. For example, if you are advising an individual who is involved in negotiating the terms of a partnership agreement which have not yet been agreed, you will be less certain as to the amount of time you will be involved in completing the transaction:

> 'As I mentioned at the start of the interview, my firm charges my time at £100 plus VAT per hour. It is difficult to estimate how much of my time will be taken up during the negotiations, and so it is impossible to give you a precise estimate of the overall costs. It may well amount to over £1,000 but I will report to you regularly about the costs as the matter progresses.'

There are many situations, particularly those involving potential litigation, where it may not be possible to give a realistic overall cost of the matter. In such cases, you should explain this to the client and instead give the best information possible about the cost of the next stage of the matter. For example, in a case where the client has decided that he would like to defend legal action taken against him, you might advise the client as follows:

> 'As I mentioned at the start of the interview, my firm charges my time at £100 plus VAT per hour. Clearly, the cost will depend on how much time is involved and this in turn depends on whether the case can be settled. It is impossible, at this stage, for me to give a realistic estimate of the costs involved in taking this matter to full trial if it does not settle. We have agreed that the next step will be for me to instruct a barrister to provide an opinion on the likelihood of your defence succeeding in court. In my experience, the cost of my time in preparing the instructions to the barrister and the barrister's fees in providing such an opinion is likely to be in the region of £2,000 plus VAT. Before instructing the barrister, I will need you to provide me with £1,000 which I will hold pending payment of the costs I incur on your account. Once we have the opinion, we can meet again to discuss whether you wish to proceed with your defence and I will, at that time, be in a better position to advise you further as to the likely costs.'

In all cases when you are giving an estimate, you should consider whether either of the following assurances should be offered to the client: reassurance that you will keep him or her informed regularly as to how the costs are mounting during the matter; or perhaps agreeing a ceiling figure for costs, with the client's agreement being needed before costs beyond this figure are incurred.

If you anticipate the client having to pay disbursements then you must mention this and explain how much they are likely to amount to and when the client will be expected to pay for them.

The client should be reassured that detailed information relating to costs will be confirmed in the follow-up letter (see **11.8.10**).

Next contact

Make it clear which of you is to make the next contact. Does your client expect to hear from you or vice versa?

At the same time, tell your client whether you think that another face-to-face meeting will be necessary and (if so) why and who will organise it.

For example:

> 'So we've agreed that I shall do nothing until you let me know how much you want to offer to Mr Jones. I shall then write to his solicitors offering that sum in full and final settlement.
>
> Obviously, if they confirm in writing that he accepts, that will broadly be an end of the matter.
>
> On the other hand, if he rejects the offer and continues with the court action, I shall need to arrange another meeting with you to give more detailed consideration to the strength of the evidence in support of your defence.'

11.8.8.3 Skills summary

(1)   Summarising.

(2)   Explaining.

11.8.9 Parting

When the interview is over, you should accompany the client back to the reception area.

The parting should be friendly, courteous and (as far as possible) reassuring.

11.8.10 After the interview

After the interview, the notes you have taken during the interview should be used to produce a full written record of the interview as soon as possible, whilst your memory is still fresh.

In most cases, you will have promised to send the client a follow-up letter. This letter should be drafted and sent in good time after the interview. The letter is effectively confirming your understanding of the instructions you have received. It should confirm the advice you gave and the follow-up action that both you and the client agreed to take. It should contain the detailed costs information that you promised the client during the interview, and provides a convenient opportunity to deal in writing with client care issues and may include a copy of your firm's terms of business. Further advice on drafting letters can be found in **Chapter 1**.

The notes taken during the interview, together with your full attendance note, the follow-up letter, copies of the client's proof of identity papers and the client care information sheet signed by the client during the interview should all be placed on the client's file.

11.9 THE SECRET OF SUCCESS – PRACTICE

The principles set out in this chapter seek to provide something for everyone.

If you have never interviewed a client then the structure and skills that are outlined here will provide a firm foundation for you to prepare for your first interview. By reviewing how that interview went, you will begin to hone your skills and gradually, with further practice, develop a manner and technique with which you feel comfortable, safe in the knowledge that it is based on sound principles.

If you are already used to interviewing clients then reading this chapter may have made you evaluate the skills and techniques that you employ with a view to improving your personal style.

CHAPTER 12

NEGOTIATION AND ALTERNATIVE DISPUTE RESOLUTION

LEARNING OUTCOMES

After reading this chapter you will be able to:

- identify your predominant negotiation style
- understand the pros and cons of different negotiation styles
- set out the core preparation you would undertake prior to negotiating
- identify the key stages in a negotiation
- select the most appropriate forum for a negotiation
- explain the different types of ADR available
- understand basic negotiation strategy and tactics.

12.1 INTRODUCTION

It is essential that lawyers add value in negotiation if they are to serve their clients well. To add value requires an understanding of the principles of good negotiation and regular practice in implementing the techniques and tools involved. Much recent research has been done into how we make decisions and how we persuade others. This research now informs our understanding of how best to negotiate. In the rest of this chapter we consider some of the basic principles. There are also examples and exercises.

Negotiation is a process by which two or more parties attempt to come to an agreement which meets their needs and provides as much of what they want as possible. Skilled negotiators are aware that negotiation is a subtle art. It is not a simple battle of wills where one side must succeed at the expense of another. Using principled interest-based negotiating techniques, it is often possible for both sides to achieve a solution which satisfies their needs and delivers much of what they want, ie a genuine solution acceptable to all the parties.

Set out below is a summary of some of the essentials of good negotiating practice which will be explored in more detail in this chapter:

(a)   Full preparation, including mastery of all relevant facts and law, and identification of your best alternative to a negotiated agreement ('BATNA' – see **12.4.4** below).

(b)   Use of objective standards of reference, eg market standards, expert reports, audited accounts etc.

(c)   Adoption of an interest-based approach whereby you seek to identify the interests of the other side and better to understand their needs and wants.

(d)   The ability to identify gaps in your information or understanding and to ask questions to uncover this information, together with good listening skills.

(e)   The ability to develop trust with the other party or parties to encourage information sharing and seek creative solutions.

(f)   Observance of high ethical standards.

(g)   The ability to manage your emotions and to be flexible in your choice of negotiating style.

12.2   THE ETHICS OF NEGOTIATION

To practise effectively, it is essential not only to understand the professional and ethical rules which apply but to uphold them. To be an effective negotiator, you must be an ethical negotiator, not simply because you are bound to do so by a professional code of ethics and behaviour, but also because any failure to uphold the highest ethical standards will diminish your effectiveness as a negotiator. You will lose the trust of your client and of the other side if you breach ethical standards. Negotiation is based on establishing trust between the parties. Once lost it is extremely hard to rebuild. Familiarise yourself with all the relevant Code of Conduct provisions and try to anticipate any possible areas of difficulty.

You must never lie or exceed your client's instructions. However, you have no duty to volunteer information which is adverse to your client's position. If asked a direct question on such a point you cannot lie, but you can refuse to answer, offer no comment or attempt to deflect the question (eg by offering a partial answer or by parrying with a counter-question). However, it is likely in such circumstances that the other negotiator will guess what the true position is, and it may have been tactically wiser to have made an admission.

12.3   NEGOTIATING STYLES

12.3.1   Categories

Some writers group negotiators into two general styles with labels such as hard/soft or aggressive/co-operative.

However, such categorisation may be a misleading division of a myriad of different styles. **Figure 1** demonstrates this by charting two characteristics of the negotiator which are not necessarily mutually exclusive but which can be integrated with each other to widely varying degrees.

Figure 1

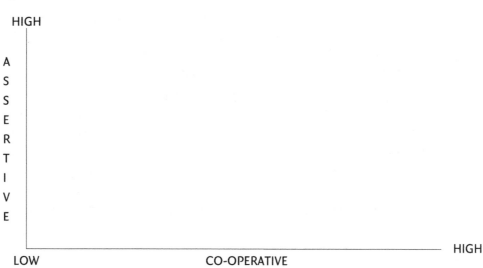

How assertive are you? Mark your point on the vertical axis. How co-operative are you? Mark your point on the horizontal axis. Mark on the graph where your two points meet.

This analysis recognises that everybody's style is different: there are hundreds of points on the graph. However, although it gives a general indication of a person's predominant style, the analysis has inherent drawbacks. First, self-analysis is not always accurate. Secondly, it fails to recognise that you can and should vary your style according to the needs of a particular negotiation. Effective negotiators are highly flexible and will vary their style according to the merits of the case they are pursuing and the style adopted by the other negotiator.

Figure 2

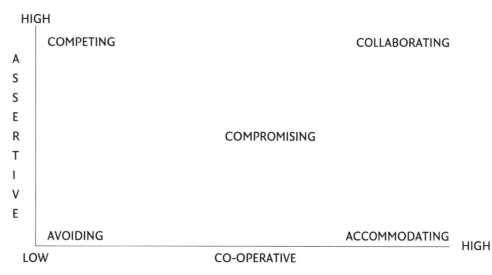

Figure 2 shows the same chart divided into five broad styles, any one of which may be used according to the circumstances.

It is important to:

(a)   know the potential strengths and weaknesses of your own predominant style;

(b)   learn to vary your own style; and

(c)   be able to identify, and react appropriately, to the style of the other negotiator.

12.3.2 Avoiding

The avoiding style is low both on assertiveness and co-operativeness. It is sometimes used by those who are facing actual or potential legal action, or a proposed term in a transaction, against which they have little or no argument. They hope that, if they ignore the problem, it will either go away or circumstances will change in their favour.

It is also an approach that might be adopted by the solicitor on one side if he or she knows the other side has a deadline to meet. He or she will be trying to put off the real negotiations until the other side is under severe time pressure, knowing that this will then put him or her into a strong position.

The appropriate response to an opponent who adopts an avoiding style is to press ahead as quickly as possible, perhaps by imposing time limits or by pursuing alternative courses of action which force him or her into serious talks, for example by issuing and serving proceedings.

12.3.3 Accommodating

A person adopting an accommodating style is keen to accept the other side's proposals and reach agreement. It is sometimes a style which results from the negotiator's personality.

It may be consciously adopted, however, if the other side has grossly misjudged the parties' positions. Even in these circumstances, it might, in some cases, be wiser not to take advantage of the other side's error particularly when the parties will have an ongoing relationship.

12.3.4 Compromising

It is vital that negotiators should have the capacity to compromise; otherwise, deals would never be made and disputes would never be settled. The important question for a negotiator is how and when to compromise. Factors which frequently motivate compromise include avoiding:

(a)   the uncertainties of trial (on liability or quantum, eg, when a witness fails to come 'up to proof');

(b)   the possible publicity arising out of litigation;

(c)   the delay involved in going to trial;

(d)   the emotional stress that continued litigation could involve;

(e)   the legal costs of going any further – even if you win in court, you are unlikely to recover all the legal costs from the unsuccessful defendant;

(f)   the further loss of management time for a commercial client;

(g)   the transaction falling through; or

(h)   souring an ongoing relationship between two commercial parties or between members of a family.

Although compromise is necessary, a compromising style can be characterised as a readiness to 'split the difference' between the two sides positions, regardless of the objective merits. There may occasionally be good reasons for securing a deal in this way, but they do not include the easy disposal of the matter or speedier payment of your fees. Always evaluate your reasons for compromise and ensure that you are compromising when appropriate and using relevant criteria to calculate the basis on which you offer or accept compromise.

12.3.5 Competing

Competitors are unco-operative and highly assertive. They may or may not also be aggressive.

If you have a strong case and the other side is accommodating, a competing style can be highly effective.

On the other hand, if it is misused, a competing style is likely to create mistrust, distort communication, increase tension and possibly sour long-term relationships. It can provoke retaliation (the other side become aggressive or unreasonable), and settlement can be severely delayed or a proposed deal can fall apart. Given the potential dangers of this style, it should be adopted with caution.

If you are faced with competitive negotiators, try to avoid counter-productive reactions. Ignore personality and concentrate on the objective merits of the arguments. It may be helpful to ask: 'Why are they behaving like this?' There could be a number of possible reasons, each of which should generate a different response from you:

(a) Their behaviour might reflect their personality and normal style. Research/consult with colleagues to see if this is their experience. Try to separate the problem from the person as far as possible.

(b) Consider whether your own reaction or behaviour is in your client's best interests. It may be that they do in fact have a very strong case.

(c) They may have a very weak case and are therefore bluffing or over-compensating. Stay calm. Take care not to react too hastily. Bide your time until you are more certain of the objective merits of the case.

(d) They may be under-prepared. As a result, they may be worried that they are running the risk of making an error of judgement and conceding too much. They therefore over-compensate and become less co-operative and more assertive (or avoiding) in order to reduce that risk. If you suspect this to be the reason, the best tactic might be to adjourn the negotiation until they are better prepared.

(e) They may have become competitive in response to what they perceive to be your competitiveness.

Ultimately, it should be remembered that in a negotiation there are no rules or procedures which have to be followed (unless you have agreed to them), and there is no obligation to reach a settlement. The other side cannot force you into anything without your consent and vice versa.

12.3.6 Collaborating

Some people call collaboration 'problem solving' or 'principled negotiation'. It encompasses highly assertive and highly co-operative behaviour. It is often the ideal negotiating style because it gives you the best of both worlds. Assertiveness and co-operativeness are not mutually exclusive.

Assertiveness is not the same as aggression. You should aim to be sufficiently assertive to press your own client's case and to avoid being trampled on by an aggressive opponent; at the same time, you should be sufficiently co-operative to search for any possibility of a mutually beneficial solution. This is particularly important where there will be (or the parties would like there to be) a continuing business or personal relationship after the present dispute has been resolved.

Beware, however, of certain risks:

(a) Watch out for wolves in sheep's clothing, ie the pleasant negotiator who smiles a lot, flatters you, appears to be perfectly reasonable (and may pepper his or her statements with phrases like 'fair and reasonable' and 'sympathetic to your client's case'), but who on objective analysis is being competitive and offering very little. Do not jump to conclusions; try not to allow personality to influence you; concentrate on the objective merits of the case.

(b) If you are trying to adjust your own predominant style, for example to become more assertive or more co-operative, there is a danger that, as one characteristic increases, so the other decreases. Although it is possible to be high on both, it can be difficult to achieve.

12.3.7 Conclusion

Everyone has a different combination of assertive/co-operative behaviour and a different natural negotiating style. The key is to identify your natural predisposition, and to harness your strengths and be aware of your potential weak points. Concentrate on your client's objectives and treat the negotiation as a common problem rather than a battle of wills.

The rest of this chapter generally assumes a collaborative style. However, thorough preparation, self-confidence and perceptiveness are more important than personal style.

12.4 PREPARATION FOR A NEGOTIATION

12.4.1 Importance of preparation

The successful negotiator possesses many skills; these include the abilities to communicate, listen, persuade, analyse and create. These talents must, however, be supported by a bedrock of knowledge.

A thorough knowledge of the facts, the law and the procedure relevant to a particular case is vital. Without that knowledge, you lose any chance of controlling the negotiating process.

It is also essential to establish clearly your client's objectives in entering into the negotiation. What is the minimum he or she is prepared to accept? Has he or she reached this position with the benefit of all available information? If he or she is proceeding under certain misconceptions, it is part of your role to correct them.

Armed with the requisite knowledge (law, facts and procedure) and your client's instructions, a plan based on the following sections (**12.4.2–12.4.7**) should be prepared.

An effective starting point in your preparation is often to identify all the business issues which are likely to be relevant to your client. These should include consideration of money, risk, control, standards and closure. The details will vary according to the facts of each case or transaction. Set out below are examples of the sort of issues you might consider under each heading.

Money

How much will be paid by any of the parties? What will the currency be? How will the money be paid? When will it be paid? Having cash up front may be a benefit to your client that makes it worth taking a lesser amount or vice versa.

Risk

What are the potential risks for your client and how can you minimise them? Who should bear the risk and can you protect against it, eg by purchasing insurance? Risks to be considered will depend on the circumstances of each case but might include risk of insolvency/failure to pay, risk of damage to a product or of damage in transit, risk that markets might change, etc.

Control

Who will have control of the product/business? When will control be transferred? How will control be handed over? For example, in selling a business, when/how might management changes be implemented, and what handover will be required?

Standards

Who will have the power to decide whether any standards set have been reached? For example, if goods are to arrive in 'good condition', who will decide whether this has been met or not?

Will you require independent verification and, if so, who will select, appoint and pay for such services, eg if a valuation is required for goods or property?

Closure

How will the settlement/transaction be completed? At what point will liabilities cease? When will ownership pass? What rights do either party have to reject the settlement/transaction? If goods are being handed over, where will the handover take place, who will deliver and when will this take place?

Using this framework will often help you identify additional information or questions you need to ask your clients.

TRANSACTION CASE STUDY

Using the Toast & Tea transaction case (which may be found at p xii), identify what the likely business issues for the sellers might be.

Business issues for consideration if negotiating the Toast & Tea sale include the following:

- The owners of Toast & Tea ideally want £22 million but are prepared to accept £18 million. On what basis are they prepared to drop from their ideal figure?

- The owners of Toast & Tea want the transaction to proceed quickly, and as they have other investment projects presumably they will need the money quickly. You will need to identify how much money they want and what the timeframe is. Is there a deadline date by which the transaction needs to be complete? Is there a minimum amount the owners need to achieve by a particular date?

- How will the money be paid and over what period? Are the owners prepared to accept payment in instalments? How can they be sure that they will be paid the full amount? What happens if the buyer fails to make a payment? When will ownership of Toast & Tea pass? Who will manage the company during any handover period?

- Valuation of property will be important consideration in this case. Who will appoint the valuer? Who will pay the valuer? When will valuation be made? Ideally the owners of Toast & Tea will want to select their own valuer and will want to select a point of valuation when commercial property prices are most likely to be at their highest. Would they accept an average figure if both sides appoint valuers, or would they consider agreeing to the joint instruction of a valuer?

- What happens if the valuer comes back with a figure below that which the owners are prepared to accept?

- Is Florence Lowe prepared to continue in her current role? If she is prepared to stay, how long is she prepared to commit to this role, and what will her salary and notice provisions, etc be?

Identifying some of the business issues relevant to your client will help you prepare for the negotiation and identify possible gaps in the information you have. It should also help generate possible bargaining points.

12.4.2 Interests not positions

The client will inform you of his or her negotiating position; he or she wants compensation, a fixed-term contract, the removal of a tenant. You must look behind his or her stated position and try to identify his or her underlying interests. Why does the client want what he or she is demanding? Ask – or you may end up negotiating on the basis of false assumptions.

Anticipate the other side's interests. Consideration of these will help you avoid being taken by surprise and will allow you to develop a wider range of bargaining points.

In addition, once the underlying interests or unspoken assumptions are identified, it may be that the underlying interests can be satisfied in some other way and at less cost than you initially expected.

EXAMPLE

In negotiating a lease of the major unit in a new shopping mall, the landlord might demand from his or her major 'anchor' tenant absolute bars on assignment, sub-letting or change of use. The tenant might demand absolute freedom on all three. This presents an apparent impasse. However, the landlord's underlying interest might be to use the anchor tenant to attract 'satellite' tenants to the other, smaller units, while the tenant's interest might be the long-term freedom to move elsewhere. A compromise which might satisfy both parties' underlying interests would be to have a short-term restriction rather than one which lasted for the whole duration of the lease.

Looking for underlying interests is particularly important in transaction-based negotiations or multi-issue claims. It is less likely to be productive in debt collection, personal injury or other single issue, 'money only' claims. However, it should always be investigated. For example, in debt collection it may be that the creditor has an underlying interest in the survival of the debtor's business.

In a personal injury claim there may be an interest in improving future management or training procedures to avoid similar incidents.

12.4.3   Strengths and weaknesses

The logical next step after a consideration of the parties' underlying interests and identification of your BATNA is to assess the factors which support and those which undermine your client's case (ie, once you know what he or she wants, what are the chances of him or her getting what he or she wants?).

Identify your client's strengths and weaknesses and those of the other side. Perhaps your client has no pressing need to make a deal, but the other side have financial difficulties which make it vital for them to reach an agreement; perhaps your client's case is supported by strong legal precedent.

Once the other side's strengths have been identified, you can plan how to counter them. For example, can you obtain other evidence or reinterpret existing evidence?

What are the weaknesses in the other side's position? For example, will they risk court action if their main concern is to avoid bad publicity?

Expect the other side to have spotted the weaknesses in your client's case and to ask questions which could expose those weaknesses. Anticipate these questions and prepare carefully worded replies which (without lying or misrepresenting the position), as far as possible, protect your client.

You must behave ethically. Any misrepresentation would constitute professional misconduct, as well as rendering voidable any resulting agreement.

What questions could you ask to exploit your client's strengths and which probe for weaknesses in the other side's position? The phrasing of such questions should be carefully considered to make it difficult for the other side to avoid giving a straight (and it is hoped revealing) answer.

Consider whether you should use 'open' or 'closed' questioning techniques or a combination of both depending on the information you require.

To negotiate effectively you must be assertive in advancing your client's case and tenacious in seeking replies to your questions. However, this should be done within the constraints of a professional and detached approach. If the general tone of your questioning (or answers) is aggressive, sarcastic or discourteous, it is likely to sour relationships and prevent you from having productive discussions.

12.4.4 BATNA

One of the best known books on negotiation is Fisher and Ury's *Getting to Yes*. Their acronym, BATNA, stands for Best Alternative To a Negotiated Agreement. In other words, *if the negotiations were to break down and you failed to settle*, what would you be left with? What would be the true cost or value of that alternative?

In transaction cases, your BATNA could be to do a deal with a third party rather than with the other side, or not to do a deal at all. In dispute resolution cases, the BATNA would often be litigation. Exploring the available alternatives in advance can concentrate the mind wonderfully – both your own mind and your client's. Make sure that the perceived BATNA is a realistic alternative and not just a vague possibility.

Fisher and Ury recommend that you identify, evaluate and develop your own BATNA and also try to guess the other side's. Developing your own BATNA might involve, for example, pressing ahead with litigation procedures simultaneously with trying to negotiate an out-of-court settlement.

The aim of the BATNA approach to planning a negotiation is to provide you with a yardstick against which you can assess the value of any offer made in the negotiation. Identifying your BATNA helps you to decide your 'resistance point' in the negotiation (see **12.4.5.3**). It can therefore protect you from being too generous, ie agreeing to give the other side more than the value of your BATNA. It can also protect you from being too obstinate, ie rejecting a final offer which is in fact better than your BATNA.

If your client appears to have an attractive alternative available, this strengthens his or her negotiating position; it might therefore be a good tactic to make the other side aware of this alternative.

In some instances, the client may have more than one alternative course of action available. If so, you should discuss with your client the feasibility of each alternative and consider whether it is worthwhile trying to develop each alternative or to concentrate on just one.

12.4.5 Issues, priorities and variables

12.4.5.1 Isolation of separate issues

Many negotiations involve the resolution of several issues. It is a good idea in such cases to isolate each issue. One reason for doing this is that it helps to ensure that all relevant matters are covered in the negotiation.

> **EXAMPLE**
>
> Your client is a retailer who has a contract with a manufacturer for the supply of an exclusive range of golfing accessories. The client has suffered losses owing to the manufacturer failing to meet agreed supply dates. He wants compensation but is aware that the stocking of the contract goods generates a great deal of his custom.
>
> The issues are:
>
> - the claim for compensation;
> - the continuation of a profitable relationship.

12.4.5.2   Relative importance of each issue

Having identified the issues, you should discuss with your client the relative importance to him or her of each, to ensure you have a clear view of his or her priorities. In the above example, your client would almost certainly decide that the claim for compensation should not be pressed too hard if it would put at risk the continuation of the relationship.

12.4.5.3   Opening bids and resistance points

On each issue, make an assessment of the most favourable result that you would hope to achieve and the least favourable result that you would be prepared to accept.

Most favourable result ('opening bid')

To begin by making demands which are wildly optimistic and which bear no relation to the parties' positions will result in your losing credibility. You are bound to look foolish when you are unable to give sound reasons to justify your position.

The bid you make should be the highest justifiable bid, after taking into account the law and facts which support your client's case; ie, try to predict the settlement you would obtain if all the factors which support your case were accepted without any counter-arguments being put forward by the other side.

EXAMPLE

Through no fault of his own, your client has been dismissed by his employer, with two years of a fixed-term contract left to run. His salary (after tax and national insurance deductions) was £35,000 per annum. The most favourable result would be to obtain the total of lost net salary (£70,000) for the remaining two-year period. It is a bid which can be justified on a contractual basis.

You would expect your opponent to put forward arguments which support the reduction of this figure (eg, the former employee has a duty to mitigate his loss by looking for other work), but if your opponent fails to do so you could achieve a very good settlement for your client (although bear in mind that other factors may lead you to decide not to take advantage of the other side's mistakes).

This is one of the possible benefits of aiming high at the start. Another is that, if valid counter-arguments are raised, it allows you to 'come down' and offer concessions. This can be an important way of showing the other side that you have listened to and understood their case and that you are prepared to compromise. Any compromise requires 'give and take'. It allows people to save face; honour is satisfied. If, however, you refuse to move from your opening figure, the other side may perceive you as obstinate and unreasonable, and therefore may refuse to settle even when your opening figure is in fact realistic.

Generally, you should open at your final figure only if:

(a)   it is the tradition or culture in that particular field of law; or

(b)   you have a case or bargaining position that is obviously strong.

In either case, you should explain clearly to the other side that it really is a case of 'take it or leave it'.

Least favourable result that, on current information, you would accept ('resistance point')

The above process also allows you to decide on the poorest deal your client should accept, ie what settlement you would expect to negotiate if the other side put forward all the relevant counter-arguments to your client's case.

The resistance point is not a 'bottom line'; it should not be rigidly adhered to if further information which affects your client's position comes to light in the negotiation. You must be flexible enough to take on board the significance of any new information and adapt your expectations accordingly.

Deciding on the resistance point is complicated by two other factors. First, in cases where your client has an acceptable alternative course of action, the resistance point is the point below which the client is likely to receive less from the negotiation than might be obtained by pursuing the BATNA. For example, you might decide that (even after taking into account the extra costs) your client would receive more than is currently being offered by allowing the court to decide on the level of compensation.

Secondly, your client may have given you instructions not to settle below a certain figure. If you think he or she is being unrealistic, you should try to persuade him or her to adopt a more sensible position, but if he or she will not be moved, you must comply with his or her instructions.

With multi-issue negotiations, the position becomes even more complicated. You might be prepared to go below your resistance point on one issue if it means you would obtain a favourable result on another. It is important to keep the whole package in mind.

Your client's priorities are the key to the decisions you make in this area. Items which are of no great significance to your client could be conceded altogether in exchange for concessions which are of more importance to him or her.

12.4.5.4 Variables and unorthodox approaches

Another consideration in assessing the opening bid and resistance point will be the existence of 'variables'. Variables are those factors which allow for some give and take in the negotiation and which could therefore help to achieve a settlement. For example, your client might be prepared to pay a higher amount of compensation if he or she is allowed to pay by instalments rather than in one lump sum.

Other examples of variables which might be brought into play (depending on the subject matter of the negotiation) are inclusion/exclusion of costs, payment in a different currency, promises of future orders, quantity of goods (eg, buy more, but at a lower price per unit), quality of goods (eg, buy a lower grade at a lower price).

Sometimes, there may be other unconventional ways to resolve problems which have benefits for both sides. Be as creative as possible in seeking a solution.

EXAMPLE

You are acting for a business which runs a parcel delivery service. One of its business customers is threatening to take action against your client because of its failure to deliver a consignment of goods. The goods have disappeared and the customer is asking for compensation. An orthodox settlement would involve a cash payment to the customer. A different approach would be to offer to make free deliveries for that customer over an agreed period. Such an offer could represent a good deal for the customer but could still be a cheaper solution for your client compared with a cash payment (the deliveries could probably be accommodated within its regular delivery service and so would not add greatly to overall costs). This approach also gives your client a chance to rebuild the customer's confidence in its service, making it less likely that the customer will go elsewhere in the future.

12.4.6 Settlement zones

The aim of much of your preparation and of some of your questioning during a negotiation will be to attempt to identify possible settlement zones (or lack of them). You can add value as a lawyer by getting the maximum possible within a settlement zone for your client or by minimising what is paid, depending on which side you are on.

> **EXAMPLE**
>
> Use the example of the dismissed employee set out at **12.4.5.3** above. The employee's maximum expectation is £70,000. Assume that his solicitor has advised him that the least favourable result he should expect is a payment of £20,000 (taking into account the duty to mitigate loss and the current job market for the employee's skills). The employer, on the other hand, has been advised that a payment of £17,500 is probably the best result it could hope to achieve, but it is prepared to pay up to £35,000 if necessary to avoid any bad publicity. As illustrated by **Figure 3**, the possible settlement zone between the parties is £20,000 to £35,000. Where within that zone you are able to settle is a measure of how effective you have been as a negotiator. Negotiation is harder when the possible settlement zone is very narrow. By working to identify the settlement zone, you can help to speed the negotiation (saving time and costs), and in some cases you may be able to identify that there is no settlement zone and that either something must change or a negotiated settlement will not be possible.

Figure 3

Having completed all your preparation, including as far as possible making an attempt to gauge the possible settlement zone, you should identify your strategy. You should have a clear plan as to how you will conduct the negotiation. Waiting to see how the other party or parties will behave is not a strategy and should be avoided. By waiting to see the other side's approach, you risk losing the initiative. If all the parties 'wait and see', it wastes time and valuable opportunities to build rapport by implementing a clear, interest-based approach to the negotiation. The negotiation should allow for flexibility in response to new information and the attitude of other parties.

Examples of things you might consider in planning your strategy are:

• *Your opening position*

Will you take an extreme stance and pitch high, or will you start at a reasonable figure which you believe is likely to be conceded by the other side?

- *The order in which you would prefer to deal with issues*

  Is there a key issue which you need to address first? Are there issues you would prefer to keep back?

- *What disclosures to make and when*

  If there is information which may have an effect on the other party or parties, when will you reveal this information and how?

12.4.7 Opening statement

It is usually helpful to begin a negotiation with both parties making a brief opening statement setting out their expectations of the meeting and explaining their clients' status. Having identified your strategy, you are in a position to decide on the content of your opening statement.

There are several points to consider (see **12.8.3**), but a basic consideration at the preparatory stage is to decide upon the information you would want to disclose to the other side at this early point in the talks.

In most cases, the more information you communicate to the other side, the better the chance of reaching an agreement. In particular, there are usually interests which are common to both sides; these should be stressed at the start.

The sharing of information develops trust between the parties and helps to create a climate for successful talks.

There will, however, be some information that you correctly decide not to reveal, either because it is damaging to your client's position (in which case you would hope to avoid disclosing it at any stage) or because you would prefer to introduce it later for tactical reasons (eg, you intend to put it forward as a concession to the other side at the bargaining stage).

12.5 THE FORUM FOR THE NEGOTIATION

The forum for negotiation could be correspondence, telephone, a meeting or any combination of the three.

At the outset, choose the most appropriate medium for your client's case, and then be prepared to change if it proves inappropriate. For example, in many cases you might start by using correspondence, but that could later become unnecessarily rigid and time-consuming. It may be wise to suggest a meeting when you have developed a strong enough case to be able to take advantage of face-to-face contact.

12.5.1 Correspondence

Correspondence has the following features:

(a) It is capable of being orderly and reasoned, and is therefore especially appropriate at the outset of complex cases.

(b) It gives people time to think and therefore to avoid over-hasty decisions.

(c) There is a risk that certain points in a letter may be left unanswered in the reply.

(d) Some solicitors find it easier to be assertive on paper.

(e) It contains no non-verbal signals ('body language').

(f) It can lead to delay – either as a tactic, or because ambiguities or omissions are not rectified immediately.

(g) It is more difficult to trade concessions.

12.5.2 Telephone

Negotiation conducted by telephone has the following features:

(a)   It is quick and useful for resolving one point.

(b)   Make sure you are properly prepared. It is better to be the person making the call. If you are the receiver, consider saying that you will call back at an agreed time so that you have the opportunity to prepare properly.

(c)   There is no body language, but tones of voice are more noticeable. Silences are even more powerful on the telephone than in meetings. Use silence yourself, and do not be tempted to fill silences with a remark you may regret.

(d)   Some solicitors find it more difficult to be assertive on the telephone than in correspondence; and vice versa.

(e)   There is a risk that either of the parties could subsequently 're-interpret' what was said.

12.5.3   Meetings

Meetings have the following features:

(a)   They are immediate.

(b)   They give greater commitment to explore the case thoroughly and/or to settle.

(c)   Body language and silences are readily apparent and capable of use.

(d)   They are more fluid and give greater possibilities of fine movements, nuances, and the trading of concessions.

(e)   Some solicitors regard the suggestion of a meeting as a sign of weakness; others regard it as a sign of strength.

Some solicitors are uncomfortable with face-to-face meetings because of the possibility of making an inadvertent slip or of accidently agreeing a weakness. If, however, a meeting would objectively be in the client's best interests, you should try to overcome any fears by thorough preparation and practice which will increase your self-confidence.

12.6   OTHER CONSIDERATIONS BEFORE A MEETING

12.6.1   Are you ready to negotiate?

Do not be forced into premature negotiations, which will needlessly increase costs. It is usually advisable to defer talks until you are in possession of all the information you can reasonably expect to collect.

12.6.2   Venue

In some fields of law, there is a tradition that meetings will take place at the offices of the seller or claimant. What if you have a choice? What are the factors to bear in mind?

Having the meeting at your own firm's premises gives you the feeling of control. You have full access to your papers and to the office's secretarial, catering and other facilities. Also, you do not have to suffer the time, cost and general inconvenience of having to travel.

Attending a meeting at the other side's offices might therefore be a disadvantage. However, the travelling time can sometimes enable you to arrive fresher and more fully prepared. Also, enabling the other side to feel at ease in their own offices might induce them to be more collaborative.

A third possibility is to agree a neutral venue.

12.6.3   Agree the time and length of the meeting

As a matter of courtesy to the other side, you should inform them of the time you can devote to the meeting on the agreed date. It is also important for you to determine how long the other side has so that you can manage time when planning and undertaking the negotiation.

12.6.4   Attendance at the meeting

How many people from each side will be attending? Find out their names and roles in advance. If a number of people will be attending, who will chair the meeting – the host, the person who suggested the meeting, or someone else?

Will clients also be present? Often, they are present at transaction-based negotiations but not at litigation-based meetings. Sometimes clients sit in separate side-rooms or make themselves available for telephone calls or faxes in order to give instructions to their solicitors during the meeting.

It may be a good idea to have clients present at the meeting so that an agreement can be hammered out there and then, particularly if you think:

(a)   a lack of communication has been a major problem between the respective clients; or

(b)   your client is being unrealistic; or

(c)   the other solicitor is exacerbating the problem (eg, not settling a case which his or her client wants to settle or giving his or her client overly optimistic advice); and

(d)   you can trust your own client (preparation of roles is vital); and

(e)   you trust the other solicitor not to seek to undermine your authority in front of your own client.

Conversely, you might not wish to have clients present where there are personality clashes between the different clients or where you have an intimidating client who might hamper progress.

12.6.5   Seating arrangements

Who will sit where? What ambience do you want to try to create? Sitting face to face across a table from each other is more likely to appear adversarial, whereas seating placed at a 90 degree angle is likely to appear more collaborative.

12.6.6   Clarify the purpose of the meeting

Is the meeting to be exploratory only, or is there a possibility of settling? If the latter, check that those attending will have authority to settle on behalf of their respective clients.

12.6.7   The agenda

In a multi-issue case, try to agree the agenda with the other side in advance.

If possible, try to arrange the order of issues on the agenda in a way which will enable you to test their negotiating pattern and their willingness to trade concessions before reaching an item which is of critical importance to your own client.

12.6.8   Which party should make the first bid?

In some fields of law, the issue of which person makes the first bid is determined partly by tradition. For example, in property transactions, the solicitor acting for the landlord or seller draws up the draft lease or contract. In litigation, if the claim is for a liquidated sum (eg, a contractual debt), the opening bid belongs to the claimant. If the claim is for unliquidated damages, in certain cases (eg, personal injury claims) there is an argument that the claimant should simply wait until the defendant makes an acceptable Part 36 offer or payment.

Where the position is not clear cut, the advantages of going first are that it allows you to exert an immediate and powerful influence and it shows confidence. The disadvantage is that, if you are underprepared, you risk misjudging the bid.

Even if you don't wish to make the first bid, you might still want to make the first opening statement in order to establish the tone of the negotiation.

12.6.9 Final preparation for the meeting

Re-read the file, and refresh your mind on key documents, facts, dates and names.

Make sure that you know your client's position on the issues and on all the possible variables. If no agenda has been agreed, prepare one now.

12.7 OVERVIEW OF A NEGOTIATION

Negotiations should be clearly structured. Decide upon the best process and agree it with the other parties. Adopting a clear process will help ensure that all parties feel that the negotiation is fair and will assist in establishing an effective structure and tone. You should not start negotiating until you have clearly identified the process. We recommend that you invite all parties to make a preliminary opening statement, then allocate time for discussion of each point on the agenda. It may be necessary to organise separate meetings for different parties to the negotiation. A clear time frame should be adopted and provisional timings set for adjournments. As with interviewing and advising, structure and management skills are closely related to good communication skills.

12.8 THE OPENING

12.8.1 Setting the tone

The opening phase of a negotiation is important for two reasons. First, it creates the climate for the negotiation. Patterns, styles and pecking order establish themselves early and are difficult then to change.

Secondly, energy and concentration are high at the outset of the negotiations but later may deteriorate.

12.8.2 Ground rules

The host of the meeting should, after effecting any necessary introductions, confirm the ground rules for the meeting, for example:

(a)   the purpose of the meeting;

(b)   whether or not it is 'without prejudice' and/or 'subject to contract';

(c)   the likely length of the meeting;

(d)   the agenda; and

(e)   who will make the first opening statement.

12.8.3 Your opening statement

Proper, well prepared opening statements are a great help to most negotiation meetings. They:

(a)   help to avoid unintentional false assumptions from hindering the communication process;

(b)   help to reinforce the tone established at the outset of the meeting;

(c)   provide structure and order (an analogy can be drawn with court trials – the advocates' opening addresses set the scene; cross-examination, etc comes later);

(d)   help everyone to 'settle down';

(e)   remind everyone of the background, the areas of agreement, and the areas of dispute.

Unless you have sound tactical reasons for not following them, there are some general rules relating to opening statements.

12.8.3.1 Do:

(a)   say how long your statement will take if it is likely to be more than two or three minutes;

(b)   if your opening statement is going to contain a bid, explain your reasoning *before* disclosing the actual bid. This increases the chances of the other side listening properly to your reasons. Otherwise, they will be thinking about the figure and their response rather than your reasons;

(c)   present your case concisely and confidently;

(d)   use collaborative tone, posture and gestures (unless you have decided to adopt a competitive style);

(e)   observe carefully the other side's verbal and non-verbal reactions;

(f)   remember the one-third rule (see **10.1**).

12.8.3.2   Don't:

(a)   express your assumptions of the other side's interests and priorities, as this could annoy or antagonise them. Allow them to make their own case in their opening statement;

(b)   allow them to interrupt or side-track you;

(c)   speak for too long.

12.8.4   The other side's opening statement

12.8.4.1   It is important that you:

(a)   listen carefully – use all possible listening techniques (see **10.2.1**);

(b)   concentrate on identifying their underlying interests;

(c)   evaluate their style;

(d)   remain non-committal on their proposals and arguments – indicate understanding, if you can, without indicating agreement;

(e)   take brief notes (this can be a useful way of concealing your immediate reactions).

12.8.4.2   At the end of their opening statement:

(a)   seek clarification if necessary. Do not allow pride to deter you – you must be sure you understand exactly what they are saying. Negotiations can easily break down because of simple miscommunication;

(b)   summarise;

(c)   stress areas of agreement;

(d)   make sure that they have told you the whole of their 'shopping list' to reduce the risk of being ambushed later by a last-minute demand.

Avoid mentally drafting or rehearsing your own rebuttal, as this will hinder your listening and understanding of their case, and do not interrupt.

12.9   THE MIDDLE PHASE: DISCUSSION AND BARGAINING

Statements generate resistance

Questions generate answers

Silence generates discomfort, answers, new suggestions.

(adapted from a passage in *Getting to Yes* by Fisher and Ury)

I don't go in to do all the talking. Quite the opposite.

I go in to do the listening because that's the best bit.

(insurance company chief claims inspector, quoted in *Hard Bargaining* by Hazel Genn)

12.9.1   Discussion

During the discussion:

(a)   Demonstrate that you have heard and understood what the other side has said even if you do not agree with them.

(b)   In the middle phase of a negotiation, you should probe the other side's case with a mixture of appropriate open and closed questions. You could question any of the following:

    (i)   any assumptions you think they might be making;

    (ii)   their underlying interests or needs ('Why does your client want … ?');

    (iii)   whether or not there may be other ways of meeting those interests;

    (iv)   the criteria or evidence to justify their bid ('What criteria did you use to arrive at … ?', 'What evidence have you got to support … ?', 'Where did you get that evidence from?');

    (v)   their interpretation of the law or of the facts; or

    (vi)   analogous or comparable circumstances or cases they have had.

(c)   Do not ask two questions at once.

(d)   Give them time to answer – do not be tempted to fill a silence too quickly.

(e)   Listen and observe carefully when they answer. Was there any hesitation, uncertainty or discomfort?

(f)   If necessary, rephrase crucial questions so that all the angles are covered.

(g)   Do not allow them to use diversionary tactics such as answering a question with a question, or changing the subject. Be courteous but firm.

(h)   Spell out the weaknesses of their position calmly and firmly.

(i)   Be prepared to answer their questions with a judicious mixture of firm replies, silences and counter-questions. Try to maintain a confident tone of voice and posture.

(j)   Review the progress of the discussions at appropriate intervals. If there is an impasse, or one aspect is taking too long, consider the following:

    (i)   summarise – this will give you the opportunity to stress the areas on which you have already reached agreement and so reinforce the climate for agreement; it will also give you time to think and, if appropriate, to try to redirect the negotiation;

    (ii)   defer further discussion of the particular topic until later in the negotiation;

(k)   explore the possibility of settling issues on the basis of objective criteria. For example, you might agree to accept the opinion of an independent expert as a way to resolve the problem. An advantage of this approach is that neither party will feel cheated by the other; another is that you are more likely to achieve a fair result, which can have particular benefits where the parties will have an ongoing relationship.

12.9.2   Bargaining

Generally, you will have agreed to a meeting (other than a purely exploratory meeting) only if both parties are prepared to compromise, ie to bargain.

Although you might bargain item by item or clause by clause in multi-issue cases, try to keep the whole package in mind. It might be sensible not to finalise an agreement on any particular issue until the shape of the whole agreement is clear (including, for example, costs).

Keep searching for variables, for example: time for payment; payment in a different currency; a promise of future orders or the grant of options; performance-related payments; performance in stages.

Bargaining involves the trading of concessions. Compromise is achieved by both parties moving from their original positions. On the assumption that the other side have aimed high, you should be cautious about accepting their first offer.

A competitive negotiator might refuse to concede anything to you for some time, and then concede only small amounts, slowly and at irregular intervals, and of diminishing amounts.

Such a strategy is clearly designed to lower your expectations. However, if in fact there is a significant margin between that negotiator's opening bid and resistance point, the strategy carries the risk of a relatively sudden but very late climb-down (eg, a 'door-of-the-court' settlement). If you suspect that this strategy is being used against you, consider abbreviating the negotiation and press ahead with your BATNA (see **12.4.4**) – for example, by pressing ahead with the litigation if you are representing a claimant or making a Part 36 payment if you are representing a defendant.

When you are offered a concession, it is a question of judgement whether you express appreciation for it, or emphasise the lack of cost to them or both.

When making a concession, emphasise the cost to you of it and try to give a reason for it. For example, you can often relate it to something the other side have said in the negotiation. Your concession can thus demonstrate that you have taken their point and responded accordingly, rather than appear to be arbitrary.

In order to avoid 'giving away' a concession with nothing in return, or in order to try to move the negotiation forward, always consider offering conditional or hypothetical concessions: 'We could move on X, but only if you could move on Y'; 'I have no authority from my client on this point, but what if X ...?' Although these statements might be interpreted to mean that, if pushed, you would be prepared to concede unreservedly, it is a risk that parties have to take in the dynamics of a negotiation.

Make sure you take appropriate notes and, in particular, keep a record of all concessions or agreements.

12.9.3 Adjournments

Adjournments can be very useful.

The length of an adjournment will depend on its purpose. It could be for as little as 10 minutes, for example in order to have a brief strategy review (on your own, with a colleague, or with your client), or for as long as several weeks or months in order to await the availability of further evidence.

Other reasons for suggesting an adjournment include:

- alertness waning;
- to help resolve an impasse or deadlock;
- to allow a heated atmosphere to cool down; or
- to try to 'close the deal' during the relative informality of a refreshment break.

12.9.4 Resolving deadlocks

In cases of deadlock, the following actions should be considered:

- defer an item on the agenda;
- search for variables;
- adjourn; or
- refer to an alternative dispute resolution ('ADR') process (see **12.13**).

12.10 THE END: CLOSING A NEGOTIATION

12.10.1 When?

The timing of the close of a negotiation will depend on a cost–benefit analysis. How much more do you think you can achieve? Compare the expected achievements against the cost to the client in terms of time, money and stress. Will further negotiation be cost effective? This analysis needs to be conducted at regular intervals. Beware of a variation of Parkinson's Law: 'Negotiating expands to fill the time allotted to it.'

12.10.2 How?

A number of tactics may be used to signal to the other side that you see the end in sight.

(a)   'Last rites' – summarise the position reached, emphasising the concessions you have made and the extent and reasonableness of your movement: 'We have reached our final position.'

(b)   Use a refreshment break to suggest informally that the end is near.

(c)   Give a deadline or ultimatum.

(d)   Make a concession and express it as a final gesture to settle.

(e)   If the gap between the parties is small, check your BATNA to see whether you could move further or try to induce the other side to do so. Alternatively seek to find criteria or principles upon which you could agree to divide or accommodate the difference.

(f)   If there is one outstanding point, you might be able to agree that the point be adjudicated by an agreed independent third party.

12.10.3 The agreement

Do not allow the euphoria of reaching agreement to distract you from other important and immediate tasks, such as:

•   confirming what has been agreed;

•   preparing an immediate agreed written summary;

•   ensuring that details are clarified in order to avoid later disputes; and

•   preparing a list of actions to be taken (if appropriate) by both sides.

12.11 'DIRTY TRICKS'

The phrase 'dirty tricks' is used loosely, and is not necessarily confined to misconduct. You need to be aware of such tricks, not so that you can use them, but in order both to be able to recognise them when they are used against you and, if possible, in order to counter them. They include the following.

12.11.1 Surprise attacks

Surprise attacks can take the form of sudden changes in tactics or demands, intimidation, withdrawal of offers or emotional outbursts. They are often designed to throw you off balance, undermine your confidence, and create anxiety and a desire to placate or settle quickly.

Try to remain unperturbed. Try not to retaliate. If you find it difficult to continue to focus on the merits of the case, consider questioning the other side's tactics openly or calling an adjournment.

12.11.2 'Good guy, bad guy'

The 'good guy, bad guy' tactic is sometimes used by a negotiating team of lawyers, or a solicitor who wishes to portray his or her client as hard and uncompromising.

The aim of the tactic is to capitalise on the relief felt at evading the 'bad guy'. Again, you should try to continue to focus on the merits of the case and ignore the personalities of the negotiators as far as possible.

12.11.3 Feinting

Feinting is where the solicitor seems to attach great importance to one particular item. He or she then concedes it in order to 'soften you up' for another item in which he or she expresses little interest but which is, in fact, far more important to his or her client.

Do not take things at face value; always try to ascertain the other side's interests.

12.11.4 False deadlines

False deadlines can sometimes be tested by saying, 'We might be able to offer more, but we will not know until after [the date of the deadline]'.

Question and research any reasoning given for imposing a deadline you suspect is being used as a tactic.

12.11.5 Limited authority/reneging on 'agreements'

Always make sure at the time of the agreement that it is explicit whether or not the solicitor has the authority to settle and whether the agreement is final, and record the position in writing. If you do not, you may think that a case has been settled only to receive a letter stating, for example: 'I reported on our provisional agreement. My client is fairly happy with it, but there is just one matter …'.

12.11.6 Last minute demands

Make sure you obtain all the other side's demands at the outset.

This will make it less likely that they will surprise you with a sudden new demand.

12.11.7 Environmental controls

If the seating arrangements or environment of the meeting room make you feel uncomfortable, you should immediately and politely ask for them to be changed.

12.11.8 Lying

Try to take accurate notes of key points without being distracted from the negotiation. If you can later prove that the other side lied during the negotiation then the settlement could be rescinded for misrepresentation, and where a solicitor knowingly lied, the matter could be reported to The Law Society as professional misconduct.

12.12 ALTERNATIVE DISPUTE RESOLUTION

12.12.1 What is it?

Alternative dispute resolution (ADR) is not a term of art: it includes any process of dispute resolution other than litigation, arbitration or traditional negotiation between the parties or their solicitors.

The commonest form of ADR is mediation, but other processes – including adjudication, conciliation, early neutral evaluation and expert determination – also come under the umbrella of ADR.

The object of ADR is to provide a process which efficiently and effectively resolves a dispute. Which particular process or which combination of processes is best, will depend on the circumstances of each case.

The essential ingredients of ADR are:

(a) It is a voluntary, private process. The parties cannot be forced to use ADR; if they do use it, they can control the mechanics and rules of the process; and they can withdraw from it at any time unless and until they make a contractually binding out-of-court settlement or agreement.

(b) There is a third party neutral (often a mediator) who facilitates settlement, often by 'shuttlecock' diplomacy, but who has no power to order or impose a solution on the parties.

In essence ADR is intended to be an efficient and structured form of negotiation involving a third party. It can thus be interposed between traditional negotiating and litigation (or arbitration): if traditional negotiating fails, try an ADR process; if that fails, then either stalemate or litigation (or arbitration) remains.

12.12.2 Types of dispute resolution

12.12.2.1 Conciliation

Conciliation is similar in process to mediation but the third party neutral tends to take a more activist role in putting forward terms of settlement. The Advisory Conciliation and Arbitration Service (ACAS) offers free conciliation for many types of employment dispute.

12.12.2.2 Early neutral evaluation

A preliminary assessment of facts, evidence or legal merits. This form of ADR is often used to help avoid further litigation or serve as a basis for further negotiation.

12.12.2.3 Expert determination

An expert independent third party is appointed to decide the dispute. This process is often similar to neutral fact finding and will frequently be restricted to certain issues.

12.12.2.4 Complaints and grievance procedures

Generally the first port of call for any complainant. It is usually important to exhaust the provisions of any relevant schemes before proceeding further.

Ombudsman schemes (eg, Parliamentary Ombudsman, Estate Agents Ombudsman)

Ombudsmen are independent, impartial adjudicators who consider complaints about maladministration in particular areas (often public services/government departments). Schemes vary but often combine elements of neutral fact finding, mediation and adjudication.

Regulators

Regulators are watchdogs who generally oversee the way complaints are handled (eg, OFWAT, the water regulator). They are generally free but tend to focus on how a complaint or grievance was handled.

12.12.2.5 Mediation

> Mediation, with recognition in the UK under the Civil Procedure Rules since 1999, is a flexible process conducted confidentially where a neutral person actively assists the parties in working towards a negotiated agreement of a dispute, with the parties in ultimate control of the decision to settle and the terms of resolution. (Tony Allen, solicitor and Director of the Centre for Effective Dispute Resolution (CEDR))

Mediators are neutral third parties who facilitate a settlement between the parties in a dispute. They act as brokers or facilitators. Mediators do not advise on the law or the merits of the case. They seek to foster agreement between the parties themselves. At present there are no statutory qualifications required to mediate, but in practice mediators generally require some form of training and accreditation. There are a number of organisations which provide qualifying courses which are recognised by the Legal Services Commission, including CEDR and the School of Psychotherapy and Counselling.

The use of mediation has been actively promoted by the civil courts through a number of important cases.

In the landmark case of *Dunnett v Railtrack plc (in Railway Administration)* [2002] EWCA Civ 303, Railtrack had attempted to protect its costs position by making a modest Part 36 offer to Mrs Dunnett. Despite winning the appeal, Railtrack was not awarded its costs. In his judgment Brooke LJ remarked on the efficacy of mediation and its potential benefits: 'A mediator may be able to provide solutions which are beyond the powers of the court to provide'.

He also highlighted the potential consequences of failing to give adequate consideration to ADR:

> It is hoped that any publicity given to this part of the judgment of the court will draw the attention of lawyers to their duties to further the overriding objective in the way that it is set out in Part 1 of the Rules and to the possibility that, if they turn down out of hand the chance of alternative dispute resolution when suggested by the court, as happened on this occasion, they may have to face uncomfortable costs consequence.

The case of *Halsey v Milton Keynes General NHS Trust* [2004] EWCA Civ 576 established that mediation should be considered whenever appropriate. Whether a refusal to participate in ADR is unreasonable will be determined having regard to all the circumstances of that particular case. Factors which the court considered as likely to be relevant include:

(a)   the nature of the dispute;

(b)   the merits of the case;

(c)   the extent to which other settlement methods have been attempted;

(d)   whether the costs of the ADR would be disproportionately high;

(e)   whether any delay in setting up and attending the ADR would have been prejudicial; and

(f)   whether the ADR had a reasonable prospect of success.

Case law has continued to underline the increasing importance of ADR. In *Burchell v Bullard* [2005] EWCA Civ 358, the comments of Ward LJ confirm its status:

> *Halsey* has made plain not only the high rate of successful outcome being achieved by mediation but also its established importance as a track to a just result running parallel with that of the court system ... The court has given its stamp of approval to mediation and it is now the legal profession which must become fully aware of and acknowledge its value.

The recent case of *Laporte v The Commissioner for the Police of the Metropolis* [2015] EWHC 371 (QB) has again reinforced the *Halsey* principles and pro-ADR stance of the courts.

Although usually used in the litigation field, ADR may also be used in commercial transactions. First, a commercial contract could incorporate an ADR clause, ie, a non-binding (but influential) promise that if any dispute later arises between the parties, they will refer that dispute to an ADR process before resorting to litigation or arbitration. Secondly, if parties are negotiating the terms of a transaction and reach an impasse on one particular term, they could agree to refer that one item to an ADR process.

12.12.3   How and when should you consider ADR?

With civil litigation in particular, consideration of ADR has now become an essential part of case evaluation and strategy. Knowing that it should be considered in most cases, you must carefully decide what might be the most appropriate method of dispute resolution in each particular case.

The following should form part of your analysis:

(a)   Is ADR an option?

    (i)   Is the other side willing to take part?

    (ii)   Can ADR provide your client with the result they seek? (For example, if they want a public hearing or a judgment about who is legally right or wrong, then litigation may be the best option.)

    (iii)   Certain types of case are not suited to ADR, eg:

        where a legal, commercial or other precedent needs to be set;

        where summary judgment is available and likely to be granted;

        where one of the parties requires emergency relief, eg an injunction or other form of immediate protection;

where publicity is actively sought; or

where there is no real interest in settlement.

(iv) ADR is particularly suitable in cases where:

costs are likely to be disproportionate;

the parties are deadlocked in settlement negotiations;

the case is likely to be particularly long/complex;

there are multi actions involving common parties;

the issues involved are particularly sensitive; or

the parties are anxious to avoid publicity.

(b) What method of ADR is appropriate?

(i) What method is most likely to meet the client's objectives?

EXAMPLE

Your client is pursuing a claim for medical negligence against the local NHS trust. If his or her prime objective is to bring the problem to the attention of those managing the hospital and to prevent it happening again, then using the Health Service Ombudsman would be an ideal choice. If the prime objective is to obtain maximum compensation, then this option is less suitable.

(ii) What are the client's resources/how does he or she want the dispute managed? You need to consider the comparative cost of the available options, the length of time likely to be involved and the impact on your client's business/life.

12.12.4 The advantages

Like traditional negotiating, ADR can be quicker, cheaper and more private, and produce more flexible terms of settlement, than litigation or arbitration.

The third party neutral:

(a) may provide a view that is perceived by both parties as being more objective;

(b) by shuttlecock diplomacy may be able to identify potential solutions that neither party alone could see; and

(c) has a better chance of preserving relationships between the parties.

This last point can be very important in commercial or family disputes, but is less so where neither party has any intention of continuing any future relationship with the other.

12.12.5 The disadvantages

(a) One reason why ADR is relatively quick and cheap is that the evidence is not investigated or examined as thoroughly as in litigation or arbitration: instead, only what are thought to be the key issues and interests are explored. Parties cannot have it both ways, ie, a wide, in-depth investigation which is also quick and cheap. In each case, it is a question of choosing the lesser of two evils.

(b) Because ADR is a voluntary process, it is not appropriate, as we have seen, when one party needs immediate judicial relief.

(c) Likewise, ADR is unlikely to resolve 'non-genuine' disputes, for example where a defendant is clearly stalling for time and refusing to admit liability simply in order to hang on to his or her money for as long as possible.

12.12.6 A note about arbitration

'Arbitration is the settlement of a matter at issue by one to whom the parties agree to refer their claims in order to obtain an equitable decision' (*Shorter OED*). Arbitration differs from

ADR in that, as with litigation, the parties are passing control of the outcome of the dispute to a third party or parties.

Arbitration has been an alternative to litigation through the courts for centuries. It was used as early as the thirteenth century by English merchants who preferred to have their disputes resolved according to their own customs rather than by public law.

Arbitration is a huge specialist subject and encompasses a wide range of different institutions and procedures. It varies from informal to court-like proceedings. It is used particularly to resolve commercial disputes, often in an international context.

SUMMARY

- You must prepare fully in order to negotiate effectively.
- Preparation should include identification of:
  - your BATNA;
  - your client's objectives;
  - the optimal process for the negotiation;
  - any information you would like to obtain;
  - any independent/objective expertise or information that may be relevant;
  - what you know about the other side, their needs and likely position;
  - a clear strategy for the negotiation;
  - a plan for how to deal with problems or difficult tactics;
  - a clear agenda and endgame.

- Be self-aware and learn to adapt your predominant style to best advantage.
- Develop a clear strategy and implement it, but be flexible in your approach and style.
- Look behind stated positions and seek mutual gain.
- Maintain high ethical standards and develop trust for the best long-term results.
- Understand the different types of ADR, and be prepared to advise your client as to the most appropriate forum for any dispute.

ADVOCACY

LEARNING OUTCOMES

After reading this chapter you will be able to:

- identify the skills required of an advocate
- understand the purpose of opening and closing speeches
- explain the three stages in the questioning of a witness at trial
- identify the advocate's ethical duties
- make appropriate representations in a contested bail application
- prepare and present an effective plea in mitigation
- explain the nature of interim applications and make appropriate submissions.

13.1 INTRODUCTION

In its widest sense advocacy is the art of influencing outcomes. It is about convincing others: the art of persuasion. In this general sense, it is a valued accomplishment in many areas of life. This chapter is, however, concerned with the specialised meaning of the word as used by lawyers; in its legal context, advocacy is the art of conducting cases in court.

There are many reasons why advocacy is a skill worth studying. You may wish to become an advocate and, if you do, you will want to do the best possible job for your client. Also, understanding the task of the advocate in presenting a case for court is central to understanding the litigation process. Without such an understanding, you will struggle to give realistic, cogent and confident advice to clients. Even if you do not appear as an advocate, you may want to instruct one. By understanding advocacy, you will be better able to prepare the case for others to present. You will also be better placed to evaluate the advocates you see and recommend one who is best suited to speak on your client's behalf. Advocacy is not just important in the courtroom. It is often useful, and sometimes vital, in client interviewing, in negotiation and in meetings, client seminars and public lectures. Even if later you decide not to practise law, the principles of advocacy will be useful in whatever you do. Advocacy is about persuading people, and you cannot go through life without, on occasions, needing to persuade. Advocacy is a valuable skill to have – a transferable skill, a lifelong skill.

In answer to the question, 'Are good advocates born or made?', most people would say, 'They're born. Advocacy is not one of those things which can be taught'. Many lawyers would probably say the same. Skilled advocates are seen as being eloquent, articulate and able to think on their feet: all qualities which at first sight seem to be innate rather than acquired. Undoubtedly, some advocates are more naturally gifted than others, but many of these so-called gifts can be acquired through hard work and practice. Perhaps the worst mistake is to assume that good advocacy is simply a matter of flair, and little else. The advocate who demolishes an opponent's witness in cross-examination rarely achieves this by jumping to his or her feet and firing off the first thing that comes into his or her head: a great deal of thought and preparation will have gone into every aspect of the challenge he or she makes.

This chapter gives a basic introduction to advocacy. For those who wish to practise as advocates, it represents the first stage of a continuous learning process. However, others may never appear before a court as an advocate at any stage of their professional careers. Even so, the skills covered in this chapter will prove useful in any situation where effective oral presentation is required.

13.2 SKILLS

The skills of an advocate divide into oral skills and organisation skills.

13.2.1 Oral skills

Advocates are skilled talkers: this is an obvious point which should never be overlooked. Within the stylised atmosphere of the courtroom, the task of the advocate, subject to the rules of professional conduct, is to talk his or her way to the best result that can be obtained for his or her client. The three major oral skills are as follows.

13.2.1.1 Presentation

Every advocate needs to be a good storyteller, especially when he or she is opening a case on behalf of either the prosecution or the claimant. It is not generally realised that a criminal court, in particular, may know next to nothing about the facts of the case it is about to try or the issues involved; it therefore needs to be put in the picture in a way which will engage its interest.

13.2.1.2 Argument

Every advocate also needs to be a good persuader. Much of an advocate's time will be spent addressing the court with a view to persuading it to find in favour of his or her client. Argument may be as to the overall issue of guilt or liability, or as to a subsidiary issue such as bail, the grant of an interim order, or a point of law.

13.2.1.3 Questioning witnesses

The questioning of witnesses is the skill which young advocates tend to find the most complex and difficult to master. English trials are characterised not only by their adversarial nature but also by the fact that much evidence is still given orally. The ability to extract the relevant evidence from your own witnesses by means of examination-in-chief (especially important in criminal cases) and to challenge the testimony of an opponent's witnesses in cross-examination is still seen as the most important attribute of the experienced advocate.

In the course of a civil or criminal trial, all three of the above skills will be exercised, but in many other situations advocacy will consist almost exclusively of presentation and argument. This is particularly true of the vast majority of chambers applications in civil cases, because evidence will almost invariably be given by witness statements. Bail applications and pleas in mitigation in criminal cases also involve very little questioning of witnesses.

13.2.2 Organisation skills

In addition to the oral skills, a good advocate also draws upon other back-up skills which are exercised outside the court room. When an experienced advocate is performing in court, it all seems effortless: he or she has all the facts at his or her fingertips, nothing seems to throw him or her off his or her stride, and witnesses are examined and cross-examined incisively and in a logical sequence. On top of this, he or she manages to maintain the appearance of being calm and dignified at the most crucial moments, and never loses his or her temper. At all times, he or she is courteous to the court, his or her opponent, and the most recalcitrant witnesses. To the uninitiated, it may look easy, but this level of competence is achieved only by hard work and experience. It is also dependent upon the advocate having thoroughly prepared and organised the case beforehand.

The most important organisation skills are set out below: there is nothing magical about any of them – in fact some of them may appear positively mundane – but no advocate can do without them.

13.2.2.1 Fact gathering and analysis

No advocate can begin to prepare a case until he or she has thoroughly mastered its facts. Until this is done, it is impossible to analyse its strengths and weaknesses. Ignorance of the facts will also make it far more difficult to perform adequately in court. For example, when cross-examining a witness, it will often be necessary to fire a sequence of rapid questions in order to try and shake his or her testimony. The task will be made immeasurably easier if the advocate's mastery of the facts is such that there is little or no need to refer to prepared notes before proceeding to the next question. Many readers will have seen US courtroom dramas on television in which advocates never use notes. In real life, they are trained to memorise the whole case file. Although UK courtroom style is very different, advocates should try to rely on notes as little as possible.

13.2.2.2 Knowledge of the relevant law

It is essential to research the relevant substantive law. The advocate must also develop a detailed knowledge of the law of evidence and the relevant procedural law. So far as evidence is concerned, it will always be necessary to study the relevant facts carefully in order to analyse:

(a) what the issues are;

(b) which issues are in dispute;

(c) who has the burden of proof; and

(d) what admissible evidence is available to prove or disprove those issues.

However, that is not enough: you will also need to memorise as much of the law of evidence as you can since an evidential problem may arise unpredictably during the course of a trial. Advocates rarely have time to look the law up in advance of raising an objection.

Similarly, procedural points have a habit of cropping up unexpectedly: an advocate's effectiveness will be greatly enhanced if his or her level of knowledge is such that these can be identified as soon as they arise.

13.2.2.3 Handling paperwork

In some respects, handling paperwork is the most neglected organisation skill of all, but it is in fact one of the most important, especially in civil cases. Even quite simple cases can end up producing masses of papers, some of which may need to be referred to at some time during a case. It is important therefore not only to devise a system which enables a required document to be located at a moment's notice, but also to know the contents of every document. This is particularly vital in chambers applications in civil proceedings so far as witness statements are concerned. The master or district judge may intervene by suddenly asking a question on a particular issue. The advocate should immediately be able to refer him or her to the relevant paragraph in the appropriate witness statement.

The ability to handle paperwork is also important in civil trial advocacy with rules requiring pre-trial exchange of witness statements and experts' reports.

13.3 THE BASICS

This section contains a simple checklist to assist in preparation of a case. It also deals with wider aspects of court behaviour and protocol.

13.3.1 Preparation

Good advocacy depends on planning and preparation at every stage. In particular, the order in which you address each task needs to be carefully considered so as to achieve the maximum benefit. The following checklist should always be followed.

13.3.1.1 Master the relevant facts

If the facts are simple, try to commit them to memory. In more complicated cases, prepare a written chronology for reference purposes which should ideally then be memorised as far as possible.

13.3.1.2 Analyse the facts

By applying the appropriate substantive, evidential and procedural law, you should be able to identify the following:

(a)   the legal issues in dispute. Consider in this context whether there are any submissions you will need to make, for example as to admissibility;

(b)   the factual issues in dispute. Identify what findings of fact the court will have to make if your client's case is to succeed;

(c)   develop a 'theory' of the case consistent with your client's instructions. The more plausible the case advanced, the more likely it is to succeed.

Based upon the analysis above, plan objectives for each stage at which you will be called upon to speak or examine witnesses.

13.3.2 Presentation

Although presentation has been categorised as a specific oral skill, every aspect of the advocate's courtroom role in effect involves conducting a presentation, not only of the client's case but also of the advocate himself or herself. The following list sets out a number of presentational rules which should always be followed:

(a)   Maintain eye contact with the person whom you are addressing.

(b)   Never read from a prepared text.

(c)   Be aware of 'body language'. The way in which an advocate behaves can affect the court's perceptions of his or her case. Try always to bear the following points in mind:

   (i)   Stand still. Advocates who are nervous have a tendency to sway from side to side.

   (ii)   Stand up straight when in open court. Make sure you know your case well enough to avoid frequent references to your papers.

   (iii) Do not speak with your hands in front of your face. This is another common mannerism when a speaker is nervous. Be especially conscious of this trait in chambers proceedings where advocates remain seated.

   (iv)   Keep your hands and arms still (within reason). Although arm and hand gestures can sometimes be an effective means of emphasising a point, they should be used sparingly.

(v)   Keep your emotions under control. To be an effective advocate, you will need to be able to hide all kinds of feelings. For example, never appear shocked because a witness says the opposite to what you expect. Learn to sail on unperturbed through the most stormy waters.

(d)   Speak slowly in a clear, low tone. If you are anxious, you are likely to speak quickly and in a high voice. In particular, always 'watch the judge's pen'. You are hardly likely to be persuasive if the court cannot keep up with you. The same rule applies when taking the court through documents; it takes time for the court to read them and digest their contents.

(e)   Do not be afraid of pauses. What may seem to the advocate to be a long gap in presentation is often not even noticed by the court.

(f)   Avoid being long-winded and unnecessarily repetitive. These are both traits which suggest that you have not prepared the case very well.

(g)   Know your court. All your planning must be with a view to persuading the court of the strength of your case. It is perhaps obvious but nevertheless important to realise that, for example, a judge will need to be addressed differently from a lay magistrate. Tailor your style to suit your audience.

(h)   Be honest and courteous. At all times, bear in mind the need to build and maintain your reputation with the court. The advocate who loses the court's trust is of no use to his or her client. Always be scrupulously courteous to the court and to your opponent, even if you are disappointed with the way your case has gone.

(i)   Dress appropriately. Check whether you need to be robed. In general, robes are not required in the magistrates' court or hearings in chambers. However, robes are required at all other open court hearings (*Practice Direction (Court Dress) (No 4)* [2008] 1 WLR 357).

13.3.3   How to address the court

Nothing reveals an advocate's lack of experience more than a failure to adopt the correct mode of address. The following list should therefore be committed to memory:

Court	*Mode of address*
High Court Judge	'My Lord' or 'My Lady' as appropriate
Circuit Judge	'Your Honour'
Recorder	'Your Honour'
District Judge of the High Court or County Court	'Sir' or 'Madam' as appropriate
District Judge of the magistrates' court	'Sir' or 'Madam' as appropriate
Master of the Supreme Court	'Master'
Supreme Court Costs Judge	'Master'
Magistrates (lay and stipendiary)	'Sir' or 'Madam' as appropriate.

In the magistrates' court, 'Your worships' is technically incorrect, but is frequently used and indeed preferred by many lay benches.

A particular problem is whether it is appropriate to address the court in the second person singular ('You'). In the case of district judges, masters and magistrates, it is perfectly permissible provided 'Sir' or 'Madam' is interposed at appropriate intervals. For example, in a plea in mitigation to a bench of lay magistrates, it would be perfectly appropriate to proceed as follows:

> Madam, there are three matters relating to the defendant's involvement in these offences that I should like to draw to the attention of you and your colleagues. First, Madam, there are two specific aspects of the pre-sentence report to which I should like to refer you ...

High Court and circuit judges pose more of a problem. As a general rule, 'you' should be substituted by 'Your Lordship(s)', 'Your Ladyship(s)' or 'Your Honour(s)' as the case may be. For example, in the Crown Court before a circuit judge, the previous address would begin:

> May it please Your Honour, there are three matters relating to the defendant's involvement in these offences that I should respectfully like to draw to Your Honour's attention. First, Your Honour, if I might be permitted to draw Your Honour's attention to two specific aspects of the pre-sentence report ...

To those who are unfamiliar with courtroom protocol, this version may sound unnecessarily obsequious. Nevertheless, this is the level of courtesy expected and you depart from it at your peril. The odd 'you' or 'your' here and there may be acceptable, but do not take risks until you are experienced and know your court.

13.3.4 How to refer to your opponent

It is equally important to extend all the appropriate courtesies to your opposing advocates. Choose from 'My friend' or 'The prosecution/defence' or 'Mr/Ms/ Mrs/Miss Smith'. The term 'My learned friend' is traditionally reserved for barristers, although this is no longer a hard and fast rule. If you are opening the case, you should always ascertain the name of your opponent, since it is a normal courtesy to introduce him or her to the court. For example: 'Sir, my name is Mr Jones and I appear to prosecute this case and my friend Ms Smith appears on behalf of the defendant.'

13.3.5 Three golden rules when addressing the court

As well as knowing how to behave in court, an advocate must be able to create an impression of being experienced. Failure to observe the following will tend to reveal precisely the opposite.

13.3.5.1 Do not give evidence yourself

Not only is this improper, it also suggests over-involvement in the client's case. Avoid phrases such as 'My client tells me ...' or 'I happen to know that ...'. However, it will often be necessary to put the client's views to the court, for example in a civil chambers application or a plea in mitigation in a criminal case. In chambers applications, the phrases 'I am instructed that' and 'my instructions are' are perfectly acceptable, but in criminal cases they are sometimes interpreted as being coded messages that the advocate does not believe a word the client is saying. Phrases such as 'I have discussed this with my client and he wants you to know' or 'My client wishes me to inform you' are more appropriate.

13.3.5.2 Do not give your opinion

Avoid using phrases such as 'In my opinion ...' or 'I think ...'. When an advocate wishes to persuade the court to adopt his or her view of the case, phrases like 'I submit' or 'I would seek to persuade you' or 'I would urge you' are more appropriate. The important thing to remember is that the only opinion that counts is that of the court.

13.3.5.3 Object rarely, but quickly

There is an enormous temptation, especially when you have thoroughly researched a case, to object at every opportunity. Indeed, this often impresses the client. However, it will not endear an advocate to the court unless the point is one of substance. Do not object unless the point advances your case or diminishes that of your opponent. Be alert: the decision to raise an objection will often be a split-second one, especially if it involves the issue of whether an inadmissible question has been put to a witness.

13.3.6 Five golden rules when questioning witnesses

Although the examination of a witness is as much an art as a science, the following are basic rules for questioning witnesses whatever the nature of the proceedings.

13.3.6.1 Keep your questions short

Formulate questions so that, ideally, they do not exceed 10 words. If the question is convoluted, there is a risk that neither the witness nor the court will be able to follow it. Nothing takes the wind out of an advocate's sails more than being asked to repeat or rephrase a question because it is incomprehensible.

13.3.6.2 Ask one question at a time

For reasons similar to those given above, it is essential to refrain from asking multiple questions. The last thing you want is for your opponent to rise to his or her feet and say, 'Madam, I wonder if my friend would be kind enough to indicate to the witness which question he wants him to answer first'.

This means that a quite simple point may often need to be broken down into several questions before it can effectively be put to a witness. For example, if you are seeking to extract a concession from an identification witness that he was standing 50 feet away, it was dark and it was raining, etc, you may need to ask a whole series of short questions in order to succeed in this objective.

13.3.6.3 Know your objectives in respect of each witness

This applies as much to your own witnesses as to those of your opponent, but is particularly important when planning a cross-examination.

13.3.6.4 Try to avoid asking questions in cross-examination to which you do not know the answer

This rule should not be taken too literally because sometimes one has no choice but to probe. The main thing is to ensure that you are never floored by the unexpected. For example, let us assume that you are cross-examining an identification witness on the issue of where he was standing at the time of the incident. If you were simply to ask 'Where were you standing?', you would have no control over the answer. Contrast:

> Q. You said earlier that you were standing on the corner of Main Street and Underwood Road, didn't you?
>
> A. Yes.
>
> Q. And there's no dispute, is there, that that is about 50 feet from the incident you say you saw?

Even if the witness says 'No', you have much more control over where to proceed from there. Alternatively, if you can easily prove that the witness was standing 50 feet away, you could quite safely ask the question 'Where were you standing?', because you know that if the witness were to reply 'About 6 feet away', you would have plenty of ammunition with which to contradict him or her.

13.3.6.5 Know when to stop

There is always a danger in going on for too long, but it is particularly important not to fall into the trap of asking one question too many. It is a great temptation to press on when you have a witness 'on the run'. However, that is the time to pause and reflect briefly upon whether, having secured some favourable concession, it might not be wiser to refrain from cross-examining further.

For example, if you have managed to extract from the identification witness referred to above concessions that she was standing 50 feet away, it was dark and it was raining, it is a great temptation to then say with a final flourish, 'So how can you be so sure it was the accused that you saw?'.

This is the one question you (and your client) may live to regret!

13.3.7   Witnesses: court formalities

There are a number of matters of court protocol concerning witnesses of which you need to be aware, especially since it will be your task to explain them to your client and other witnesses before they give evidence.

13.3.7.1   Criminal cases

In a criminal case, witnesses other than the defendant should be asked to stay out of court until called.

If the defendant is to give evidence, he or she must be called before other defence witnesses unless the court directs otherwise.

Witnesses may refresh their memories from their written statements prior to being called to give evidence. Other parties must be informed if this has taken place.

13.3.7.2   Civil cases

In a civil case, witnesses may sit in court throughout the hearing. If the advocate wishes to exclude witnesses from court, he or she must apply for an order to that effect.

The claimant and defendant are both usually called first by their advocate.

Witnesses may refresh their memories from their written statements prior to being called to give evidence. Other parties must be informed if this has taken place.

13.4   OPENING THE CASE

This section considers opening speeches in all types of proceedings. Although the length and purpose of such speeches may vary widely, they are all vitally important. They provide the advocate with an opportunity to make the first impression. This may be vital, as the court or tribunal may know little or nothing about the case it is about to try. For example, in a criminal trial before magistrates, the bench will probably know nothing about the case other than details of the charges.

13.4.1   Criminal trials in the magistrates' court

The prosecution always have the right to make an opening speech before calling their evidence. In simple trials, this right is sometimes waived. If the prosecutor does open, he or she will usually:

(a)   introduce himself or herself and his or her opponent to the court;

(b)   take the bench briefly through the charges;

(c)   outline the facts of the case and the evidence that he or she intends to adduce in order to prove the charges; and

(d)   explain the law, where necessary.

The opening speech requires the advocate to be a good storyteller so that the relevant incidents are brought to life. If there is an item of evidence for which admissibility is in dispute, the prosecutor should make no mention of it when opening, leaving admissibility to be determined at a later stage.

Defence advocates rarely make an opening speech before calling their evidence, because by doing so they lose the right to make a closing speech. Since the prosecutor may make a closing speech, the defence advocate will usually take advantage of having the last word.

Apart from the right to make speeches, either advocate may at any stage make a submission on a point of law. In particular, the defence may submit that there is no case to answer at the close of the prosecution case. In such an event, the opposing advocate always has a right to reply.

13.4.2   Civil trials

The claimant's advocate has the right to open (unless, unusually, the burden of proof of all issues lies on the defendant). As judges now have power to dispense with opening speeches, their use may decline, but the practice of handing in a written 'skeleton argument' to the judge in lieu of an opening speech is likely to increase. As in criminal cases in the magistrates' court, if the defendant's advocate elects to make an opening speech, he or she is not entitled to make a closing speech except with leave of the court.

The purposes of the advocate's opening speech in a civil trial will be to:

(a)   introduce himself or herself and his or her opponent to the court;

(b)   indicate the nature of his or her claim, for example, 'Your Honour, this is a claim for damages for breach of contract';

(c)   summarise the areas of dispute between the parties;

(d)   outline by reference to the statements of case the alleged facts of the case (nothing which cannot be proved should be asserted), indicating areas of dispute;

(e)   introduce the evidence, including any matters contained in agreed documents;

(f)   summarise the legal principles involved, indicating areas where a ruling will have to be made.

13.5   EXAMINATION-IN-CHIEF

Examination-in-chief is in many respects more difficult than cross-examination because an advocate should always be seeking to succeed on the strengths of his or her own case rather than on the weaknesses of his or her opponent's. Accordingly, the way your own witnesses give their evidence has a vital bearing on the overall impression that your case creates in the mind of the court.

13.5.1   The characteristics of examination-in-chief

Although, with one exception, advocates have a complete discretion as to the order in which witnesses are called, it is usual in civil cases for the claimant or defendant, as appropriate, to be called first. In criminal cases, the prosecutor will usually call the victim first, but the defence advocate is obliged to call the defendant before other witnesses as to fact unless the court directs otherwise (Police and Criminal Evidence Act 1984, s 79). The advocate calling the witness will, as a matter of courtesy, begin by announcing each witness in turn, for example, 'Your Honour, I now call the claimant, Margaret Brown'.

The principal objectives of examination-in-chief are:

(a)   to present the witness's evidence in a logical sequence (usually chronologically or by topic);

(b)   to cover all the relevant issues upon which the witness is able to testify; and

(c)   to anticipate matters likely to be raised in cross-examination.

The major characteristic of examination-in-chief (and what makes it so difficult for the advocate) is that the witness must, so far as possible, be left to tell his or her own story with minimal prompting from the advocate. In order to achieve this objective, leading questions are not generally permitted.

Although there is a degree of controversy over what constitutes a leading question, the generally accepted definition is that it is a question which suggests its own answer by seeking to put words into the witness's mouth. For example, if an advocate was seeking to establish that a witness saw the defendant, James Smith, in The Mitre public house at midday on Monday, 21 August (all of which is in dispute), it would not be permissible to ask, 'Did you see James Smith in The Mitre public house at midday on Monday, 21 August?'.

Instead, the advocate would need to proceed by means of a number of non-leading questions as follows:

> Q.   Can you remember what you were doing on Monday, 21 August? (This question is arguably leading, but probably not objectionable.)
>
> A.   Well, let me see. Oh yes, I went into work in the usual way.
>
> Q.   Did you stay there all day? (non-leading)
>
> A.   No, I went out for an early lunch.
>
> Q.   About what time was that? (non-leading)
>
> A.   Oh, about ten to twelve I think.
>
> Q.   And where did you go? (non-leading)
>
> A.   A pub called The Mitre.
>
> Q.   Did you see anyone there you recognised? (non-leading)
>
> A.   Yes, I saw James Smith ...

and so on. As can be readily appreciated, this technique requires the advocate to prepare very carefully in advance to ensure that he or she is able to guide the witness through his or her evidence without resorting to prompting.

The technique also requires stamina, since it may take time even to elicit a simple set of facts in this way. The only three occasions on which leading questions are permitted by way of exception are:

(a)   when the witness's evidence relates to a matter that is not in dispute;

(b)   where a denial is invited from the witness; and

(c)   on those rare occasions when a witness is declared to be hostile.

An example of exception (a) above would arise if the only dispute was as to the date on which the witness saw James Smith:

> Q.   Do you recall an occasion when you saw James Smith in The Mitre public house? (leading, but not disputed)
>
> A.   Yes.
>
> Q.   And can you remember when that was? (non-leading)
>
> A.   Yes, it was on Monday, 21 August.

The advocate should always check in advance with his or her opponent as to what matters can be led to the witness. Matters such as name, address and occupation may always be led, but some advocates prefer to ask witnesses to state these details in their own words to help put them at their ease.

An example of exception (b) would be if Mr Smith's advocate was seeking to extract a denial from his client. It would then be permissible to proceed as follows:

> Q.   Mr Smith, were you in The Mitre on Monday, 21 August at midday? (leading)
>
> A.   No, I was not.

Exception (c), namely the hostile witness, is rarely encountered.

13.5.2   The witness who does not come up to proof

13.5.2.1   Criminal cases

If the witness displays an unwillingness to tell the truth at the instance of the party calling him or her, the court may declare the witness to be hostile. This allows the advocate who has called him or her to ask leading questions and, with leave, any previous inconsistent statement made by the witness may be put to him or her (Criminal Procedure Act 1865, s 3). Such a statement may be used not only to discredit the witness's testimony but also to prove the truth of anything contained in the statement (Criminal Justice Act 2003, s 119).

In most cases, however, the witness's failure to say what the advocate is hoping for is the result of forgetfulness, incompetent examination-in-chief or a poorly-taken statement. In such a situation, witnesses cannot be cross-examined. The advocate can only try to repair the damage by calling additional evidence which supports his or her case. The problem of the forgetful witness may also be avoided if a note of his or her earlier evidence is available (see **13.5.4**).

13.5.2.2 Civil cases

The position of the hostile witness in civil cases is broadly similar to that in criminal cases (see Civil Evidence Act 1968, s 3).

If the witness is not declared hostile, the advocate's options are limited in the same way as in criminal cases (but see **13.5.4**).

13.5.3 Exchange of witness statements

The exchange of witness statements in civil proceedings has made a fundamental difference to examination-in-chief. If a party has served a witness statement and wishes to rely at trial on that witness's evidence, the party must call that witness to give oral evidence unless the court orders to the contrary. The witness's statement will stand as his or her evidence-in-chief unless the court orders otherwise. This means, in cases involving exchange of witness statements, that examination-in-chief has been reduced to:

(a)   formally calling the witness and establishing his or her name and address;

(b)   asking the witness to identify his or her statement; and

(c)   asking the witness whether the contents of the statement are true.

13.5.4 Introducing documents and real evidence

Documentary evidence may be introduced for a variety of reasons. The term 'document' includes items such as photographs, tape-recordings, video films and computer data. From an evidential point of view, it is important to remember, not only that a document's authenticity must be established, but also that its contents must be admissible for the purpose for which they are tendered. The rules differ materially in criminal and civil proceedings.

13.5.4.1 Criminal cases

A witness must normally be called to prove the authenticity of any document which is to be adduced in evidence. Although documents cannot be agreed (contrast the position in civil cases), in practice many documents, such as agreed plans of traffic accidents, are routinely admitted. Copies of the documents are generally sufficient (see Criminal Justice Act 1988, s 27). A police officer will normally be called to prove the authenticity of a defendant's written confession. This will be done by asking the officer to identify the defendant's signature and recount the circumstances in which the statement was made. If accepted, the original will be admitted as an exhibit. The police officer will then normally be invited to read the defendant's written confession to the court. Although most interviews with suspects are now tape-recorded, the written summary of the interview will basically be proved in the same way.

The other commonly encountered document is the 'memory refreshing document'. The basic rule is that a witness may refresh his or her memory in the witness box from any document which was made or verified by him or her at an earlier time and 'his recollection of the matter is likely to have been significantly better at that time than it is at the time of his oral evidence' (Criminal Justice Act 2003, s 139(1)).

Police officers, in particular, will frequently ask for leave to refresh their memories from notes contained in their pocket books, but other witnesses may also be permitted to refer to their original statements.

Real evidence consisting of other objects, for example a weapon, must likewise be proved by a witness who can show that they are what they purport to be and that they are relevant to the issues. It will also be necessary to prove that an appropriate chain exists which links the object to the defendant.

13.5.4.2 Civil cases

In theory, a witness must be called on to prove the authenticity and originality of each document which is to be adduced in evidence. However, in civil cases, documents are almost invariably agreed. They will usually be put in as one or more agreed bundles by the claimant's advocate in the course of his or her opening speech. Furthermore, the use of documents is inextricably bound up with the rules as to disclosure, expert evidence and exchange of witness statements, all of which are outside the scope of this chapter.

The rules relating to the use of contemporaneous notes to refresh the memory and the court's discretion to allow the witness to leave the witness box to read his or her statement are the same as in criminal cases. These rules have effectively been overridden in cases where there are exchanged witness statements.

13.6 CROSS-EXAMINATION

Effective cross-examination is generally regarded as representing the highest level of advocacy. The skilled advocate, by harrying his or her opponent's witnesses with probing questions, can effectively demolish the other side's case. However, it is an art hedged with misconceptions, most of which derive from watching too many fictional courtroom dramas. The aggressive language and sarcastic manner that are characteristic of the television soap opera are usually inappropriate in the real world.

13.6.1 Defining objectives

Advocates should always give careful thought to what they hope to achieve by cross-examination. In order to do this effectively, it will be necessary to develop a 'theory' of the client's case. This theory should be a plausible version of the events, consistent with the available evidence and the client's instructions which, if accepted, will result in the court finding in the client's favour. Once the advocate has developed this theory, he or she will find it easier to work out his or her tactics.

Another point to be borne in mind is that, whatever tactics are to be adopted, the cross-examining advocate must always 'put his or her case' to his or her opponent's witnesses. In other words, the advocate must confront his or her opponent's witnesses with all aspects of the client's case which conflict with their evidence. This need not be done directly. One often hears advocates saying, 'I put it to you that …', as if it were an essential ritualistic device. However, it is possible to be more subtle than this. For example, using the illustration at **13.5.1**, if Mr Smith's advocate needed to put to the witness that it was in fact on 22 August that he saw his client in The Mitre, it would be permissible, but inadvisable, simply to state, 'I put it to you that you are mistaken; it was on 22 not 21 August that you saw Mr Smith in The Mitre, wasn't it?'.

If the answer were to be, 'No', that would be the end of the matter.

Suppose, however, that the cross-examining advocate knew that the witness regularly went to The Mitre at that time: the client's case could be expressed more effectively in the following way:

> Q.   It's true, isn't it, that you regularly go to The Mitre for lunch?
> A.   Yes.
> Q.   At about the same time each day?
> A.   Yes.

Q.   Around midday?

A.   Yes.

The cross-examiner could continue by trying to establish that there was nothing special about 21 August, before suggesting to the witness that he had in fact got the day wrong and that he had seen the defendant on a different day.

In other respects, the cross-examiner has considerable freedom of manoeuvre in deciding how to structure his or her cross-examination. There are four main questions to consider.

13.6.1.1 Should I cross-examine at all?

It may well be that, unless the advocate needs to put the client's case, it is better to ask no questions at all. This is especially so if a witness has not directly damaged the case. Cross-examination may increase the risk of eliciting unfavourable material that would otherwise not come out.

13.6.1.2 Are there any favourable matters that I can extract?

It is far better for an advocate to get a witness on his or her side, rather than to confront him or her. For example, in a case involving disputed identification, try gently to elicit concessions from the witness that it was, for example, dark and raining at the time, rather than suggest aggressively that his or her evidence is worthless.

13.6.1.3 Is there any way in which I can discredit the witness's evidence?

Witnesses can, and often do, make mistakes or erroneous assumptions that may be exposed by cross-examination. Very few witnesses deliberately give false evidence. This always needs to be borne in mind when probing for weaknesses. Again, an indirect rather than a confrontational approach is likely to yield better results. Exposing inconsistencies by reference to a previous inconsistent statement is a particularly effective method. It is governed by special legal rules which are outside the scope of this chapter.

13.6.1.4 Is there any way in which I can discredit the witness himself or herself?

It is rare for the advocate to find himself or herself in a position to insinuate, for example, that the witness is biased. It is a particularly risky tactic when done on behalf of a defendant in a criminal trial because of the dangers of falling foul of s 101(1)(g) of the Criminal Justice Act 2003. In any case, the tactic should never be adopted unless there is independent evidence available to substantiate the allegations.

The above four questions are not mutually exclusive: a cross-examining advocate may wish to adopt those parts of a witness's testimony which favour his or her client whilst challenging other parts which do not. This is a highly skilled and complex operation.

13.6.2 The technique of cross-examination

The major difference between examination-in-chief and cross-examination is that the advocate cross-examining is permitted to ask leading questions. This is a particularly valuable right since it enables him or her to retain tighter control of the witness than is the case with non-leading questions. However, leading questions should not be used to excess since this may give the impression that the witness is being brow-beaten. The tactic can, however, be particularly effective when an advocate wishes to expose inconsistencies or illogicalities. The trap can be set by asking the witness a series of non-leading questions on peripheral matters as a preliminary to confronting him or her with weaknesses or inconsistencies in his or her testimony by means of a series of tightly controlled leading questions. This is a highly skilled exercise.

Two general examples will suffice. Suppose that you were trying to discredit the testimony of an identification witness. There would no doubt be a number of matters which you had thoroughly researched beforehand, such as where he or she was standing, how far away he or she was from the incident, the time of day, the weather conditions, etc. You would no doubt wish to keep tight control of this part of your cross-examination by means of leading questions. However, it might also be appropriate to probe into what the witness had been doing beforehand by means of non-leading questions. For example, you might ask, 'Now Mr Smith, you say you were on your way home when you witnessed this incident; where were you coming from?'. The answer might be, 'I'd been down The Mitre for a drink'.

Not all cross-examinations will yield such promising results, but it can be seen that much useful information can be gleaned from peripheral matters by means of non-leading questions without running any risk to your case.

A second example might be in the case of a witness whom an advocate wished to confront with a previous inconsistent statement. It might be appropriate to begin by inducing him or her by means of non-leading questions to embellish his or her story still further before confronting him or her with the inconsistencies. This is a particularly effective technique where the allegation is that the witness is biased.

13.7 RE-EXAMINATION

Once cross-examination is completed, the advocate who called the witness has the right to re-examine. That right is limited in that: first, he or she may deal only with matters raised in cross-examination; and, secondly, leading questions are not permitted. Very few advocates are skilled re-examiners. It is a sophisticated art. As a general rule, it is most unwise to re-examine unless you are absolutely certain as to your objectives. Its principal function is to repair any damage done in cross-examination by giving the witness an opportunity to explain or qualify his or her previous answers. It is useful where, for example:

(a)   cross-examination has confused the witness;

(b)   the cross-examiner has attempted to impeach the witness's credit;

(c)   the cross-examiner has elicited only partial details of an incident which appears to favour the opponent's case.

13.8 CLOSING THE CASE

Closing a case can be more difficult than opening, because a greater degree of improvisation is required. An opening speech can be worked out in detail beforehand: by the time an advocate rises to make a closing address, all the evidence will be before the court and the case may look very different by then. However, it is rare that the central issues will have changed, only the details. It is absolutely vital, therefore, to have identified the likely issues and evolved a 'theory' of the case in advance. It is only in this way that a closing address can deal with all the outstanding issues in a coherent and persuasive manner. It is important to remember that, just as the advocate who opens the case has the advantage of the first word, so the closing speaker is the last advocate the court will hear before retiring to consider its verdict.

13.8.1 Who closes the case?

13.8.1.1 Criminal cases

In magistrates' court trials, both the prosecution and the defence may make final speeches. The prosecution may make a final speech where the defendant is represented or if the defence introduce evidence other than that of the defendant. The defence will have the final word.

13.8.1.2 Civil cases

Except where the defendant began or where the defendant calls no evidence, the advocate for the claimant has the last word in a civil case. If the judge says that he or she does not wish to hear a closing speech, the claimant has probably already won.

13.8.2 The purpose of the closing speech

13.8.2.1 Criminal cases

Be brief. Magistrates' courts are very busy places and you will be well advised to confine yourself to the essential points which advance your client's case. However, the experienced advocate will not allow himself or herself to be rushed. If you need a few moments to compose yourself and go over your notes, do not hesitate to ask for them. You should always cover:

(a) any relevant points of law;

(b) the key issues in dispute;

(c) any part of the evidence which weakens the prosecution case and strengthens that of the defence.

Avoid saying too much about the burden and standard of proof. Magistrates need little reminding of this. It is better to concentrate on those parts of the evidence which genuinely raise a reasonable doubt.

13.8.2.2 Civil cases

The position in civil cases is broadly similar to that in criminal cases, except that an advocate must always be aware that he or she is addressing a judge, not magistrates. Modify your style accordingly. Since civil trials still take place on the statements of case, a closing speech which follows the issues raised by the statements of case will greatly assist the court. Judges are particularly grateful to advocates who not only summarise the issues that are still outstanding but also emphasise the essential findings of fact which the judge will have to make in order to decide the case.

13.9 ETHICAL ISSUES

An advocate's reputation with the court is his or her most valuable asset. An advocate who has lost the court's trust through some piece of unethical conduct is a liability. All advocates should be familiar with Chapter 5 of the SRA Code of Conduct 2011.

13.9.1 Criminal cases

13.9.1.1 Duties of the prosecution advocate

The duties of the prosecution advocate are:

(a) to ensure that all relevant facts and law are before the court;

(b) to make available to the defence any evidence which is inconsistent with the evidence which a prosecution witness gives at the trial.

13.9.1.2 Duties of the defence advocate

The duties of the defence advocate are:

(a) to say on a client's behalf all that the client would properly say for himself or herself;

(b) to keep confidential all information received about a client and his or her affairs which the client wishes to keep confidential;

(c) to ensure that the prosecution discharge the onus placed upon them to prove the guilt of the accused. The defence advocate is entitled to put the prosecution to proof even if the defendant has admitted his or her guilt;

(d) to disclose to the prosecution and to the court all relevant cases and statutory provisions relating to the case, even if unfavourable to the defence. However, unfavourable evidence need not be disclosed;

(e)   not to participate in a positive deception of the court. A solicitor may not continue to act for a client who misleads the court (eg, by giving a false name, or giving evidence which the advocate knows to be untrue) unless the client is prepared to reveal the truth;

(f)   not to act for two or more clients whose interests are in conflict, even if invited to do so by the court.

13.9.2   Civil cases

Advocates for the claimant and the defendant are bound by the same rules which are:

(a)   to ensure that all relevant facts and law are before the court;

(b)   to say on a client's behalf all that the client would say properly for himself or herself;

(c)   to keep confidential all information received about a client and his or her affairs which the client wishes to keep confidential;

(d)   where relevant, to ensure that the opponent discharges the onus placed upon him or her by the burden of proof;

(e)   to disclose to the court all relevant cases and statutory provisions relevant to the case, even if not favourable to the client. The advocate may then seek to show that decisions which are against him or her are erroneous, not binding, per incuriam or distinguishable. As in criminal cases, the theory is that unfavourable evidence need not be disclosed. However, the rules as to disclosure and exchange of witness statements are such that, in practice, both parties may be required to disclose such evidence;

(f)   not to participate in a positive deception of the court. A solicitor may not continue to act for a client who misleads the court (eg, by giving evidence which the advocate knows to be untrue) unless the client is now prepared to reveal the truth;

(g)   not to act for two or more clients whose interests are in conflict.

13.10   CRIMINAL CASES: BAIL AND MITIGATION

A detailed study of criminal advocacy in bail applications and pleas in mitigation is outside the scope of this chapter. However, a very basic guide to the skills required is set out below. Because most criminal advocates will begin their careers with a simple bail application or plea, it is often erroneously assumed that this is 'easy' advocacy. Nothing could be further from the truth: there is nothing easy about a situation in which the client may face a period in custody if his or her advocate fails him or her.

13.10.1   Bail

The skills of the advocate will be required only when the application is opposed. Although bail is always ultimately a matter for the court, it will normally be granted as a matter of course unless the prosecution object. Since defendants have a right to bail prior to conviction, it is customary for the Crown Prosecutor to begin by formally setting out his or her objections by reference to the prescribed criteria in Sch 1, Pt I to the Bail Act 1976. The objections will almost invariably be based on an assertion that there are substantial grounds for believing that the defendant will either abscond and/or commit further offences while he or she is on bail. The risk of the defendant interfering with witnesses or otherwise obstructing the course of justice is also frequently advanced as an objection.

The task of the defence advocate is twofold. First, he or she should seek to put forward arguments which tend to minimise the risks adverted by the Crown Prosecutor. Thus, for example, if the prosecution claim that there is a substantial risk of the defendant absconding, this might be rebutted by arguing that:

(a)   the defendant is pleading not guilty and the evidence against him or her is weak;

(b)   the defendant's record (if he or she has one) reveals that he or she has never absconded whilst on bail in the past;

(c)   even if he or she is convicted, the likelihood of a custodial sentence is remote.

These are very general illustrations: each case must be dealt with on its own facts. Whatever the facts, thorough preparation is always essential.

Secondly, the advocate must neutralise any substantial risks by putting forward a sensible package of conditions, such as a surety combined with a condition of residence, which will be sufficient to persuade the bench that it can afford to take a risk and grant bail. Although s 4 of the Bail Act 1976 is supposed to secure a right to bail, in reality if a prosecutor raises substantial grounds for withholding bail, the defence advocate has a difficult task upholding that right. An effective application therefore requires as much advance preparation as the circumstances permit. The Crown Prosecution Service (CPS) should always be approached (in advance if practicable) in order to obtain as much information as possible about both the offence and the defendant.

If possible, you should obtain detailed instructions from the client concerning his or her personal circumstances and the existence of any potential sureties. It may be that this will avoid a contested application altogether. If you can produce an appropriate package of conditions to the CPS before the hearing, you may be able to persuade it to withdraw its objections. So far as the actual application itself is concerned, an advocate should always bear three things in mind:

(a)   Structure the application in such a way that each prosecution objection is countered in a logical sequence, and conclude with any package of conditions you wish to put forward.

(b)   Keep the application as short as circumstances permit and remember that courts usually have a long list of cases to hear.

(c)   Tailor the application to the individual client. Magistrates are often offered the same platitudes whatever the nature of the application, such as, 'My client strenuously denies the charge, has a fixed address and instructs me that he has been offered work on a building site'. The statement may be true, but it is vitally important to interest the court in your client's personal circumstances. It might therefore be more appropriate to explain a little more about why your client's denial is so significant. For example:

'Sir, if I might begin by referring you to the case against Mr Smith, you will see that it is tenuous in the extreme. The evidence consists solely of hotly disputed identification evidence ...'

and so on.

PROSECUTION PAPERS – GARETH DAVIES

Charge: Inflicting grievous bodily (Offences Against the Person Act 1861, s 20)

The defendant, Gareth Davies, is jointly charged with Stephen Jones. Last night he assaulted Phillip Bennett, outside the Seagull fish and chip shop in High Street, Weyford.

At about 11.15pm Bennett was outside the fish and chip shop waiting for his friends who were inside the shop. He saw Stephen Jones and Gareth Davies walking along High Street from the direction of Market Street. Both Jones and Davies used to be regulars at Cindy's nightclub in the High Street where Bennett works. Some two weeks earlier Bennett banned them because of an incident at the nightclub.

When they saw Bennett they crossed the road and started talking to him, trying to persuade him to lift the ban. At first the conversation was good natured and then things changed. Jones became more and more aggressive and despite Bennett's attempts to calm him down Jones punched Bennett hard in the face. Bennett fought back but he fell over. Whilst on the ground he was hit at least a dozen times on the face and arms. He was also punched and kicked in the chest and stomach. The punches were coming from his left and right and Bennett now saw that Gareth Davies was involved. He could not be sure which of the two men was more responsible but he is sure both were involved. The assault finished when a friend of Bennett's, John Bevan, intervened.

Bevan, who also works at Cindy's, knows both Jones and Davies. He said that he was inside the fish and chip shop heard a commotion outside, rushed out and saw Bennett being attacked by both Jones and Davies. He managed to break it up and then Jones and Davies ran off.

The police were called and both Jones and Davies were arrested about half a mile away. On arrival at the police station both men were found to be under the influence of alcohol. They were unfit to be interviewed and left in the cells to sleep.

Jones denied the offence in interview. He said he was defending himself having been attacked by Bennett. He denied causing all of Bennett's injuries saying that Davies must have caused them.

When interviewed at 9.30am today Davies denied any involvement in the offence saying all he did was to try to pull Jones off Bennett. He said that Jones was the one that was responsible for causing all the injuries to Bennett. When told that Jones had put the blame onto him Davies said 'I'll get him for this. He'll regret saying that. You wait until I catch up with him.'

As a result of the attack Bennett suffered a deep cut above his left eye; cuts and bruises to his face; a bleeding nose; grazes to his hands and knees; bruises to his stomach and arms; a broken nose and a broken left arm. Bennett was treated at Weyford General Hospital and released earlier today.

Jones, who has no previous convictions, was granted unconditional bail. He is due to appear before Weyford Magistrates' Court in seven days time.

Previous convictions:

4 years ago	ABH	Fined £500; Compensation £70
	Absconding	Fined £100
3 years ago requirement	Criminal damage	Community sentence with a supervision
	Absconding	Fined £75
18 months ago	ABH	3 months' imprisonment

Antecedents:

Aged 27, married (separated from his wife), unemployed, previous employment all casual – barman, bouncer etc. After his marriage break-up some three months ago he has slept on friends' floors and in their spare rooms. He is staying with friends at the moment but has to move out by the end of the week. Previous offences all alcohol related.

The case will be adjourned for advance disclosure of the prosecution case. Apply for a remand in custody for seven days.

DEFENCE PAPERS

Mr Davies says:

I live with friends at 36 Town Lane, Weyford.

THE OFFENCE

I am charged jointly with Stephen Jones with inflicting grievous bodily harm on Philip Bennett. I wish to plead not guilty.

Last night I went out for a drink at the Ship public house in the High Street and met Stephen Jones there. I used to go out with him a lot. We used to go to Cindy's Nightclub but about two weeks ago we both got banned by the bouncer there called Philip Bennett. Stephen got hammered and started hitting on some girls who didn't like it. The girls complained and Bennett became involved. There was an argument and Stephen threatened him. I wasn't involved but because I was with Stephen I got barred as well.

After having a few pints in the Ship we were walking along the High Street on the way home. We saw Bennett outside the Seagull fish and chip shop with a group of girls and Stephen said that we should try to persuade Bennett to let us back into Cindy's. I told him that it wasn't a good idea but before I knew it Stephen had crossed the road and was talking to Bennett. I thought that Bennett would tell Stephen to get lost but he seemed quite happy to talk to him. The girls then went into the fish and shop and one of the girls recognised Stephen from the night we'd been banned from Cindy's and said something like 'Not you again, you tosser' and then Stephen lost it. He started to argue with Bennett about how out of order Bennett had been to ban him from Cindy's and then he punched Bennett in the face.

I didn't want to get involved. With my record I didn't want any trouble but I knew that things were getting out of hand. Bennett had fallen to the ground and Stephen was now kicking him. I tried to pull Stephen off Bennett but he just kept laying into him on the ground. Another man, who works with Bennett called John, then came out of the fish and chip shop and managed to get Stephen off Bennett. Stephen then ran off and I chased after him.

The police later arrested us. I was fed up with Stephen's behavior and when they put us into the police van we had a bit of an argument. He always seems to be getting into trouble. When I arrived at the police station I was given some written rules about my rights and asked if I wanted a solicitor, but I didn't see the need, I hadn't done anything wrong.

I told them what had happened. I suppose I was a bit aggressive about Stephen during the interview. In fact I think I said that I'd sort him out but I didn't mean it. He basically put all the blame on me – I suppose he was afraid of getting a criminal record and decided that the best thing to do was to land me in it.

We were both charged but I was refused police bail. Stephen was granted police bail.

Personal background

I am aged 27. I left school when I was 16 and have done casual jobs as a bouncer, barman and general labourer. I am currently unemployed. I've lived in the Weyford area for about ten years. I married five years ago but split up from my wife about three months ago when our tenancy came to an end. After we split up I've slept on friends' floors, and in their spare rooms. I'm staying with friends now but they've told me that I have to move out by the end of the week.

My parents live in Scotland and will not put me up even if I wanted them to. The last time I got into trouble I stayed at Weyford Bail Hostel.

Four years ago my marriage hit a bad patch and I began to drink. Drink is at the root of all these offences. I pleaded guilty to them all.

The ABH some four years ago took place in a pub. I'd been drinking and watching the football when this bloke said something I didn't like about my team. I lost my temper and got into a fight with him.

The first absconding offence was a mistake – I got the dates mixed up. I was arrested under a warrant.

The criminal damage offence was when I thought my wife had left me. She went to stay at her mother's. I'd had a few pints at the pub and went round to see her but she wouldn't let me in. I lost my temper and ended up smashing a few of the windows. I didn't attend court on time because I overslept and turned up about three hours late.

I continued to drink and the last offence was also committed whilst drunk. Someone picked on me in a pub. I defended myself but overdid it. It was about that time that I decided I had to pull myself together. I went on an alcohol awareness course run by a local charity and my drinking is now under control.

Mr Davies wishes you to apply for bail on his behalf.

PROSECUTION SUBMISSIONS

Sir, the prosecution oppose bail because, if released on bail, there are substantial grounds for believing that the defendant will fail to surrender to custody, interfere with witnesses or otherwise obstruct the course of justice and commit offences whilst on bail. I shall deal with each of these grounds in turn.

The first ground of objection is failure to surrender to custody. This was a serious, unprovoked attack on Mr Bennett.

At about 11.15 last night the victim, Mr Bennett, was outside the Seagull fish and chip shop in the High Street, Guildfleet waiting for his friends who were inside the shop. He was approached by Mr Davies and his co-defendant Mr Jones. Both men are known to Mr Bennett as he banned both men from his place of work, Cindy's nightclub, some two weeks ago. Mr Jones tried to persuade Mr Bennett to lift the ban. At first the conversation was good natured but then Mr Jones became more and more aggressive. Mr Bennett tried to calm him down. Then Mr Jones punched Mr Bennett hard in the face. Mr Bennett fought back but he fell over. Whilst on the ground Mr Bennett was hit at least a dozen times on the face and arms. He was also punched and kicked in the chest and stomach. The punches were coming from his left and right and Mr Bennett could see that not only was Mr Jones involved but Mr Davies too. He couldn't be sure which of the two men were responsible but he is sure that both were involved. The assault finished when a friend of Mr Bennett's, John Bevan, intervened. Both Mr Jones and Mr Davies ran off.

The police were called and both men were arrested. On arrival at the police station both men were too drunk to be interviewed and they were left in the cells to sleep. Earlier this morning Mr Davies was interviewed and denied any involvement in the offence.

The strength of the evidence against Mr Davies is strong. Not only does Mr Bennett identify Mr Davies as being involved but Mr Bevan does too. Mr Bevan, who works with Mr Bennett at Cindy's nightclub, also knows Mr Jones and Mr Davies. He said that he heard a commotion outside the fish and chip shop, rushed out and saw Mr Bennett being attacked by both Mr Jones and Mr Davies.

If convicted the defendant is likely to receive a custodial sentence for this offence. As a result of the attack Mr Bennett suffered a deep cut above his left eye; cuts and bruises to his face; a bleeding nose; grazes to his hands and knees; bruises to his stomach and arms; a broken nose and a broken left arm. Mr Bennett was treated at Weyford General Hospital and released earlier today. What makes a custodial sentence even more likely in this case is the defendant's list of previous convictions. He has two previous convictions for offences of violence; an assault occasioning actual bodily harm some five years ago for which he was fined £500 and another assault occasioning actual bodily harm some eighteen months ago for which he received three months imprisonment.

As can also be seen from the defendant's list of previous convictions, he already has two previous convictions for failing to surrender to custody. This was also in respect of an offence of violence which the defendant faced. When seen in the context of the current offence, this must raise substantial doubts that the defendant will surrender to custody.

Another factor which may lead the defendant to fail to surrender is his lack of community ties. He is unemployed and since the breakdown of the defendant's marriage some three months ago he has been sleeping on friends' floors and in their spare rooms. He is staying with friends at the moment but has to move out by the end of the week. The defendant therefore has no permanent address, nor any employment to keep him in the Weyford area.

The second objection to bail being granted is that the defendant may interfere with witnesses or otherwise obstruct the course of justice. Mr Davies is jointly charged with Mr Jones. In his interview Mr Jones denied all involvement in this offence. He said that he was defending himself having been attacked by Mr Bennett. He denied causing all of Mr Bennett's injuries saying that Mr Davies must have caused them. When told in his interview that Mr Jones had put the blame on him Mr Davies said 'I'll get him for this. He'll regret saying that. You wait until I catch up with him.'

The third objection to bail being granted is that the defendant may commit offences if released on bail. Sir, this is a defendant with a history of violent offending. The defendant has been convicted of two offences of violence in the past four years. All these offences appear to be connected with alcohol. You may recall Sir that this offence was alcohol related too.

Sir, for the reasons that I have outlined the prosecution oppose bail being granted to the defendant and invite you to remand the defendant in custody for seven days.

DEFENCE SUBMISSIONS

Sir, I wish to apply for conditional bail on behalf of Mr Davies. Any concerns that you may have about whether Mr Davies will fail to appear, interfere with witnesses or otherwise obstruct the course of justice or commit further offences whilst on bail can be more than adequately dealt with by granting Mr Davies bail with conditions.

I shall deal first with the allegation that Mr Davies will fail to surrender to custody if released on bail. The charge Mr Davies faces is a serious one, this makes it all the more likely that Mr Davies will attend the next court hearing. When interviewed by the police Mr Davies denied any involvement in the offence saying all he did was try to pull Mr Jones off Mr Bennett. Mr Davies intends to plead not guilty to this offence. He is anxious to clear his name and does not wish to worsen the situation by failing to surrender.

The prosecution evidence is not strong. Mr Bennett claims that both Mr Jones and Mr Davies were involved in this offence. The prosecution allege that Mr Bennett was punched by Mr Jones and then Mr Bennett fought back but he fell over. He was then hit, punched and kicked to the body. Presumably Mr Bennett was protecting his head, as anyone would do, whilst defenceless on the ground. It is unlikely that Mr Bennett would be able to say for certain that he saw Mr Davies hit, punch or kick him. The evidence of Mr Bevan should also be treated with caution. He works with Mr Bennett and is a friend of his. It is only natural that his evidence may be favourable to Mr Bennett. It is noticeable that the prosecution failed to mention any independent evidence to support their version of events.

The prosecution argue that, should Mr Davies be convicted, he will receive a custodial sentence because of the seriousness of this offence and his record of previous convictions. Sir, a custodial sentence is not inevitable in this case. The prosecution allege that his offending is alcohol related. If that is the case, then the court may consider a community sentence to help him address any alcohol problem that he may have. Mr Davies does have two previous convictions for similar offences. The first was some four years ago and did not result in a custodial sentence and the last was some eighteen months ago. Following his custodial sentence Mr Davies decided to pull himself together and has kept out of trouble.

The prosecution seek to place reliance upon the defendant's previous convictions for failing to surrender to bail. This must be placed in context. Mr Davies did not actively abscond. His first failure to surrender was a mistake on his part. He thought that he was due to appear in court at a later date. His second failure to surrender was due to his oversleeping. He attended court about three hours late. Sir, you will see that both offences resulted in the imposition of fines which indicate that these were not the most serious examples of failing to surrender to custody. I would urge you to give little weight to the prosecution's arguments on this point.

The prosecution also suggest that Mr Davies' lack of community ties mean that he is likely to abscond. Mr Davies has lived in the Weyford area for about ten years. He is currently unemployed but has been employed locally as a bouncer, barman and general labourer. Until some three weeks ago he was living in rented accommodation with his wife. Unfortunately they have now split up and he has been sleeping on friends' floors and in their spare rooms. I have liaised with the Probation Service this morning and should Mr Davies be granted bail there is a place available for him at the Weyford Bail Hostel.

The second ground raised by the prosecution is that Mr Davies will interfere with witnesses or otherwise obstruct the course of justice by interfering with his co-defendant, Mr Jones. When Mr Davies was told what Mr Jones had to say, Mr Davies was upset. Mr Jones is someone whom Mr Davies regards as a friend and Mr Davies cannot understand why Mr Jones is implicating him in this offence. Mr Davies was also upset by the police keeping him in the cells overnight when he believed he was fit to be interviewed. He was tired and emotional when he made those comments about Mr Jones. He did not mean them and has no intention of seeking to influence Mr Jones's evidence.

The third ground of objection raised by the prosecution is that Mr Davies will commit further offences if released on bail. I would submit that this is not the case. Mr Davies intends to plead not guilty to this offence. In addition, Mr Davies does not have a lengthy list of previous convictions. He has five convictions spread over a four-year period and these do not constitute substantial grounds for believing that Mr Davies will offend again.

Sir, for the reasons that I have set out I would ask you to grant conditional bail to Mr Davies.

There are a number of conditions that I would invite you to consider imposing to remove any concerns you might have as to Mr Davies' willingness to attend court on the next occasion. You might wish to consider imposing a condition that Mr Davies reside at the Weyford Bail Hostel and report to Weyford Police Station on a regular basis. I would submit that the imposition of such conditions would remove any substantial grounds for believing that Mr Davies would fail to attend court on the next occasion.

For the reasons that I have outlined, I do not consider that the prosecution have established substantial grounds for believing that Mr Davies would obstruct the course of justice. However, if you should have any concerns with regard to this, I would submit that any such concerns may be addressed by imposing a condition that Mr Davies does not contact or associate with Mr Jones.

Finally I submit that the prosecution have failed to establish substantial grounds for believing that Mr Davies will commit further offences if released on bail. Should you have any concerns Sir, then any such concerns may be addressed by imposing a curfew or a condition that Mr Davies should not enter any licensed premises or the Weyford town centre other than for the purposes of employment or to see his solicitor.

Sir, unless I can be of any further assistance, those are my submissions.

13.10.2 Pleas in mitigation

As with bail applications, advance preparation is essential. Courts can sentence only on the basis of information, and although the sentencing court may have a written pre-sentence report (PSR) available (this is mandatory when the court is considering a custodial sentence or certain types of community penalty), there will often be a great deal of further relevant background information which the defence advocate may put before the court. The Criminal Justice Act 2003 places the seriousness of the offence at the forefront of the matters to which the court must have regard when passing sentence. Nevertheless, the court is not precluded from considering the circumstances of the individual offender by way of mitigation. A useful starting point in the magistrates' court is to consult the sentencing guidelines published by the Sentencing Council, and in particular the Magistrates' Court Sentencing Guidelines.

The following points should always be considered when preparing a plea:

(a) Thoroughly research the realistic sentencing options available, referring, where appropriate, to relevant statutory or judicial guidelines.

(b) Take as full a written statement as possible from the client, dealing with the circumstances both of the offence and of the client.

(c) Obtain an up-to-date copy of the client's criminal record, and deal thoroughly with the circumstances of any offences which the court may regard as being 'aggravating'.

(d) If a PSR has been ordered, try to contact the Probation Service in advance of the case to see if it will discuss its contents informally.

(e) Arrive at court in plenty of time so that you can discuss your mitigation speech with the client and obtain his or her approval of your proposed course.

(f) When called upon to address the court, invite them to read any PSR first.

(g) When the court has read the PSR, begin your speech by dealing with matters which affect the seriousness of the offence. Then go on to deal with matters of offender mitigation, referring where appropriate to the PSR. Never read paragraphs of the PSR aloud, because the document is confidential. Instead, invite the court to consider the appropriate paragraph. For example:

'Madam, you will recall that Mr Smith's family history is dealt with at the top of page 2 of the pre-sentence report. I would particularly draw your attention to the matters dealt with in paragraph 3 ...'

and so on.

(h) Conclude by 'showing the court the way home'. In other words, if you can suggest a realistic sentencing option which the court can take, you are not only discharging your duty to the client, but you are also assisting the court. Sentencing an offender is never easy, and anything which helps the court discharge this onerous duty will be gratefully received.

GARETH DAVIES

Following the contested bail application Davies was released on bail with conditions. The prosecution subsequently obtained CCTV footage and witness statements from Philip Bennett, John Bennett and three other witnesses who were in the Seagull fish and chip shop. The prosecution evidence showed that Jones and Davies were both involved in the assault. At the next court appearance the defendants decided to enter guilty pleas and the case was adjourned for the preparation of pre-sentence reports. Jones was granted unconditional bail and Davies bail with conditions.

Gareth Davies says:

I was not telling the truth when I made my earlier statement. I did assault Bennett. My initial reaction was to pull Jones off him but then I decided to give him a good hiding. I decided to get my own back for unfairly banning me from Cindy's by punching and kicking him whilst he was on the ground. I was drunk at the time. I now realise that it was a foolish thing for me to do and I am sorry for my actions. I do have an alcohol problem. My wife has been telling me for years that I have a drink problem. I took no notice of her. I have been drinking heavily since I left my wife. I want to get back together with her and I need to address my offending which is associated with my drinking. She is now staying at her mother's house.

Pre-sentence report:

BLANKSHIRE
PROBATION SERVICE   Chief Officer: John Evans

This is a Pre-Sentence Report as defined in Section 158 of the Criminal Justice Act 2003. It has been prepared in accordance with the requirements of the National Standard for Pre-Sentence Reports. This report is a confidential document and has been prepared for these proceedings only. Its value on other occasions and for other purposes will therefore be limited.

PRE-SENTENCE REPORT

COURT	Weyford Magistrates'
NAME	Gareth Davies
AGE	24
ADDRESS	Weyford Bail Hostel
	27 Carter Street
	Weyford
	Blankshire
	WE2 1HA
PETTY SESSIONS AREA	Weyford
OFFENCE(S)	GBH (s 20)
OFFICER PREPARING THIS REPORT	Enid Barton
TITLE:	Probation officer
REF CODE:	JEW/DF/11224/M4/5/010/N/MEBP/W02

34 Bennetthorpe   Tel: (00002) 730099
Weyford WE2 6AD   Fax: (00002) 730220 (General)
Fax: (00002 730720 (Divisional Manager)

PRE-SENTENCE REPORT ON GARETH DAVIES

INTRODUCTION

1. This report is based upon two interviews with Mr Davies; one at Weyford Bail Hostel and one at my office. I have read the prosecution papers and seen a copy of Mr Davies' previous convictions. I have also liased with Mrs Davies, Mr Davies's solicitor and Mr Williams the manager of the Weyford Bail Hostel.

OFFENCE ANALYSIS

2. Mr Davies inflicted grevious boldily harm on another man outside the Seagull fish and chip shop in the High Street, Weyford. Mr Davies's co-defendant punched the victim in the face. There was a fight. The victim then fell over and Mr Davies together with his co-defendant punched and kicked the victim to his head and body whilst the victim was lying on the ground. The assault finished when a friend of the victim intervened. Mr Davies was under the influence of alcohol at the time of the offence and was not fit to be interviewed by the police until the following morning.

3. Mr Davies told me that he knew the victim and disliked him. The victim worked at Cindy's nightclub in Weyford and had, some two weeks before the offence, banned Mr Davies from the nightclub. Mr Davies's co-defendant Stephen Jones was drunk and made some unwanted advances towards a group of girls in the nightclub. The girls complained to management and the victim became involved in handling the complaint. Mr Jones then had an argument with the victim in which he threatened him. Mr Jones was banned from the nightclub and since Mr Davies was with Mr Jones he was banned too even though he was not involved. Mr Davies felt that his banning from the nightclub was unwarranted.

RELEVANT INFORMATION ABOUT THE OFFENDER

4. Mr Davies has appeared in Court for sentencing purposes on three previous occasions. His offending began four years ago and consists of assaults occasioning actual bodily harm, criminal damage and absconding. The assaults and criminal damage offences were all committed whist he was under the influence of alcohol.

5. Eighteen months ago Mr Davies was sentenced to 3 months' imprisonment. He found the experience of prison a chastening one and he told me that he was determined to keep out of trouble as a result. He believes that his offending is alcohol related. He went on an alcohol awareness course run by Addiction, a local charity, and found the course useful. From the enquiries I have made the course was not an intensive one and since alcohol abuse appears to be at the root of his offending then such a course is unlikely to prevent him committing offences in the future.

6. Mr Davies is one of five children and he originates from Scotland. He is literate and numerate but tells me that he left school with no qualifications. During his last two years at school he increasingly played truant because, he says, he was bullied. Shortly after leaving school he met a woman who is now his wife, Carolyn Davies. She originated from Weyford and Mr Davies moved to Weyford to be near her. After going out together for about five years they married. Mr Davies tells me that his marriage was a happy one but his wife felt that he had an alcohol problem which he failed to acknowledge. Some three months ago he split up from his wife believing that his wife was having an affair with another man.

7. Since leaving his wife he has been sleeping on friends' floors and in their spare rooms. During these proceedings Mr Davies has been living at the Weyford Bail Hostel. I understand from the manager of the hostel, Mr Williams, that since his time there Mr Davies has been a model resident.

8.   Mr Davies still has feelings towards his wife. He was accompanied by his wife when he attended our second interview. He now believes his wife when she says that she was not having an affair. They intend to get back together and are looking for rented accommodation together in Newtown. Mrs Davies is in full-time employment as a waitress.

9.   Whilst on remand Mr Davies has been making attempts to obtain work. He has attended three interviews for different types of manual work. He did have a job for a short while in a timber yard but he was sacked because he turned up for work after lunch under the influence of alcohol.

10.   It is very unfortunate that Mr Davies has not been able to hold down a steady job since he seems to have great difficulty in structuring his time. He is in good health although he drinks to excess when he has the money to do so and I feel that this has caused many of his problems.

11.   Mr Davies accepts that he has an alcohol problem and he is making efforts to control it. He says that he has reduced his alcohol intake and is feeling healthier for it. He realises that his lack of formal qualifications is hindering his search for employment. However, because he did not enjoy school he is reluctant to return to an educational environment. He accepts that he is unlikely to be bullied at his age. He says that he lacks the motivation to study.

12.   At the time of the interview Mr Davies was in receipt of income-based job seeker's allowance.

RISK TO THE PUBLIC OF RE-OFFENDING

13.   Mr Davies is a gregarious man, although his manner can easily seem aggressive. I believe that many of his problems relate to his alcohol problems. The harm inflicted on the victim was intentional. As the court mentioned when adjourning for sentence, Mr Davies was fortunate that the victim did not sustain more serious injuries as a result of the assault. Since Mr Davies has an alcohol problem and difficulties controlling his temper, which he acknowledges, there is a high risk that Mr Davies will cause further harm in the future.

14.   I have no concerns as regards the possibility of deliberate self-harm in the community. Mr Davies presents himself as a fairly confident individual and I suspect that he will cope easily if his offending were to result in a custodial sentence.

CONCLUSION

15.   Mr Davies seems genuine when he says that he is determined to address the causes of his offending. I feel that he could benefit from a community sentence with the two following requirements:

- Supervision requirement

- An alcohol treatment requirement (Addressing Substance Related Offending – ASRO)

I have discussed these requirements with Mr Davies and he has agreed to co-operate with the Probation Service. He has been assessed as suitable.

A supervision requirement would focus on increasing his employability and encourage him to improve his educational qualifications or secure training. The alcohol treatment requirement would address his alcohol problem.

16.   If the court is of the view that a custodial sentence must be imposed, I am required to identify and comment upon any adverse effects of custody. Since Mr Davies has experience of a custodial setting, is currently looking for accommodation and is jobless, I can identify no major concerns.

Since Mr Davies would benefit from requirements designed to address the causes of his offending the court may consider that a suspended sentence is more appropriate. Such a disposal would also enable Mr Davies to find work, thereby placing him in the position to pay compensation to the victim. Mr Davies has no savings and therefore any compensation ordered by the court would have to be paid by instalments.

Signed: *Jason King*   Dated: _ _ 20__
             Probation Officer

PLEA IN MITIGATION

Sir, I understand from your legal advisor that you have had the opportunity to read the pre-sentence report prepared by the Probation Service.

Clearly, Sir, this is a serious matter, and you may be minded to impose an immediate custodial sentence on Mr Davies. I hope to persuade you that a more suitable method of disposing of this case would be for you to impose a community sentence as recommended in the report.

I shall begin by addressing the circumstances of the offence, I shall then provide you with details of Mr Davies's personal circumstances, before concluding by addressing the requirements of the community order which I hope to persuade you to impose.

Sir, Mr Davies pleaded guilty to this offence and accepts the version of events outlined to you by the prosecution. He expresses remorse for his actions.

Once Mr Davies saw Mr Jones fighting with Mr Bennett he foolishly became involved. His motivation for becoming involved was Mr Bennett banning him from Cindy's nightclub. The banning arose as a result of Mr Jones becoming drunk at the nightclub and Mr Jones making some unwelcome advances to a group of girls. The girls complained to the management and Mr Bennett became involved. Mr Jones began an argument with Mr Bennett and threatened him. Mr Davies played no part in the incident but since he was with Mr Jones he was banned as well. Mr Davies felt aggrieved by the way he had been treated by Mr Bennett. He felt angry and upset. When he saw Mr Jones fighting with Mr Bennett he decided to get his own back and whilst Mr Bennett was on the ground he punched and kicked him several times to the face and body. No weapon was used by Mr Davies. Whilst the banning from the nightclub should not condone Mr Davies's later actions, it does help to explain why Mr Davies acted in the way he did. There was another factor which influenced his behaviour that night: his excessive consumption of alcohol, a factor which I shall return to later.

Sir, Mr Davies is 27 years of age. He has lived in the Weyford area for some ten years. He is currently unemployed though he has been employed for much of that ten year period as a bouncer, barman and general labourer. Whilst on bail for this offence Mr Davies did manage to get a job for a short while in a timber yard. He lost his job because he has been drinking at lunchtime. Mr Davies realises that it was a foolish thing for him to have done. He tells me that he went to a local public house because he was depressed and wanted to drown his sorrows. He is still looking for employment but realises that in the present economic climate jobs are hard to come by and he regrets throwing away what could have become a permanent job at the timber yard.

Sir, Mr Davies does have previous convictions for offences of violence and criminal damage.

His offending began some four years ago when his marriage was in difficulties and he started to drink to excess. He was convicted of an assault occasioning actual bodily harm following an argument in a public house. Mr Davies had been watching some football. A supporter from another team said something derogatory about the team that Mr Davies supported. Mr Davies lost his temper and there was a fight.

The criminal damage occurred at a time when he thought that his wife had left him and his wife went to stay at her mother's house. Following a few pints to drink Mr Davies went round to see his wife. She would not let him into the house because he had been drinking. Mr Davies lost his temper and an angry and drunk Mr Davies picked up some stones, threw them at the windows breaking them.

Mr Davies's last conviction was some eighteen months ago. He was out drinking in a public house. He says that someone attacked him and in defending himself he used excessive force. The court considered the offence serious enough to merit a custodial sentence. Mr Davies coped with prison life but realised that he had an alcohol problem.

On release from prison he decided to address what he considered to be the cause of his offending: his drinking. To his credit Mr Davies sought help and he went on an alcohol awareness course run by the local charity Addiction. He reduced his alcohol consumption and things were progressing well. Then he mistakenly thought that his wife was having an affair with another man. He left his wife some three months ago and started to drink heavily again culminating in this offence.

Mr Davies and Mrs Davies are now back together again and are looking for somewhere to live. Until they do so they intend to stay with Mrs Davies's mother.

Sir, there is a theme running throughout Mr Davies's offending. That theme is the misuse of alcohol. All his offences are alcohol related. The pre-sentence report says that unless he addresses his alcohol problem the risk of his re-offending is high.

As you will be aware one of the five purposes of sentencing is the reform and rehabilitation of offenders. The sentence suggested by Mr King in his pre-sentence report is a community order comprising a supervision requirement and an alcohol treatment requirement. Such an order would give him the help and support that he needs to overcome his alcohol problem.

I would submit that the imposition of an immediate custodial sentence, whilst achieving the goal of punishing Mr Davies, would not prevent Mr Davies from re-offending. He was sentenced to a term of imprisonment some eighteen months ago and on release thought that he could address the issue himself. He managed to keep out of trouble but Mrs Davies has informed me that throughout this period his alcohol consumption was a constant source of tension between them. Mr Davies thought that he had his drinking under control. Mrs Davies thought that he was still drinking to excess; a view that Mr Davies now belatedly accepts. You will be aware Sir that many offenders who receive prison sentences offend again because prison fails to address the root causes of their offending.

Sir, should you feel that a community sentence is inappropriate then perhaps a suspended sentence would be appropriate. In imposing such a sentence you can make a supervision order and an alcohol treatment order. This would satisfy the need to punish Mr Davies, but also the need to prevent him from offending in the future. Should Mr Davies re-offend or fail to comply with the terms of the suspended sentence then he knows that a custodial sentence is inevitable.

You will also be aware Sir that another purpose of sentencing is the making of reparation by offenders to those affected by their offences. I would submit that such a purpose could be satisfied in this case by the making of an order that Mr Davies pay compensation to Mr Bennett. Should you order compensation to be paid, or should you order that Mr Davies pay the cost of the prosecution then Mr Davies would ask for time to pay. He has no savings and is currently in receipt of income-based job seeker's allowance.

Sir, in conclusion, I would urge you to adopt the sentence recommended by Mr King in his report, namely a community sentence incorporating a supervision requirement and an alcohol treatment requirement. In addition Mr Bennett is in a position to make a payment of compensation to Mr Bennett.

Unless, Sir, you have any questions, that concludes my submissions on behalf of Mr Davies.

13.11 CIVIL CASES: INTERIM APPLICATIONS

13.11.1 Key characteristics

It is particularly important to master the skills relevant to interim applications in civil cases because trainee solicitors have full rights of audience. An interim application is any application made to the court before the trial of the claim. In the High Court, those interim applications requiring a hearing will be dealt with by a master (in the central office in London) or a district judge (in the district registry). In the county court, these will be dealt with by a district judge. All interim applications, whether in the High Court or the county court, share a number of common features:

(a)   There are no 'live' witnesses. With rare exceptions, all the evidence will be in witness statement form. Hence, the principal tasks of the advocate are to present his or her case and to argue for the order sought.

(b)   Advocates are seated (except for some applications before a master).

(c)   The proceedings are heard in public (unless the court otherwise directs).

13.11.2 Preparing for the application

Although the subject-matter of an application may vary considerably from case to case, there are a number of steps which should always be taken:

(a)   Try to agree as much as possible in advance.

(b)   Make sure all relevant witness statements are served before the hearing. Although the court may be prepared to accept a late witness statement, it will result in your client being penalised in costs.

(c)   Make sure that you have mastered the facts of the case and that you are familiar with the contents of the statements of case and witness statements. You may find it useful to prepare a written chronology of the case including the key events and steps in the action from issue of proceedings to date. It is not uncommon for the master or district judge to deal only with those particular points in the case which he or she considers need arguing. Your grasp of the facts and documentation therefore needs to be such that you can locate them instantly. If the case is a complex one, consider handing to the master or district judge a written chronology which you have agreed with your opponent.

(d)   The master or district judge should have a copy of the court file. However, you will need to ensure that you have copies of any relevant documents to hand to the master or district judge, should the court file be incomplete.

(e)   Prepare brief notes. Although you should never read out your submissions, it will help you to have a list which sets out the points that you intend to raise. Focus on the main facts to be addressed. You might use a highlighter pen on copy documents (not the originals) for this purpose. Write in the margin of a copy witness statement a brief summary of what each paragraph contains. An example of such a note in a contract case might be, 'Para 3 – Summarises the dispute as to time of delivery'.

(f)   Make sure you have read and flagged the relevant passages in the Civil Procedure Rules 1998 and Practice Directions.

(g)   Have a very clear idea of the order you want the master or district judge to make. If you are making the application, you should attach to the application notice a draft of the order you propose (except in the most simple applications).

(h)   Work out in advance any relevant interest calculation and costs order the master or district judge is likely to make. Also consider whether the master or district judge should make any directions for the future conduct of the claim.

(i)   Consider the prospect of an appeal should your application be unsuccessful. An application for permission to appeal may be made to the master or district judge at the end of the hearing.

13.11.3   Conducting the application

Whether the claimant or the defendant is the applicant, the party whose application it is will begin. The order of speaking will be the same whether the proceedings are in the High Court or the county court.

13.11.3.1   The applicant's case

If you are representing the applicant, the procedure is as follows.

(1)   Formally introduce yourself, your opponent and the application and identify any relevant document on the court file to which you intend to refer

For example:

> 'Good morning, sir, my name is Mr Holtam and I am from Collaws.
>
> I represent the claimant, David Mills. Miss Gibson, from Evans and Co, represents the defendant, Christopher Marlow.
>
> The claimant's application today is for summary judgment in a debt claim arising out of ...'

You should then check that the district judge has all the documents you intend to refer to on the court file.

The master or district judge will not have copies of the correspondence between the parties or their solicitors. You should refer to such correspondence only if it is exhibited to a witness statement.

You should then ask the master or district judge if he is familiar with the facts of the case or whether a brief summary would assist, and proceed accordingly.

(2)   Concisely identify the issues (legal and factual) for the court to decide and, by reference to the documents, highlight the relevant facts

State the issues clearly before taking the master or district judge through the documents. Argue for the order sought on the basis of the issues you have identified from the documents.

Take the master or district judge through the documents at a sufficiently slow pace to enable him or her to digest their contents. It is not normally necessary to read them out verbatim; you should merely refer to paragraphs and summarise their effect. If the master or district judge has read the papers, your summary can be quite concise. More detail is needed where the papers have not been read. Refer to any exhibits in a way which ties them in with and explains the contents of the relevant witness statement. You do not need to refer to matters that are not in dispute between the parties.

Anticipate and deal with all disputed matters revealed by your opponent's evidence.

(3)   Succinctly refer to the relevant law and/or procedure

Apply the relevant law when highlighting the relevant facts. Explain simply which Rule you are relying on and apply it to the facts of the case.

(4)   Conclude submissions for the order sought

Emphasise what you consider to be your best points and explain briefly why you are entitled to the order sought. Be prepared to address the court on an alternative or 'second best' order if you think the court is not prepared to grant the order you really want.

Make it clear to the master or district judge that you have finished your application. For example, 'Sir, unless I can help you further, that concludes my application'.

13.11.3.2   The respondent's case

The respondent's case will be structured differently as the court should by now have been taken through most of, if not all, the evidence. Nonetheless, the respondent's case follows a similar model.

(1)   So far as necessary, identify any relevant document on the court file to which you intend to refer

The applicant should have introduced you, and therefore there is no need for you to introduce yourself again. If the applicant failed to introduce you, then you should introduce yourself.

You should identify the documents that you will be relying on as a basis for your response, for example, 'Sir, in opposing this application I will be relying on the same documents as my friend but, in addition, the Defence'.

(2)   By reference to the documents, concisely identify and deal with issues (legal and factual) for the court to decide, highlight relevant facts and address the applicant's submissions

You should identify what you want the court to do and why.

The applicant should have already taken the master or district judge through the statements of case (if appropriate) and the evidence. Take the master or district judge to the relevant paragraphs in the statements of case and the witness statements which support your arguments. Present a positive case in support of your opposition to the order sought by the applicant. Do not just reply to the points made by the applicant. While making your submissions and presenting your positive case, deal with each of the applicant's points.

(3)   Succinctly counter the applicant's arguments on the relevant law and/or procedure

Reply to the legal points raised by the applicant. Distinguish, if possible, the applicant's authorities and introduce any you rely on.

(4)   Conclude submissions against the order sought

Briefly emphasise why the order requested by the applicant should not be made (or at least, if it is made, why it should only be in modified form). Stress the effects of making the order on the claim and, if it be the case, that the application is an attempt to blur the real issues and/or to prevent them being properly decided by the court after hearing oral evidence.

Make it clear to the master or district judge that you have finished your opposition. For example, 'Sir, unless I can assist you further, those are the grounds upon which I oppose the order sought'.

13.11.3.3   The applicant's final word

The master or district judge will normally invite the applicant to respond to matters raised by the respondent.

The applicant should deal with the points made against him or her preferably in the same order in which they were put. This can be done very briefly if it is a point which has already been dealt with by the applicant earlier. If it is a new point, face it squarely and be quick to point to any evidence or document that supports your assertions. Encapsulate why the court should make the order you seek.

MARKS (TRADING AS MARKS ROOFING) V MASTER BUILDER HOMES LTD

You will find on the following pages:

(1) Chronology

(2) Claim Form

(3) Part 24 Application Notice

(4) Claimant's witness statement in support of the application

(5) Defendant's witness statement opposing the application

(6) Claimant's witness statement in reply

Richard Marks is a roofing contractor and the owner of Marks Roofing. He has carried out work before for Master Builder Homes Limited. He entered into a contract to provide flat roofing for 50 double garages for Master Builder Homes Limited at a total cost of £75,000 plus VAT. Master Builder Homes Limited was attracted by the competitive price and Richard Marks's agreement that the roofing would be completed by November 2016.

The work was completed by the deadline and so far as the Claimant was aware there were no difficulties. Richard Marks has been pressing for payment but Master Builder Homes Limited has refused to pay anything despite several reminders.

A Claim Form endorsed with the Particulars of Claim has been issued out of the Weyford District Registry of the High Court claiming the £75,000 plus VAT and interest. An acknowledgement of service has been filed indicating that Master Builder Homes Limited intends to defend the claim. An application notice pursuant to CPR Part 24 has been issued on behalf of Richard Marks. You have a copy of the supporting witness statement together with Master Builder Homes Limited's witness statement opposing the application. You also have a copy of the Claimant's witness statement in reply.

You may assume that both Claimant and Defendant have served upon each other a statement of costs for the hearing at least 24 hours in advance. They have agreed their respective figures for costs subject to an order being made by the court.

(1) CHRONOLOGY

Marks v Master Builder Homes Limited

2016

7th March	Contract entered into for the construction of 50 garage roofs at agreed price of £1,500 per garage plus VAT.
20th April	Claimant enters site and commences work.
27th October	Work completed.
5th November	Claimant renders invoice for £90,000 (including VAT); payment due no later than 5th December.

2017

20th January	Reminder sent.
10th February	Reminder warning of legal action in event of non-payment by 18th February.
20th February	Claimant instructs solicitors.
27th February	Solicitors write letter before claim.

13th March	Claim form issued and served by 1st class post.
27th March	Defendant's solicitors acknowledge service and give Notice of Intention to Defend.
3rd April	Claimant's solicitors issue Part 24 notice of application.

Claim Form

In the	HIGH COURT OF JUSTICE QUEEN'S BENCH DIVISION WEYFORD DISTRICT REGISTRY
	for court use only
Claim No.	OM1527
Issue date	13 March 2017

Claimant

Richard Marks (trading as Marks Roofing), 17 Easthope Road, Westleigh, Blankshire BN1 2DP

SEAL

Defendant(s)

Master Builder Homes Limited, Crown House, Jubilee Square, Easterham, Blankshire BE2 1RE

Brief details of claim

The claim is for £75,000 plus VAT (£90,000) for work done and materials supplied by the Claimant to the Defendant between 20 April 2016 and 27 October 2016.

Value

The claim is for a specified sum of £90,000 plus interest of £2,054.08.

Defendant's name and address	Master Builder Homes Ltd Crown House Jubilee Square Easterham Blankshire BE2 1RE		£
		Amount claimed	92,054.08
		Court fee	4,602.70
		Solicitor's costs	100.00
		Total amount	96,756.78

The court office at

is open between 10 am and 4 pm Monday to Friday. When corresponding with the court, please address forms or letters to the Court Manager and quote the claim number.

N1 Claim form (CPR Part 7) (01.02)   *Printed on behalf of The Court Service*

	Claim No.	OM1527

Does, or will, your claim include any issues under the Human Rights Act 1998?   ☐ Yes   ☑ No

Particulars of Claim (attached)(to follow)

The Claimant's claim is for £75,000 plus VAT at 20% being the sum due from the Defendant to the Claimant for work done and materials supplied by the Claimant to the Defendant at their request in connection with the construction of 50 garage roofs at the Defendant's Bishopwood Housing Development between 20 April 2016 and 27 October 2016 at the agreed price per roof of £1,500 plus VAT.

Particulars

5 December 2016

To account rendered 75,000
VAT at 20%   15,000
                     £90,000

1. The Claimant claims the sum of £90,000.
2. Interest pursuant to the Late Payment of Commercial Debts (Interest) Act 1998. For the purposes of the Act, both parties acted in the course of a business. The statutory interest began to run from and including 6 December 2016 at 8% over the reference rate of 0.5% then in force, totaling 8.5% per annum. Interest due to the date of issue is £2,054.08 (6 December 2016 to 13 March 2017 inclusive being 98 days) and continuing until judgment or sooner payment at the daily rate of £20.96.
3. Compensation for late payment pursuant to the Late Payments of Commercial Debts (Interest) Act 1998 in the sum of £100.

Statement of Truth
*(I believe)(The Claimant believes) that the facts stated in these particulars of claim are true.
* I am duly authorised by the claimant to sign this statement

Full name   Richard Marks

Name of claimant's solicitor's firm   Collaws Solicitors

signed   *Collaws*   position or office held_____
*(Claimant)(Litigation friend)(Claimant's solicitor)   (if signing on behalf of firm or company)
*delete as appropriate

Collaws Solicitors
4 College Rd
Christlethorpe
Guildshire
CE1 4DZ

Claimant's or claimant's solicitor's address to which documents or payments should be sent if different from overleaf including (if appropriate) details of DX, fax or e-mail.

Application notice

For help in completing this form please read
the notes for guidance form N244Notes.

Name of court High Court of Justice Queen's Bench Division, Weyford District Registry	
Claim no.	OM1527
Warrant no. (if applicable)	N/A
Claimant's name (including ref.)	Richard Marks trading as Marks Roofing
Defendant's name (including ref.)	Master Builder Homes Ltd
Date	3 April 2017

1. What is your name or, if you are a solicitor, the name of your firm?

   Collaws Solicitors

2. Are you a   ☐ Claimant   ☐ Defendant   ☑ Solicitor

              ☐ Other *(please specify)*

   If you are a solicitor whom do you represent?   The Claimant

3. What order are you asking the court to make and why?

   Summary judgment pursuant to CPR Part 24, rule 24.2(a)(ii) and (b) because the defendant has no real prospect of successfully defending the claim and there is no other compelling reason why the case should be disposed of at trial.

4. Have you attached a draft of the order you are applying for?   ☑ Yes   ☐ No

5. How do you want to have this application dealt with?   ☑ at a hearing   ☐ without a hearing

              ☐ at a telephone hearing

6. How long do you think the hearing will last?   [ ] Hours   [20] Minutes

   Is this time estimate agreed by all parties?   ☑ Yes   ☐ No

7. Give details of any fixed trial date or period   N/A

8. What level of Judge does your hearing need?   Master

9. Who should be served with this application?   The Defendant

10. What information will you be relying on, in support of your application?

☑ the attached witness statement

☑ the statement of case

☐ the evidence set out in the box below

If necessary, please continue on a separate sheet.

Statement of Truth

(I believe) (The applicant believes) that the facts stated in this section (and any continuation sheets) are true.

Signed _Collaws_ _____ Dated 3 April 2017 _____

Applicant('s Solicitor)('s litigation friend)

Full name Richard Marks _____

Name of applicant's solicitor's firm Collaws Solicitors _____

Position or office held _____
(if signing on behalf of firm or company)

---

11. Signature and address details

Signed _Collaws_ _____ Dated 3 April 2017 _____

Applicant('s Solicitor)('s litigation friend)

Position or office held _____
(if signing on behalf of firm or company)

Applicant's address to which documents about this application should be sent

Collaws 4 College Road Chrislethorpe Guildshire CE1 4DZ Postcode		If applicable	
		Phone no.	01453 765431
		Fax no.	01452 765432
		DX no.	DX: 1032 Chrislethorpe
		Ref no.	MC/TP

E-mail address	mcharlton@collaws.co.uk

2

(4) CLAIMANT'S WITNESS STATEMENT

Claimant

1st

R Marks

3 April 2017

IN THE HIGH COURT OF JUSTICE   Claim Nº OM1527
QUEEN'S BENCH DIVISION
WEYFORD DISTRICT REGISTRY

BETWEEN   RICHARD MARKS
                    (TRADING AS MARKS ROOFING)   Claimant

and

MASTER BUILDER HOMES LIMITED   Defendant

CLAIMANT'S WITNESS STATEMENT IN SUPPORT OF
APPLICATION UNDER CPR PART 24

I, Richard Marks, of 17 Easthope Road, Westleigh, say as follows:-

1. The statements of fact in this statement are made from my own knowledge. I am the owner of the business Marks Roofing which specialises in providing flat roofing and I am the Claimant in this case.

2. On 7 March 2016 the Defendant engaged me to provide and construct the roofs on 50 double garages for houses forming phase 1 of the Defendant's development at an estate at Bishopswood, Westerfield. I gave them a written quotation which Paul Walters, their managing director verbally agreed. I didn't keep a copy.

3. I agreed to build the garage roofs for £1,500 plus VAT per garage. I built all of the garages between 20 April 2016 and 27 October 2016. However, despite numerous written and telephone requests the Defendant has failed to pay for this work. The amount I am owed is set out in the Particulars of Claim in this action.

4. I believe that the Defendant has no real prospect of successfully defending my claim and there is no other compelling reason why this case should be disposed of at a trial.

I believe that the facts stated in this witness statement are true.

Signed: *Richard Marks*

Dated: 3 April 2017

(5) DEFENDANT'S WITNESS STATEMENT

Defendant
1st
P Walters
9 April 2017

IN THE HIGH COURT OF JUSTICE
QUEEN'S BENCH DIVISION
WEYFORD DISTRICT REGISTRY

Claim Nº OM1527

BETWEEN

RICHARD MARKS
(TRADING AS MARKS ROOFING)

Claimant

and

MASTER BUILDER HOMES LIMITED

Defendant

**DEFENDANT'S WITNESS STATEMENT OPPOSING
CLAIMANT'S APPLICATION UNDER CPR PART 24**

I, Paul Walters, Managing Director of Master Builder Homes Limited, whose registered office is at Crown House, Jubilee Square, Easterham, say as follows:-

1. I am an employee and Director of the Defendant in this case and I am authorised by the Defendant to make this witness statement on its behalf. The statements of fact in this statement are made from my own knowledge.

2. I have read a copy of the witness statement of Richard Marks made on 3 April 2017 on behalf of the Claimant and for the reasons set out below I deny that the Defendant is indebted to the Claimant as alleged or at all.

3. The Defendant builds high quality executive housing and is presently developing an estate at Bishopswood, Westerfield. I agree that the Defendant engaged the Claimant to provide and construct the roofs on garages for the houses forming phase 1 of this development. They contracted to build 50 double garage roofs at an agreed price of £1,500 plus VAT per garage. The contract between us was purely oral. This is not unusual with contractors such as Richard Marks who we have used a lot in the past.

4. It was an implied term of the agreement between the parties that the Claimant would carry out the work in a proper and workmanlike manner and with all due care and skill and that any materials supplied would be of satisfactory quality and reasonably fit for their purpose.

5. In breach of these implied terms the roofs provided and constructed by the Claimant have the following defects:-

Plots 3, 4, 8	Garage roofs leak due to insufficient bitumen being applied. Damp has penetrated the timber joists, so roofs require stripping, joists replacing and roofs re-laying.
Plots 10, 33, 42, 48	Garage roofs suffer from puddling and will require stripping off and completely re-laying.
Plots 21, 22	Bitumen has been applied carelessly so as to mark and deface the rendering on the adjacent houses.
Plots 9, 14, 23, 28	Timber joists have twisted and warped so as to split the felting and leave gaps between the roof and supporting walls, so roofs require stripping, joists replacing and roofs re-laying.

    I would estimate that the total cost of putting these defects right is in the region of £30,000 inclusive of VAT.

6. Quite apart from the cost of repairs referred to in paragraph 5 herein, the Defendant has suffered damage as it has been unable to offer these plots for sale and has been deprived

of the profit therefrom. All the houses in phase 1 of the development are to be sold at £350,000 each. The budgeted net profit on each plot is £40,000. Furthermore, the poor condition of so many garages has given the whole development a bad reputation.

7.   The Claimant has been well aware that these defects have existed since 11 February 2017 when I telephoned him in response to his letter of 10 February in which he threatened legal action. I informed him that he would get nothing until the defects were put right to which he replied that he did not know what I was talking about.

8.   For the reasons set out above, I deny that the Defendant is indebted to the Claimant as alleged or at all, or alternatively the Defendant is entitled to claim damages by way of set-off that amount to a sum in excess of the sum claimed. Accordingly I would ask that the Claimant's application be dismissed.

I believe that the facts stated in this witness statement are true.

Signed: *Paul Walters*

Dated: 9 April 2017

(6) CLAIMANT'S SECOND WITNESS STATEMENT

Claimant

2nd

Richard Marks RM1

28 April 2017

IN THE HIGH COURT OF JUSTICE   Claim Nº OM1527
QUEEN'S BENCH DIVISION
WEYFORD DISTRICT REGISTRY

BETWEEN   RICHARD MARKS
                    (TRADING AS MARKS ROOFING)   Claimant

and

MASTER BUILDER HOMES LIMITED   Defendant

CLAIMANT'S WITNESS STATEMENT IN REPLY

I, Richard Marks, of 17, Easthope Road, Westleigh, say as follows:-

1.   The statements of fact in this witness statement are made from my own knowledge.

2.   I have read a copy of the witness statement of Paul Walters made on 9 April 2017 on behalf of the Defendant.

3.   I dispute Paragraphs 5 and 6 since until 15 March 2017 I was wholly unaware that the Defendant was dissatisfied with any of the completed garages. I have never been given an opportunity to inspect the alleged defects and am therefore unable to comment either upon their existence or the alleged cost of effecting repairs.

4.   I deny the contents of Paragraph 7. I have never spoken to Paul Walters on the telephone. I refer to a copy of a letter dated 14 March 2017 marked "RM1" which is the first intimation I have ever received about this particular problem.

5.   I accordingly ask that this Honourable Court awards me summary judgment.

I believe that the facts stated in this witness statement are true.

Signed: *Richard Marks*

Dated: 28 April 2017

IN THE HIGH COURT OF JUSTICE   Claim N° OM 1527
QUEEN'S BENCH DIVISION
WEYFORD DISTRICT REGISTRY

BETWEEN   RICHARD MARKS
              (TRADING AS MARKS ROOFING)   **Claimant**

                        and

       MASTER BUILDER HOMES LIMITED   **Defendant**

This is the exhibit marked "RM1" referred to in the witness statement of Richard Marks made this 28th day of April 2017.

Signed: *Richard Marks*

Dated: 28/4/2017

MASTER BUILDER HOMES LIMITED

Crown House
Jubilee Square
Easterham
EH6 8DL

Tel: 01409 255600
Fax: 01409 123321

Richard Marks   14 March 2017
Marks Roofing
17 Easthope Road
Westleigh
WT7 5AC

Dear Richard,

Phase 1 - Bishopswood

I have received court papers from your solicitors and frankly I am disappointed. We have always had an excellent working relationship and I am sad to see it threatened by legal action which, as we both know, benefits no-one but our lawyers.

We have had big problems with the roofs on plots 3, 4, 8, 9, 10, 14, 21-23, 28, 33, 42 and 48. I cannot really see how you can push for payment until these are rectified, the plots are unsaleable until then.

You also know just how tough things are in the industry at the moment. It is no secret that sales are at an all time low and I cannot afford any delays in getting all the plots on the market. Bishopswood is getting a reputation with local surveyors and estate agents as a problem estate and you know how damaging that can be.

Please contact me as to when you can start on the roofs. Needless to say I expect you to do this free of charge since it is your responsibility to complete the job properly.

Yours sincerely

Paul Walters

CLAIMANT'S SUBMISSIONS

Master, my name is Mr Holtam from Collaws Solictors and I represent the Claimant Richard Marks, trading as Marks Roofing. Miss Gibson of Swallows and Co, acts for Master Builder Homes Ltd.

This is the Claimant's application for summary judgment in a debt action concerning a contract in which the Claimant agreed to construct 50 Garage roofs at the Defendant's Bishopswood Housing Development.

Master, do you have the bundle of documents?

[The master replies that he does have the bundle of documents.]

Master, are you familiar with the facts of the case or would a brief summary assist?

[The master replies that he is familiar with the facts and a brief summary is not required.]

Thank you Master.

The legal issue in this case is whether the defendant has a real prospect of successfully defending the claim at trial.

The purported defence is that 13 of the 50 garage roofs installed by the Claimant are defective. The defendant alleges that some of the roofs leak, some suffer from puddling, some have resulted in the rendering on adjoining houses being defaced and some have warped timber joists.

Master, you will see from the particulars of claim that the garage roofs were constructed between April and October of last year at the agreed price per roof of £1,500 plus VAT. The total amount claimed is £90,000 plus interest.

Master, I shall now take you to the witness statement of Mr Marks.

Paragraphs 2 and 3 set out the contractual terms and in paragraph 3 you will see that despite numerous written and telephone requests for payment the amount is still outstanding.

In his witness statement Mr Walters, at paragraph 3, agrees the terms of the contract and in paragraph 5 gives evidence of the alleged defects. The alleged defects are disputed and the defects alleged in relation to plots 21 and 22 are not defects to the garage roofs at all and can be easily remedied by cleaning. Mr Walters estimates that the total cost of putting these defects right is in the region of £30,000 inclusive of VAT and yet the total cost of installing the 11 allegedly defective flat roofs was only £19,800 inclusive of VAT. Even if what the Defendant says is true the figure for the repairs seems excessive. It is interesting to note that no detailed breakdown of how the figure of £30,000 is calculated is provided by Mr Walters.

In paragraph 6, Mr Walters states that he has been unable to offer these properties for sale and that he has been deprived of profit as a result. Master, there is nothing stopping the Defendant offering these properties for sale. They can be shown to potential purchasers and the Defendant can assure potential purchasers that any defects will be remedied before they move into the houses. Also, as is well known, house prices have fallen since these houses were built and it is highly unlikely that these houses would now sell for £350,000. There is no independent evidence produced by Master Builder Homes of the current market value of these houses. It is unlikely that the Defendant will make a £40,000 profit on these houses in the present climate. The Defendant has not been deprived of the profit from the sale of these houses as a result of the alleged defects. Even if the defendant makes a profit, the profit has merely been delayed not extinguished. It is submitted that the Defendant is looking to the Claimant to compensate him for the depressed state of the current housing market.

In paragraph 6 Mr Walters states that the poor condition of so many garage roofs has given the estate a poor reputation. This is difficult to comprehend as the 11 houses with the alleged defects have not been offered for sale. The poor reputation of the development must therefore be due to the other houses that are being offered for sale; a matter which is outside the Claimant's control.

In paragraph 8 Mr Walters refers to a telephone conversation. It is the Claimant's case that no such telephone conversation took place.

Master, you will see that Mr Marks has filed a witness statement in reply.

In paragraph 3 you will see that it was not until 15 March that Mr Marks knew Mr Walters was dissatisfied with his work. In paragraph 3 Mr Marks produces RM1: the letter he received from Mr Walters. In his letter Mr Marks refers to how tough things are in the industry at the moment. This reinforces the submission that I made earlier. The Defendant is looking to blame Mr Marks for matters which can be explained by the difficult market conditions in the property industry at the moment. Master, you will see that no reference is made to the alleged telephone conversation between Mr Walters and Mr Marks that was referred to earlier. There is no reference to it because no such conversation took place.

Master, you have the discretion under CPR 24.2(a) and (b) to enter summary judgment for the Claimant. The Defendant has no real prospect of successfully defending the claim at trial and there is no other compelling reason why this claim should go to trial.

The Claimant has discharged his burden of proof.

The Defendant alleges that some of the garage roofs are defective. The garage roofs were completed on 27 October 2016 yet he leaves it until a letter dated 14 March 2017 to bring the defects to the attention of the Claimant. Surely if there had been defects then this would have been brought to the attention of the Claimant when they were first discovered.

The Claimant has been denied the opportunity of inspecting the alleged defects. Again if there were such defects then you would expect the Defendant to be keen to show them to the Claimant. There is no independent expert evidence to support Mr Walters' contention that the garage roofs are defective.

Neither is there any supporting evidence for Mr Walters' contention that the garage roofs would cost some £30,000 to repair which is much more than the garage roofs cost to install in the first place. The Claimant contends that the Defendant is looking for someone to blame for the fact that this development has failed to sell. This is not the fault of the Claimant but a sign of the difficult market conditions in the property industry at the moment.

Unless I can assist you further Master, I invite you to award summary judgment for the Claimant.

DEFENDANT'S SUBMISSIONS

I intend to refer to the same documents as Mr Holtam.

Mr Holtam was correct when he identified the legal issue for you to decide namely whether the Defendant has a real prospect of successfully defending the claim at trial.

It is the Defendant's case that there is a defence with a real prospect of success at trial. The defence is that 13 of the garage roofs have problems. These include leaking roofs, puddling, the careless application of bitumen and warping. The garage roofs will need attention at significant cost.

Master, from the particulars of claim you will see that there was one contract for the construction of 50 garage roofs.

The only dispute that the Defendant has with the evidence contained in Mr Marks' witness statement opposing the application is contained in paragraph 3. In paragraph 3 Mr Marks states that despite numerous written and telephone requests the Defendant has failed to pay for this work. Master, there were only two written reminders and no telephone reminders for payment before Collaws were instructed.

The Defendant's defence is contained in Mr Walters' witness statement.

Mr Walters in paragraph 3 gives evidence of the terms of the contract which are not in dispute. There was one contract for the Claimant to provide 50 garage roofs.

The contract contained the implied terms mentioned in paragraph 4 of Mr Walters' witness statement.

Paragraph 5 outlines the breaches of those implied terms.

The Defendant agrees with Mr Holtam's assertion that the roofs to Plots 21 and 22 are not defective. However that does not absolve the Claimant from responsibility for careless application of bitumen to those Plots.

Mr Walters' estimate of the cost of putting these defects right is in excess of the original cost of the garage roofs. The cost is more because the existing roofs have to be stripped, joists replaced and the roofs re-laid; much more work than if the roofs had been properly installed by the Claimant. A detailed breakdown of how the £30,000 figure is calculated can be provided in due course.

The Defendant's decision not to offer these plots for sale is a simple one. No one would buy these houses with such obvious defects. Market conditions are such that any minor defect, let alone more serious ones such as these, will discourage potential purchasers from making offers.

Paragraph 7 refers to a telephone conversation that did take place between Mr Walters and Mr Marks on 11 February 2017.

Master, I shall now address Mr Marks' witness statement in reply.

Paragraph 3 is disputed. It is the Defendant's case that Mr Marks did know of the defects as a result of the telephone conversation of 11 February.

Master, Mr Holtam was correct when he said earlier that under CPR 24.2(a)(ii) and (b) you have the power to award summary judgment if you conclude that the Defendant has no real prospect of successfully defending the claim at trial.

This contract to provide garage roofs is a contract for the supply of goods and services. The Supply of Goods and Services Act 1982 contains implied terms that the garage roofs should be of satisfactory quality and reasonably fit for purpose and that the installation should be undertaken with reasonable care and skill. The Claimant has breached those implied terms under sections 4 and 13 of the Act.

The Defendant has a defence with a real prospect of success at trial. There was one contract to build 50 garage roofs. Only 37 were completed properly. Eleven of the garage roofs have defects and the construction of two others resulted in the careless application of bitumen to adjoining houses. Consequently the Defendant is entitled to withhold payment until the contract is successfully completed. The Defendant will also be counter-claiming for the loss of profit arising from the Defendant's inability to sell these houses. Such a counterclaim will exceed the amount that the Claimant is pursuing in this action.

The Defendant invites you not to exercise your discretion to award summary judgment in this case and to dismiss this application.

Unless I can assist you further Master that concludes my submissions.

CLAIMANT'S SUBMISSIONS IN REPLY

Master, you have the power to award summary judgement for the whole or part of the claim. The Defendant has not disputed that 39 of the 50 garage roofs were successfully completed. Therefore Master, should you decide not to award summary judgment for the whole claim I invite you to award summary judgment for part of the claim. The total cost of installing 39 garage roofs amounted to £58,500 plus VAT making a total sum of £70,200.

Unless I can assist you further Master, those are my submissions.

13.11.3.4 Closing the case

The master or district judge then gives a reasoned judgment and writes his or her order in note form on the court file. This indorsement forms the basis for the order subsequently drawn up.

If appropriate, the master or district judge will give directions for the further conduct of the action. Be prepared to ask for any directions which you feel are necessary.

The party who has won usually asks for costs, and the loser is given the opportunity to reply. Be prepared to make submissions on the appropriate costs order.

13.11.3.5 Appeals

At the end of the hearing, the master or district judge may ask the parties if they wish to appeal his or her decision. An application for permission to appeal may be made to the master or district judge at the hearing. Permission to appeal may be given only where the court considers that the appeal would have a real prospect of success or there is some other compelling reason why the appeal should be heard.

13.11.3.6 Effective chambers advocacy

Although the subject matter and nature of chambers applications cover an enormous range, it is vitally important for the advocate to make his or her submissions as clearly and concisely as possible in order to help the court, especially since it hears so many applications during a working day.

13.12 CONCLUSION

Although this chapter could not deal in detail with the subject, it has provided an introduction to some of the salient features of the advocate's art. It should also have made clear the fact that many of the skills of the advocate can be acquired through study and observation. Remember that thorough preparation is the key: without that, no advocate can be fully effective, however fluent his or her oral skills may be.

BIBLIOGRAPHY

Writing and drafting

Grammar and punctuation

R Allen, *Fowler's Modern English Usage* (4th edn, 2015)

RL Trask, *The Penguin Guide to Punctuation* (Penguin, 1997)

L Truss, *Eats, Shoots and Leaves* (Fourth Estate, 2009)

Plain English

M Adler, *Clarity for Lawyers* (2nd edn, 2006)

E Gowers, *The Complete Plain Words* (1987)

Practical legal research

P Clinch, *Legal Research: A Practitioner's Handbook* (2nd edn, 2013)

J Knowles, *Effective Legal Research* (4th edn, 2016)

Oral communication skills

A Pease and B Pease, *The Definitive Book of Body Language* (2006)

Interviewing and advising

A Sherr, *Client Care for Lawyers* (2nd rev edn, 1999)

Law Society, *Client Care Practice Notes* at www.lawsociety.org.uk/support-services/advice/practice-notes

Negotiation

R Fisher and W Ury, *Getting Past No: Negotiating With Difficult People* (1992)

R Fisher and W Ury, *Getting to Yes* (rev edn, 2012)

D Kahneman, *Thinking, Fast and Slow* (2012)

D Stone, B Patton and S Heen, *Difficult Conversations* (2011)

Advocacy

K Evans, *Advocacy in Court* (2nd rev edn, 1995)

J Munkman, *The Technique of Advocacy* (1991)

SRA Code of Conduct 2011

Index